Operation Pied Piper

*The Wartime Evacuation of Schoolchildren
from London and Berlin 1938–46*

Operation Pied Piper

*The Wartime Evacuation of Schoolchildren
from London and Berlin 1938–46*

Niko Gärtner

INFORMATION AGE PUBLISHING, INC.
Charlotte, NC • www.infoagepub.com

Library of Congress Cataloging-in-Publication Data

Gartner, Niko.
 Operation Pied Piper : the wartime evacuation of schoolchildren from
London and Berlin 1938-46 / Niko Gartner.
    p. cm.
 ISBN 978-1-61735-901-9 (pbk.) – ISBN 978-1-61735-902-6 (hardcover) –
ISBN 978-1-61735-903-3 (ebook) 1. World War, 1939-1945–Education and the
war. 2. School children–England–London. 3. School
children–Germany–Berlin. 4. World War, 1939-1945–Evacuation of
civilians–England–London. 5. World War, 1939-1945–Evacuation of
civilians–Germany–Berlin. 6. World War,
1939-1945–Children–England–London. 7. World War,
1939-1945–Children–Germany–Berlin. I. Title.
 D810.E5.G64 2012
 940.53083'09421–dc23

                                                            2012020709

Printed in the United States of America

Für Walter

Homo doctus in se semper divitias habet.

(Phaedrus, Fabulae 4,21,1)

Contents

Introduction

Like the fairy tale Pied Piper of Hamelin, the somewhat ill-fitting name-sake of London's evacuation, the British and Third Reich governments took the children away. During the Second World War (WWII), when the cities would become too dangerous to live in, when air raids and blanket bombings threatened to claim civilian lives, the warring regimes initiated schemes for the evacuation of urban children into billets and camps in safer reception areas. After years of planning, the London County Council (LCC) sent away all of its schools, teachers, and some 500,000 children on the first three days of September 1939. Prior to that exodus, the Council had fought the national government over the need for evacuation, had negotiated with transport providers, had discussed their plans with London head-teachers, had appealed to parents, and had finally rolled out a scheme that it saw fit to protect the city's children and prevent panic among the adult population. In Berlin, the Nazi regime assumed that the pure mention of the word *evacuation* would trigger panic and defeatism—and consequently disguised their massive evacuation program as an extended club holiday. Participation, at least in the beginning, was voluntary, and the evacuation was advertised to parents and children as a great adventure. In the course of the war—and in the face of resentful and suspicious parents—both governments were forced to change their policies, but sustained evacuation schemes that affected millions of children and adults.

Both, the British evacuation and Third Reich *Kinderlandverschickung* (KLV) have since been subjects of major academic and popular interest in

Operation Pied Piper, pages xi–xxxi
Copyright © 2012 by Information Age Publishing
All rights of reproduction in any form reserved.

their countries—and one would assume that both countries' parallel, but in no way identical, developments hold great promise for historical comparative investigation. Still, there is a gap in the evacuations' historiography: a comparison of the enemy capitals' evacuation schemes. History of education—in defiance of the traditional historians' insistence on the allegedly unique character of historical events—has promoted comparative research for some years now. This study aims to contribute to the growing (but yet small) body of international studies in the field. This study's focus is the policy development and decision-making within local governments that were faced with major logistical and sociological challenges. Unlike previous studies, whose foci went away with the evacuees, this study will stay in the respective capitals and attempt to explain the actions and reactions of civil servants, politicians, teachers, and parents who shared the responsibility for *their* children's welfare at a time of war. Through the lens of local sources, this study will tell the story of the cities that had (or as the case may be: had not) been vacated.

This crowded introductory chapter deals with several academic considerations that need sorting out prior to diving into the actual topical work. It will introduce the research questions and key literature as well as discussing the uneven survival of sources from both cities. This chapter's purpose is also to introduce and defend the study's research design—and hopefully succeed in showing that documentary and comparative research both have long traditions, proven academic validity, and credible scientific methodologies. Furthermore, this chapter will establish relevant theoretical concepts, announce the study's limits and sort through evacuation-specific terminology.

Research Questions

In a comparative policy study of administration, the primary research questions would be technical. Who organized the evacuation at what point in time, under which circumstances, and following whose orders? What were the aims and motives of the people in charge and how far were they able to realize those ambitions? How did the planning translate into operation? What were the similarities and differences of the evacuations in London and Berlin?

A second set of questions concerns the reactions of children, parents, teachers, schools and cities. Why was evacuation never as popular as its organisers anticipated? How did the planners react to shifting perceptions of their schemes? How did education continue for those evacuated and those who stayed behind? How did the cities and their officials deal with the absence of children and their subsequent returns? What role did propaganda play in the planning and operation of the schemes?

On a more philosophical level are questions about the evacuation's place in the emotional and ideological context of its country. To what extent did the evacuation schemes embody or represent their political environment? How far were the evacuations unique to their time and place? Were the schemes unique to their countries' political system, or did strategies, rituals, and myths about the evacuation develop independent of it? How did they influence post-war reconstruction, and what place do they have in popular memory?

Generally, the success or failure of either evacuation (or both) seems an obvious research question, but measurement might be impossible. There is the problem of finding suitable parameters for the assessment of success or failure. Measuring by absolute number of evacuees from either city (assuming that it is actually possible to account for the unrecorded returnees) would only allow a superficial insight. Organizers in Berlin would judge success not only on quantity, but also on the *quality* of the evacuees: The KLV was exclusive to those Nazi ideology construed as desirable. Thus, success in Berlin would have probably been rather measured in influence over the children and detachment from their families.

Furthermore, the application of success and failure could be ultimately flawed. After all, the assumption that high numbers of evacuees are a measurement of success implies that evacuation is the *desired response to the problem*. In 1943, renowned child psychologist Anna Freud posited an opposing argument:

> The war acquires comparatively little significance for children so long as it only threatens their lives, disturbs their material comfort, or cuts their food rations. It becomes enormously significant the moment it breaks up family life and uproots the first emotional attachment of the child within the family group. (Freud & Burlingham, 1943, p. 37)

If separation from the family is more upsetting than bombing, as Freud argues, it can only be classified a success if it actually saves lives. Other motives for evacuation (recreation, health, social control) become invalid and the measurement—again—impossible, since it cannot be proven that a child remaining in an area of danger would necessarily have been killed there.

Following German historian Dietmar Süß's lead, this study will also not assess the success or failure of one country, political system or indeed evacuation scheme over the other, but rather measure policy practices and outcomes in order to find evidence for similar or diverging developments in the social order of societies in a permanent state of emergency. After all, the aerial war, bombings and evacuations had more than just local or national relevance—they became part of the complex post-war Anglo-German relationship (Süß, 2011).

A Note on the Evacuations' Historiographies

> We cannot escape the powerful hegemonic hold that World War II has on us; it is part of our everyday discourse and its presence is visible all around us in ideological, political, and academic debates as well as in myriad popular cultural relics, monuments, and memorabilia. (Crawford & Foster, 2007, p. 9)

Writing about Nazi Germany and WWII remains perilous since the level of historical investigation into that period is unparallel to any other event in the course of humankind. Adding to the over-bulging bookshelves needs justification and humility. No single study can wholly do justice to the complexity, scale, and scope of WWII—and it is prudent to point out the narrow scope and limited outlook afforded under this study's rationale. Furthermore, social history writing on any aspect of Third Reich policies demands particular care since Ian Kershaw (1999) rightly pointed to the controversy surrounding the period's uniqueness in world history: the impossible reconciliation between a highly civilized German society and the barbarism of Holocaust and total war.

German historians always need to be additionally careful since their studies instantaneously become part of a wider political discourse—occasionally even *Historikerstreite* (historians' disputes)—about the political and social legacies of Nazi regime, war, and especially Holocaust. This study aims to be part of a new generation of academic, rather than political histories that are emerging from German universities by historians too young to be overly inhibited by the elaborate moral struggles of the post-war generation. It should be clear from the outset, though, that the absence of a political agenda in this research does in no way hint to a revisionist attitude or an attempt to rewrite history in favor of an unpardonable regime. Rather, the neutral position is the result of our understanding of the historian's craft. It is our duty to find, collect, and present our findings about the past for others to use as arguments in their professions.

The *evacuation experience* in the reception areas is already well researched, but there are only a few studies dedicated to local historical research of either country's capital—and none that provides a comparison of both. In England, the evacuation is mainly treated as a nationwide phenomenon—with London's leading role acknowledged, but thrown in with events taking place in the industrial towns in the north and the major port cities in the south. In Germany, there are plenty of ambitious local studies, but none as yet specifically about Berlin.

The gap in the historiography is not only wide but also deep since many of the authors on the evacuations have been evacuees themselves or were involved in its administration. Thus, their views and accounts must be assessed against their biographical background—especially if they hide their political ambitions or missionary zeal well. Some of the publications by former evacuees are sound academic studies, but others are biased and give—in the words of Susan Isaacs— "partial answers [that] are never as good as the truth and not always better than ignorance" (Isaacs, Brown, & Thouless, 1941, p. 2).

The narrative of London's evacuation thus relies on the insider account of former LCC clerk George A. N. Lowndes (1969) as well as the celebrated academic works by Richard Titmuss (the 1950 landmark study *The Problems of Social Policy*), Peter Gosden (1976), John Macnicol and Travis L. Crosby (both 1986). From the offering of popular collections and oral histories we recommend the works of Ben Wicks (1988, 1989), Robert Holman (1995), Mike Brown (2005, 2009), Juliet Gardiner (2005a, 2005b), and John Welshman (2010), while offering a cautious note on the popular but academically flawed, revisionist studies by Martin Parsons (1998, 2008; Parsons & Starns, 2002).

Little has been published on Berlin's evacuation. Therefore, key literary contributions are former evacuees' autobiographies (Jost Hermand, 1993; Renate Bandur, 2006; the oral history collection by Claudia Bauer, 2010) and exhibition catalogues from local museums (including the impressive "Heil Hitler, Herr Lehrer!" by Norbert Franck & Gesine Asmus, 1983, but also Doris Fürstenberg, 1996). There is a good breadth of local studies from other German cities and regions—occasionally with very useful introductions of the general scheme (e.g., Gerhard Sollbach, 2002, 2006)—but the nationwide Kinderlandverschickung has only been tackled successfully by one: the imaginative researcher Gerhard Kock (1997), whose *Der Führer sorgt für unsere Kinder...* remains the landmark study on Third Reich evacuation. His study was also the first to overcome the influence of former KLV executive Gerhard Dabel's self-serving 1981 publication of sources for the *KLV e.V.* society. Most pre-1997 histories of the KLV had wholly or partially relied on the society's carefully selected, heavily edited sources—and are therefore of little use here. General histories of the Hitlerjugend—the evacuation's executive body—make little mention of evacuation, with the notable exception of Michael Buddrus' thoroughly impressive work on the influential youth organization (2003). On the wider topic of Nazi childhood and schooling we recommend the works of Geoffrey Giles (1992) and Nicholas Stargardt (2005).

It has been mentioned earlier that historians of the evacuations have done very little peeping over their own country's fences yet. There are bound to be more comparative studies now that a new generation of German social historians has broken with the heavily politicized historical discourse of the past and embraces international comparisons—a most recent example is Dietmar Süß's (2011) comprehensive social history of civilian life in air raided German and British cities. At the University of Hamburg, Carsten Kressel (1996) pioneered a comparative study of the children's evacuation in the port towns of Hamburg and Liverpool, unfortunately without offering a rationale for his choice of cities (that were really just executing plans made in the respective capitals). It remains a comprehensive study that lacks depth and detail. Kock's contemporaneous analysis has to be regarded as far superior in this respect. Kock also introduced German readers to the English evacuation—if only in a brief, attached essay that is mainly based on Titmuss' work. Since neither Kressel nor Kock have been translated yet, the best English language source on the German evacuation remains the documentary reader compiled by Jeremy Noakes (1998) that disguises itself as a humble schoolbook, but is actually a very well introduced overview of the German home front with a remarkable choice of sources, all expertly translated.

The Sources

Documentary sources from the capitals' administrations are the pillars of this study. Their explicit analyses guide, structure, and justify the overarching narrative. The retrieval, selection, and analysis of the sources require some introduction here. There has to be an asymmetrical relationship between the documentation of London's evacuation and the near simultaneous operation in Berlin. While every government and nongovernmental branch involved with London's exodus has submitted their paperwork to the official archives, the German government branches set fire to theirs when the war seemed lost. Jane Martin's laconic remark that "the politics of historical survival mean archival gaps" (Martin, 2003, p. 224) seems to be particularly true for the Third Reich. The deliberate attempt to destroy evidence of the past is not only lamentable, but also testimony to the power of archives. The perils of asymmetrical survival of sources have been summarized in Platt's seminal essay on documentary research: "When there is simply not enough data, one is tempted to over interpret what is available, and to treat it as representative of the larger class that originally existed without any knowledge that it really is so" (1981a, p. 35).

Comparative researcher Edwin Amenta confirms the validity of this observation for his discipline where "often too many hypotheses [are] chasing too few observations" (2003, p. 104). The ongoing discussion has been labeled the "messy centre" of comparative research or "paradigm wars" (Lichbach & Zuckerman, 2009, p. 17). This study needs to be sensitive to these considerations and proceed with caution.

London's evacuation is documented in its entirety in the archives of the LCC's Education Officer stored at the London Metropolitan Archives (LMA), measuring tens of thousands of pages in hundreds of folders. The deposits are not in particularly good condition, but with regards to their ready availability it seems surprising that there have been only a few published assessments since Richard Titmuss' seminal 1950 study. The bulk of sources—minutes, protocols, publications, press clippings, posters, flyers, maps, specimens of equipment, brochures, and correspondence—appears largely untouched and invites further research. In a case like this, not the scarcity of sources, but its wealth becomes the problem: making a selection from the available documents seems an impossible task. It is a necessary task, though, in order to do justice to the material by critical review instead of wholesale assessment.

The LCC was by no means the only agent involved in the schoolchildren's evacuation from London. The Ministry of Health (MoH) was officially in charge, with the Board of Education (BoE) shouldering some of the responsibilities. However, it will be shown later that there is credible evidence that the LCC was not only crucial for both the design and execution of the evacuation scheme, but that its dominant role was necessitated by weaknesses in the other agents, be it overblown bureaucracy at the MoH or the BoE's lack of authority with politicians and population. Both institutions' documents are held at the National Archives in Kew, and some of them will be utilized to complement or challenge the LCC material.

In addition, there are the documents of those who monitored the proceedings from outside the government. The English evacuation triggered widespread interest and discussion right from its commencement in 1938, resulting in a number of studies in the fields of sociology and psychology. These contemporary evacuation surveys will be used as primary source material alongside the governmental documentary sources. The University of Liverpool—who published their findings under the rather sensationalistic title *Our Wartime Guests, Opportunity or Menace?*—conducted the earliest comprehensive, if slightly premature study in 1939 (Wagner, 1940). More substantial work was carried out within the Fabian Society, who commissioned an early report (Clark & Toms, 1940) and also a later, more in-depth analysis by Fabian and LCC members Margaret Cole and Richard Padley (1940). Despite only covering the period now described as the Phoney War, their critical analysis on the nature of the evacuation as a military expedient, their poignant description of the power vacuum created by the fight for supremacy within the government, and their critique of the organizers' misjudgement of participation levels made it an important document for later historians like Richard Titmuss. Similarly influential was a major survey of London children evacuated to Cambridgeshire, conducted by the University of Cambridge in the winter of 1939–1940 under the helm of scholar and influential child psychologist Susan Isaacs and colleagues (1941). For this study, that survey is of particular relevance since the interviewees included *returnees* (children who returned home early from their billet) and their London parents, thus affording insight into attitudes towards evacuation from its intended target group. The study offers reasons for (and indeed solutions to) the government's problem of keeping children away from London by highlighting the planners' dilemma of having neglected psychological dimensions, social issues, and emotional problems in favor of timetables and logistics. Maybe some of its criticism is unduly harsh, though, since the study works with the benefit of hindsight. Largely similar, but benefiting from a longer time span of collecting data is Barnett House's study of *London Children in Oxford* (Adams & Emden, 1947), which probably started the sanguine perception of the evacuation; one of their main findings was that children preferred being away and struggled to reintegrate into their urban home.

While these contemporary studies are very valuable for this research, they come with a cautionary note: A very defensive George Lowndes remarked that these studies were issued and conducted by politically motivated researchers and reflect their then current educational ideas and position towards the government. Furthermore, they lack perspective, having been conducted so shortly after (or even during) the event and do not appreciate the emergency nature of the evacuation (Lowndes, 1969). Lowndes would have appreciated fellow LCC officer Monica Cosens' contribution to the debate. In her survey of London mothers and their very young children in the reception areas conducted in the winter of 1939, she appreciates the military nature of the evacuation: "in military operations the convenience of the civilian population cannot head the list" (Cosens, 1940, p. 3).

When the Allies advanced on Berlin in 1945, Nazi officials were industriously destroying as much evidence of the Third Reich administration as possible by burning the archives of key institutions. Among them were large parts of the Hitlerjugend's archive and one of its subsidiary offices: the *Reichsdienststelle Erweiterte Kinderlandverschickung*, the nerve center of the evacuation. Only fragments of the organization's documentation survived, leading to a patchy and incomplete picture of this part of NS history (see also Naasner & Schmidt, 1995). The scarcity of sources led historians to wrong and contradictory conclusions. Even basic facts like the actual number of children evacuated with the government scheme have long been disputed (ranging from the likely 800,000 to an incredible five million). This unfortunate situation seems to be the reason why Berlin's evacuation—unlike the evacuations of Hamburg, Hanover and the industrial west of the Reich, for example—has not yet been presented in a monograph. However, meticulous research by Gerhard Kock and recent readings of hitherto hidden or unavailable sources by authors such as Michael Buddrus have shown that the capital's evacuation can be reconstructed by a more imaginative use of sources and triangulation of the historical evidence (for example, by confirming the speculative number of evacuees with the help of account sheets from the Ministry of Finance or the size of trains provided by the Reichsbahn).

For research of Berlin's evacuation, the most promising starting point would be the national archives, the Bundesarchiv in Berlin (BA). Among their deposits is the above-mentioned, controversial collection of the KLV e.V.—but also surviving documents of the Hitlerjugend, most notably the *Mitteilungsblatt für die erweiterte Kinderlandverschickung* (in-house circular on the evacuation) and several volumes of the propaganda magazine for children in camps *Unser Lager*. While these publications provide only little information on the evacuation's operation itself, they nonetheless illustrate the propaganda that children were subjected to in the KLV camps.

The other important archive in Berlin is part of the Deutsches Institut für Internationale Pädagogische Forschung/Bibliothek für Bildungsgeschichtliche Forschung (German Institute for International Research in Education/Library of History of Education Research) that holds some KLV material within their collections donated by or salvaged from individual schools. Our additional plea for assistance that went out to some thirty Berlin schools remained largely unsuccessful. Of all those schools (that all had been around in the 1940s), only four could provide material from that period; the others never had archival deposits to begin with or had lost them in the meantime. Thorough de-nazification or indeed shame and guilt might explain the empty school archives—as does the dire need for anything burnable for heating during the cold winters of the immediate post-war period. The kind contributions by Droste-Hülshoff-Schule and Eckener Oberschule (who also holds deposits of neighboring former girls school Gertrud-Stauffacher-Schule) are all the more noteworthy—and only possible thanks to dedicated history teachers rather than a systematic culture of preservation.

Despite the restrictions imposed by the willful destruction of documents, this study can offer a wide range of sources for analysis. The evacuations will be presented with the help of internal memos, circulars, conference minutes, official instructions, official letters and private correspondence, leaflets, posters, photographs, and broadcasts. A complete listing of the sources used in this study can be found alongside the general bibliography.

Methods and Approaches

> *No researcher can be sceptical about everything at once,*
> *and it is not reasonable that he should.*
> —Platt, 1981b, p. 63

Knowing the literature and finding the sources might yet amount to nothing without a sound methodology. In history of education, "our work remains craftwork, skilled, sometimes elegant, often well researched but incoherent in its shifting agendas, theoretical concerns and epistemological assumptions" (Cowen, 2002, p. 414), or worse: "much of the History of Education is (still) unreflexive and atheoretical, and signally fails to illuminate the impact of the past on the present" (Ozga, 2000, p. 116). In this climate, it is all the more important to clarify a methodological framework early and comprehensively.

The ambition here is to place the evacuation in its context and to explain it from there. As a policy study it follows the practices of documentary research based on historical source investigation. Simultaneously, comparative research methods will contribute to this binary study by following the practices governing qualitative research. Thus, this study attempts to contribute to the potentially rewarding and not yet fully exploited history–sociology boundary crossings—even though there is potential for friction in this, since comparative education has always been more concerned with the normative *ought*, whereas positivistic and dispassionate historians have eagerly pursued the descriptive *is*, or rather *was* (Larsen, 2009).

Especially within the social sciences, there remains a lack of interest in official documents (McCulloch, 2004), with sociologists identifying more with survey and interview techniques, favoring empirical evidence and dismissing documentary records as a priori biased. Despite the efforts of some, the notion prevails that the handling of documents is the professional historian's hallmark (Scott, 1990). At the same time, the history community might think it eccentric to design a *comparative* historical study, even if it aims to assess simultaneous developments in two countries that are geographically and socially close (or rather: two European capitals with strong traditional links, roughly similar in size and cultural, economical, and political influence). There is a traditional hostility towards comparisons based on the argument that every society and its historic developments have to be unique. It is only recently that comparative historians who explicitly use social science methods to obtain insights into international and intercultural processes and structures no longer feel the need to constantly defend themselves (Siegrist, 2006; Süß, 2011).

Still, publication records show that the research communities studying comparative education and history of education do not meet often enough; there remains a division where one discipline is concerned with space and the other with time—even though there would be great benefits from more collaborative work for the understanding of influences and interactions in education. "It is essential that we should go beyond the purely local and singular, and attempt to develop connections between phenomena and problems encountered in different historical situations and in different countries and cultures" (Crook & McCulloch, 2002, p. 397).

Simultaneously, it has been convincingly argued that all historical research has always been comparative, with the *comparee* being a different time (i.e., the historian's own era) or ideal situation. Peter Burke suggests "that the two approaches, particularizing and generalizing (or historical and theoretical), complement each other, and that both of them depend on comparison, whether explicit or implicit" (Burke, 2005, p. 22). Historical analogy might even be the commonest kind of applied history, provided one acknowledges the inherent impossibility to fully explain a past event, but to be satisfied with assumptions of equivalence or correspondence; after all, "past and present are, by definition, different worlds" (Tosh, 2008, p. 62). Historical research pioneers like Adam Smith, Alexis de Tocqueville, Karl Marx, or Max Weber have all attempted cross-societal research, with John Stuart Mill contributing a methodology that remains the blueprint for most current research designs: the *method of agreement* and *indirect method of difference*. Recent commentators of Mill's work may have found fault with his reductionist explanations of causality, but especially the indirect method (where the presence of causal circumstances agrees in cases, while the absence of competing single factor explanations rules out wrong conclusions) remains a staple in comparative education (Ragin, 1987). Conscious of the ongoing discussions, we have applied a more uncontroversial research design here. A recent school of thought established comparative historical research that has "analysts ask questions about the causes of major outcomes in *particular* cases. The good of their analysis then becomes explaining adequately the *specific* outcomes in *each and every* case that falls within their argument's scope" (Mahoney & Villegas, 2007, p. 73, my italics; see also Ragin, 1987). Thus we favor the revelation of symmetries and asymmetries over predictive value judgements.

With regards to epistemology, this research follows the objectivist assumptions that always underpin positivistic research. After all, as a discipline, history seems to have overcome the "post-modernist sceptical doubts concerning the attainability of knowledge of the past" (Graf, 2003, p. 387) and once again subscribes to the idea that careful, methodological research will reveal historic facts, albeit with discursive limitations:

> [Historians] work within cultural, ideological and political parameters; some imposed, others implicit. Consequently, the stories that historians present are not value free, neutral, objective, or true. At best, they are constructed and situated truths based on historical sources…an image of the past. (Crawford & Foster, 2007, p. 7; for further discussion, see Evans, 2000; Roth & Mehta, 2002)

Central Theoretical Concepts

Since the later analysis will reference and rely on certain key concepts vital to this study, it seems prudent to propose definitions for these early on. Peter Burke suggests that historians have too long been dismissive of jargon and upheld the attitude of *gentlemanly amateurs*, while social theorists filled their science with a precise and technical vocabulary that defined phenomena in society "more precisely than their ordinary-language equivalents, and so enable finer distinctions and a more rigorous analysis" (Burke, 2005, p. 44). One central concept for history of education is that of childhood—here particularly that of interwar and wartime childhood. It would be difficult to even provide a comprehensive overview of the dramatically changing social constructions of childhood in those periods (along key discussions of children as earners or learners, of appropriate childcare and parenting, of state intervention into schooling and families, etc.) and also somewhat redundant, since Berry Mayall and Virginia Morrow have very recently and thoroughly provided just that within their study of English children's work during WWII (Mayall & Morrow, 2011). A recommendation of their work will have to suffice here.

Social Class

Class is another grand concept, and as a theoretical concept it might be the key to modern British history (Burke, 2005). This is not going to be a foolish attempt to capture all its variations, but rather a pointer to one aspect where an Anglo–German comparison needs to be particularly careful. How a society is stratified into powerful and powerless, into rich and poor, and so on, is always subject to cultural arrangements. The traditional English view seems to be that of a division into upper, middle and lower class, with wealth and property, skills and social status being qualifying criteria for belonging. Due to the slightly different set up of German society in the early twentieth century (caused by delayed industrialization, Prussia's heritage, and attempts at democracy in Weimar), going back to Max Weber's original model might be useful here: "A *social class* makes up the totality of those class situations within which individual and generational mobility is easy and typical," with the class situations being: "1. procuring goods, 2. gaining a position in life, 3. finding inner satisfactions" (Weber, 1922 /1978, p. 302). Thus the social classes are: the working class, the petty bourgeoisie, propertyless intelligentsia and specialists, the classes privileged through property and education (ibid.).

It is important to note the parity of *property* and *education* in this model, which is typical of a German society where a university professor would be considered upper class and elite, and a school teacher would automatically be considered upper middle class, irrespective of either's actual material wealth. For the study of the evacuation this will be important when discussing the German teachers' role in it: their suspicions of the anti-intellectual Nazi regime and proud autonomy from the Hitlerjugend's orders. Weber's other important distinction is that of the lower-middle classes, the petit bourgeoisie (the white collar worker, clerk, and shopkeeper) as a class of its own. This group becomes hugely relevant in the Nazi overhaul of the state. While the Weimar Republic was arguably the middle classes' (Bürgertum) attempt to monopolize political power, the Nazi regime drew its support—and subsequently favored—the petty bourgeoisie (Kleinbürger). Thus, during the 1930s, disloyal members of the intelligentsia had to surrender powerful positions in the Third Reich to loyal, but ill-equipped and ill-prepared Nazis.

Cities and Urban Population

Both London and Berlin were important political and industrial centers that had grown substantially in the hundred years prior to WWII. The two most populous European cities (although London had always nearly twice as many inhabitants than the fellow capital) had been urban settlements and administrative centers for centuries, but were subject to a real boom following the Industrial Revolution—and a diversification of their inhabitants' social statuses. Andy Green noted that the cities that grew with industrialization in the 19th century became microcosms of a dramatically changing society.

> The town became the mirror of the new society, epitomizing both its achievements and its costs. It was at once the fount of wealth and industry and a place of unparalleled misery and human degradation.... For its working-class inhabitants the town meant overcrowding, unhealthy hovels and streets made foul by open drains and contaminated air. For the middle class it meant increased anxiety as they observed the conditions of the urban working class.... Above all, it conjured up in the middle-class imagination the fearful spectre of riot and rebellion. (Green, 1990, p. 49f)

It was this fear that was partially responsible for the growing state intervention into the private lives of its citizens. While the 19th century was the time when the working class got a consciousness, it was also the time when the middle classes with their newly acquired power became conscious of the other class' existence. State schooling, free milk, and the evacuation can all be viewed against the background of the middle classes' attempt to maintain social control in the cities. Thus London in the 1930s was still subject to the tense relationship between two classes: the middle class who had the political power and self-proclaimed duty of care, and the working class who were the recipients of middle-class welfare. In Berlin, class issues were secondary to Hitler and Speer's attempts of streamlining the once vibrant and many-faceted city into the demonstrative center of Nazi power. Further specific introductions to 1930s London and Berlin can be found in Chapter 1.

State, Policy and Bureaucracy

The evasive nature of the state has been a central research topic of political and social theory. As the *apparatus of government* it has been linked to "a legally circumscribed structure of power with supreme jurisdiction over a territory" (Held, 1989, p. 11). By this definition, London more so than Berlin was subject to a dualism in state control that was exercised by the LCC locally and Whitehall nationally—after all, both city and country could be regarded as sovereign polities. Especially during the evacuation's planning stages, this power sharing would cause tension and friction—much more so than in Third Reich Berlin where the sovereignty was executed from the top, despite the country's traditional federalism.

In both cities, evacuation was a policy: a principal political decision to be turned into protocols and procedures, or to give it its more diffuse, but probably much more fitting definition: "a process rather than a product, involving negotiation, contestation or struggle between different groups who may lie outside the formal machinery of official policy making" (Ozga, 2000, p. 2). This research will show the evacuation policies to be controversial and subject to constant negotiation, modification, struggle, and public dishonesty. This policy study aims to trace how each *apparatus* planned and executed their policy in vastly differing social contexts and political climates—and what other policy decisions were affected by it. The bureaucracy was the executioner: In London this meant the civil service at the LCC, Ministry of Health, and Board of Education; in Berlin the assembled Dienststelle KLV within the NSDAP's Reichsjugendführung. Bureaucracies—administrative bodies within organizations like nation states or companies—were the result of increasingly complex forms of leadership and management brought on by industrialization and capitalism. In the early 20th century there was still an air of efficiency and rationalism about bureaucracy. Max Weber was cautiously optimistic about it being preferable to the only alternative: dilettantism ("Man hat nur die Wahl zwischen 'Brueaukratisierung' und 'Dilettantisierung'"—Weber & Winckelmann, 1980, p. 128). The question always has been: who rules the bureaucratic apparatus? Are the civil servants loyal to the government of the day, are they—as had happened in Weimar Germany—still attached to a prior government, or have they formed their own loyalties within the service regardless of the actual government? In London, Herbert Morrison, himself a dedicated administrator rather than flamboyant statesman, controlled and utilized the LCC—the city's government modeled on Whitehall—for the ambitious Labour policies of the 1930s. In Berlin, the Nazi regime had ruthlessly cleansed the state apparatus of critical or opinionated civil servants and replaced them with conformist clerks. There is no evidence that either civil service was disloyal to its political masters during the evacuation; controversies and chaos seem to have stemmed from political rivalry rather than administrative independence.

Community, Family and Citizenship

London and Berlin were heterogeneous cities with vastly differing communities. The term *community* for an interacting, but not necessarily socially or economically homogenous, population living in one location could only be applied to *quartiers* within these cities but never to the cities as a whole. This is confirmed by a new school of urban sociologists who no longer associate anonymity and isolation as the distinctive features of city dwelling, but acknowledge that cities are really a set of communities of "spontaneous, unstructured social solidarities" (Burke, 2005, p. 57, paraphrasing Turner and Durkheim). The lives of the Londoners in Chelsea and Kensington were as different (and secluded) from the ones in Poplar and Shoreditch, as those of Berliners in leafy Grunewald and decadently bourgeois Charlottenburg were from that of the inhabitants of working class districts like Wedding and Kreuzberg. However, while well-established class distinctions kept the communities apart in London—where public welfare for the paupers in the East End was improving, but still executed with condescension by the powerful middle classes and old money in the West—in Berlin the working classes had a stronger political identity (after all, they had led the 1918 revolution) and social standing. The Nazi regime favored the white- and blue-collar workers as target groups over the intellectual middle class that stood for the weak leadership of Weimar Germany. In both cities, the evacuations catered mainly to the working classes, but in London this was part of public welfare, while in Berlin the regime was very much looking after its own people.

While generic definitions of family would focus on affiliation by blood, residency, or affinity, social theory tends to see the family as a *moral community,* "an institution composed of a set of mutually dependent and complementary roles" (Burke, 2005, p. 54). How much notions of this community and its participants differed in the English social classes will be of major importance for the evacuation. While it was morally sound for middle-class families to be geographically distant (father in the City, mother in the suburbs and the children in boarding schools), working-class family members would live, work, and play in close vicinity to each other (e.g., the docks and docklands). Middle-class civil servants would find it a tough lesson to learn just how much more close-knit working class families were and how far the interdependencies in their roles went. In Nazi ideology, *family* and *family values* were important concepts—and their promotion a priority for the regime (e.g., incentives for having multiple children like the *Mutterkreuz*). At the same time, though, children on the verge of puberty would be systematically detached from their parents by one of the Hitlerjugend's branches. The party was supposed to be the children's moral community with all the allegiance and dependencies that entailed. The KLV was explicitly built on the children's emotional detachment from their parents.

Being part of a community is the essence of citizenship. According to David Held the nature of citizenship has not changed from antiquity to modern times. As a definition he proposes: "Citizenship has meant a certain reciprocity of rights against, and duties towards, the community. Citizenship has entailed membership, membership of the community in which one lives one's life. And membership has invariably involved degrees of participation in the community" (Held, 1989, p. 199).

Held points out that this definition is not to be reduced to social class alone; exclusion or inclusion in a community reflects intersectionality of other factors like gender or race as well. In London, citizenship in the 1930s would still depend on a fading notion of Empire or affiliation with a social class. The middle-class-dominated civil service were very clear on the duties expected from *its* citizens (subordinating family life to the war effort), but offered very little in terms of reciprocity. The interwar years had changed notions of citizenship away from passive and loyal subservience to a more active involvement with the national community (Myers, 1999), but still participation of the working classes in English politics only happened slowly and gradually. In Nazi Germany, a national identity or citizenship was not so much impaired by social, but by regional differences. Well aware of the diverse mentalities that occupied the rather accidental German territory, the regime keenly promoted a national, German (and racially defined) *Volksgemeinschaft* as the overruling identifier for citizenship in a way that went beyond the usual patriotism prompted by war. In Nazi ideology, other identifying features like religion, community, occupation, and political affiliation had to succumb to the greater duty of being German.

Limits and Exclusions

The most obvious restriction placed on this study, and the key to its originality, is that it does not follow the children to the reception areas. As mentioned before, there are already numerous accounts of the evacuee experience, but yet too few of the cities the evacuees left behind. Thus, the experiences of evacuees away from home will only indirectly feature here as explanations for returning or wanting to return to London or Berlin—within or outside the government schemes. The *returnees* had a major impact on the development of evacuation strategies (especially in London), and their reasons will be taken into account, but apart from that specific aspect, this research will not stray beyond the cities' boundaries.

Schoolchildren were not the only group of society that was evacuated, but for the purpose of this study they represent the ideal research topic, since their experience was in many ways more uniform than those of mothers with infants, or elderly and physically impaired adults—or indeed any civilian uprooted by the war (a third of the British population shifted geographically—officially or privately—at some point during the war—Marr, 2009). Equally, the most successful evacuation in the Third Reich was no scheme at all, but an attempt to dodge the official evacuation by making private arrangements to send children to relatives or friends in the country. Eventually, the regime accepted the nonconformists and—under the label *Verwandtenverschickung* (dispatch to relatives)—offered support with transport and billeting in order to exploit the movement in its propaganda. After all, incorporating those children meant a real boost to the numbers. Estimates show that private evacuees made up 50% of the total, whereas only close to 20% stayed in the KLV camps (Kock, 1997). The official evacuation was deliberately only for those without links to the country and the ability (or inclination) to "buy or hire safety for themselves and their dependants" (Titmuss, 1950, p. 102). For a successful comparative framework, there needs to be some uniformity in experience, which only that of schoolchildren provides. Additionally, the governments' main foci, most of the public discussion, and the media attention had always been on the official schemes for children. Thus, only those—with their comprehensive structure and available documentation—form the base of this investigation. Therefore, Andrew Marr's claim about public perception is equally true for this study: "the evacuation which really counted was the official one" (2009, p. 359).

English private schools had the opportunity to join the government scheme, but generally organized their own evacuations. London institutions would arrange to be adopted by a rural school or use alumni or parent connections to arrange accommodation in a country mansion or estate. The BoE was satisfied to be kept informed of the individual plans, so there would be no collision with regards to transport arrangements or requisitions (Gosden, 1976). David Stranack's collection of nearly 200 individual "Schools at War" (2005) shows that experiences varied greatly, but also finds unifying features: the school staff's determination to continue with education, the successful improvisation necessitated by the war, and *stiff upper lip* displayed by the youngest of Britain's elites. There is "more than one tale of schools coping admirably and philosophically with bomb-damaged classrooms and assembly halls without roofs, but when Hitler chose to drop a bomb on the playing fields and Saturday's 1st X5 rugby match had to be cancelled that truly raised the ire of the indignant English" (Stranack, 2005, p. XIII).

Gripping as the stories collected via the schools' alumni associations might be, they have no place in this study of government schemes, except to illuminate the kind of conduct the privately educated civil servants would naively expect from the children and parents from other social classes. On the German side, private schools were (and still are) extremely rare, so no mention will be made of them. There were selective and elite institutions set up by the Nationalsozialistische Deutsche Arbeiterpartei (NSDAP)—

Adolf Hitler Schulen and Napolas—but they would be evacuated, if at all, under the same system as all state schools. A reference to recent feature documentary film *Herrenkinder* (Erne & Schneider, 2009) about life in these schools will have to suffice here.

In England, overseas evacuation was—despite the comparatively low number of children actually participating—a very prominent variant of the government scheme. Organized privately by the Children's Overseas Reception Board (CORB), the prospect of sending children to safety in the Americas, South Africa, or Australia appealed particularly to affluent parents. In June 1940, CORB received 210,000 applications, but their stringent selection criteria and limited billets only led to about 2,000 children leaving England in the same month. This aspect of the evacuation created huge international press attention but was cut short by the sinking of the *City of Benares* by a German submarine on September 18, 1940. Between 73 and 83 (the number remains disputed) children died within hours, CORB seized to exist the same month, and only those daring or wealthy enough to send their children abroad privately continued the overseas evacuation (Crosby, 1986; Gosden, 1976). The German press exploited both, the fact that overseas evacuation could only be afforded by rich *plutocrats* and the carelessness of sending out ships full of children into dangerous waters. Overseas evacuation was portrayed in Berlin papers as the only evacuation happening in England, nurturing the stereotype that the British upper class criminally neglected the working class and rather sent its own children, valuables, pedigree racing horses, and dogs abroad into safety—while the NSDAP was taking particular care of the poorer sections of German society (BAZ, 24.09.1940; BNN, 14.10.1940). There should be studies of this aspect of the evacuation, but this is not it—and no further reference will be made to it.

Terminology

There does not seem to be a uniform English terminology for German institutions and policy features from the Nazi period. Some level of simplification is proposed here for general readability. Thus Nazi Germany, Third Reich, and Germany will be used synonymously. Offices and ranks/titles will be left in the original language, unless there is a well-established translation (i.e., Hitler Youth). Following Stargardt, the adjective "German" denominates the children to whom evacuation was offered, while Jewish children, despite of course also being German, are those who either emigrated, fled via *Kindertransporte*, or were persecuted in Germany. On the English side only one terminology concession applies: the terms England and Britain include Wales, but exclude Scotland and Northern Ireland, who organized and operated their own evacuation schemes independent of London.

With the evacuations subject to changes it seems useful to clarify the labels used by the administrations for different parts of it. In London there is an interrupted numeric system:

Plan I: The brief evacuation of 1,500 "handicapped" children in September 1938 as a result of the Munich Crisis

Plan II: The largest wave of the evacuation on September 1–4, 1939 (approx. 600,000 schoolchildren, mothers with infants, and other priority classes)

Plan III: was never operated

Plan IV: The second wave following the fall of the Lowlands and France on June 13–18, 1940 (approx. 100,000 schoolchildren)

Plan V: The "Trickle"—a scheme providing weekly (during the Blitz daily) departures of unaccompanied children initiated in July 1940 and suspended in November 1942. It reached approximately 64,000 children.

Plan VI: was never operated.

Plan VII: The evacuation scheme for mothers with infants and pregnant women during the Blitz. It did not affect schoolchildren and ran alongside Plan V.

Plan "Rivulet": An increase from the Trickle operated from July 1944 in reaction to the V1 and V2 attacks.

In Berlin, although there were many small changes, only the move from voluntary to compulsory evacuation created a name change.

Kinderlandverschickung: A pre-war holiday program established in the 19th century to afford poor urban children a free or subsidised holiday in the country. It has nothing to do with the evacuation and ran alongside it during the war.

Erweiterte Kinderlandverschickung (KLV): Despite its name this was the actual evacuation scheme that ran from October 1940 until the end of the war. Participation numbers are highly disputed. In the following, "Kinderlandverschickung" and 'KLV' will be used to describe the evacuation scheme.

Schulverlegung: The compulsory move of Berlin schools to reception areas ordered in autumn 1943, but only completed in April 1944—with many schoolchildren remaining in Berlin unofficially or as guests in suburban schools.

1

The Evacuations' Origins and Environments

Neither evacuation was planned and executed in a vacuum, but was influenced by the local and national political landscape, society structures, and the relationship between state and citizens. An organization of that magnitude would necessarily touch many lives and many issues. Its success would depend on the civil service's ability to organize it, the politicians' ability to convince the population of its necessity, and the urban and rural families' willingness to cooperate with it.

This chapter's purpose is to introduce the evacuations' environment. It looks at national issues (like war preparations, political and class struggles, and the organization of government) before moving on to an overview of the local situation in both capitals, including possible agents and agencies for the schemes' operation. The evacuations would have to fit in their political and social context, but they were also not invented from scratch. This chapter will also introduce prior plans and organizations that the evacuations were built on.

Operation Pied Piper, pages 1–22
Copyright © 2012 by Information Age Publishing
All rights of reproduction in any form reserved.

The State of the Nations

In England, nation building—and thus citizens' identification with the state—happened earlier than on the continent, but state schooling lagged considerably behind. Andy Green (1990, pp. 76ff, p. 110) argued the co-dependency of those developments: Precisely because citizenship had been long established in England, there was a lesser need for state schools as identity-building institutions—unlike in Prussia, where the young state was pursuing state schooling to underline Prussian dominance within the German states. In England, moves toward liberal democracy during the 19th century did not upset the stability of government, despite major changes to national and local administrations (like the 1902 Education Act). In the 1920s and 1930s, politics and public opinion focused on the aftermath of WWI, the economic crises, Irish sovereignty, the Spanish Civil War, and the 1936 abdication of Edward VIII. The royal scandal actually strengthened the position of the prime minister (then Stanley Baldwin, succeeded in 1937 by Neville Chamberlain), since his insistence on the abdication prevailed. In 1938, George VI as king and Chamberlain's Conservative government oversaw England's preparations for war. Emotionally, the multiple crises abroad led to a retreat into Englishness rather than a continuation of the Empire's grandeur; the people focused on their homes and "idealized rural landscape" in a period "where men and women in the most stable and conservative of Europe's liberal democracies became familiar with uncertainty and apprehensive of the future" (Myers, 1999, p. 313).

Dealing with Hitler's Germany proved particularly difficult for the English political class. Appeasement, now near synonymous with the name Chamberlain, has since been discussed as either the crime of *guilty men* (i.e., naïve politicians), a sensible reaction to an unpredictable German leader, or indeed the only British option at a time of economic and military inferiority. There is no space here to discuss the various revisionist and counter-revisionist views by Winston Churchill (in *Gathering Storm*, 1948), Alan Taylor, Paul Kennedy or Frank McDonough—suffice it to say that appeasement was equally contested during the late 1930s as it has been in historiography ever since. Then and now, there has been an element of myth in political thought. Politicians of the 1930s dealt in hopes and fears. Addressing a population that remembered WWI, they could summon emotional traumas and fears, making "never again!" a potent agenda for appeasement (Samuel & Thompson, 1990, p. 4). The internationalist and pacifist movements supported appeasement policies. It was the politicized working and middle classes who denounced appeasement as the illusion it was far earlier than the political elite did, thus exercising a notion of citizenship that would become important during the evacuation. It will be argued here that while the populace supported the war effort, it was not because of faith or trust in government, but rather as a compensatory power for a failing policy at the top.

Unlike the British sense of continuity, for the Germans, the first decades of the 20th century were a time of dramatic changes. Within a short time, Germans had to emotionally and economically accommodate losing WWI, the consequences of Versailles, revolution and democratization, the worldwide recession, and the political instability of the Weimar Republic that led to the rise of Adolf Hitler's NSDAP. Historians have struggled to explain the Germans' increasing public support for Hitler during the 1930s—after all, they moved from suspicious curiosity to full fledged allegiance (as displayed during the 1936 Olympic Games or party events at Nuremberg) very swiftly. In particular, social historians like Richard Evans, Ian Kershaw, Wolfgang Benz, Hans-Ulrich Wehler, or the ever-controversial Daniel Goldhagen have since come some way explaining the Germans' fascination with Fascism. Still, as a period, Nazi Germany is notoriously hard to define and explain. There is a conspicuous absence of theoretical foundations behind Hitler's state and apparatus. Marxist historian Eric Hobsbawn poignantly summarizes:

> Theory was not the strong point of [fascist] movements devoted to the inadequacies of reason and rationalism and the superiority of instinct and will. . . . Fascism cannot be identified either with a particular form of state organization, such as the corporate state—Nazi Germany lost interest in such ideas rapidly, all the more since they conflicted with the idea of a single, undivided and total *Volksgemeinschaft*, or People's Community. (Hobsbawm, 1995, p. 117; but see also Benz, 2000, p. 84, and Kohrs, 1983, p. 10)

The state formation process had thus just happened: Nazi Germany presented itself as modern and young without historical baggage save for eugenicist arguments of racial superiority. Citizenship would be emotional rather than constitutional. The absence of theoretical foundations is important, since it made it easy for the NSDAP to adapt to public opinion. The promise and later realisation of improved living standards, party organizations that structured public and (an ever decreasing) private life, and Goebbel's propaganda machinery and *Gleichschaltung* (total control over the press) are some reasons for the NSDAP's success, but they do not fully justify the enthusiasm with which Germany became antidemocratic and anti-intellectual during the 1930s. Possible explanations include the assumption that Germans were willing to trade individuality and freedom for prosperity and entertainment (there was, after all, a steady decrease of unemployment and abundant NSDAP funding for cinema, radio, and theater—Franck & Asmus, 1983). Material welfare became an important measure of stability, and the regime ensured that even in the first year of war the living standard for people in Berlin was actually higher than in previous years. The ruthless exploitation of annexed and conquered territories ensured the supply of food and goods to the capital until 1943. After that, extreme rationing began. Parks and public lawns were used to grow vegetables, and goods related to the war economy (textiles, coal) could only be bought on the thriving black market (Franck & Asmus, 1983).

The sense of belonging is crucial for the understanding of Germans in the Third Reich and this study. After all, the evacuation was built around the passionate members organized in Hitlerjugend and Bund Deutscher Mädel: party institutions that enabled (and targeted) the *petit bourgeoisie* above all to rise up, both ideologically and economically. The NSDAP sold itself as the party of the disenfranchised, and their successes with this part of the population, at the obvious expense of others, created loyal standard bearers. The majority of Germans entered the war supporting their government (by now entirely personified in Adolf Hitler), believing that war was justified and hoping that it would not be of long duration. The early successes of the Blitzkrieg in late 1939 and early 1940 seemed to confirm those sentiments—whereas the arrival of British bombers in Berlin in August 1940 took the capital's inhabitants very much by surprise.

Germany at that time was subject to somewhat parallel governments, with ministries and state officials on one side and the overpowering NSDAP with its organizations and executives on the other. Hitler and his inner circle structured and restructured the state apparatus ad hoc to suit their immediate needs. Ian Kershaw argues that most of the war was improvised on the German side, that Hitler was "powerless to prevent the governance of the Reich from slipping increasingly out of control" (2000, p. 311). The evacuation will be subject to the same power sharing problems as the rest of the state apparatus: the unresolved dualism of NSDAP and state, the overlapping spheres of competence, the improvised special authorities, the "administrative anarchy" (ibid).

The KLV might have been based on the infrastructure of charitable institutions from the Kaiserreich and Weimar Republic, but it became in design and ambition a Nazi concept. German historians now assume that there were no serious preparations for evacuation before the year 1940, which means the period under scrutiny falls completely into the war years, not the whole of the Third Reich. By 1940, any administrator not fully committed to the Nazi cause would have been removed from office and replaced by a younger, more loyal colleague who knew which party to thank for the early advancement. The evacuation might have been initiated spontaneously; it still had its roots in the work of the HJ and the ideological framework of Nazi youth policy. Part of that policy was the eradication of privacy in the name of community spirit. While British families might have seen a government scheme for their children as an intrusion into their privacy, Germans at that point were well used to leading public lives: accounting for their existence and behavior to county council, charitable organizations, and neighbors.

HJ and BdM competed with the schools for time and influence over the children. While schools remained comparatively immune to the Nazi ideology, HJ and BdM successfully indoctrinated the children with a quasi-military attitude, while upholding the appeal of a romantic, slightly rebellious youth group that provided status symbols and a sense of belonging (Huber & Müller, 1964). For the history of German childhood, the importance of these party-run youth organizations cannot be overrated. The majority of German children and young adults enthusiastically joined the HJ and supported it wholeheartedly throughout (Huber & Müller, 1964; Tofahrn, 2003). Party-organized youth activities were also generally very popular with parents. For one, HJ and BdM kept the children occupied and off the streets, but they also did a lot of charitable work that was widely appreciated. Through popular youth work and almost by stealth, the NSDAP succeeded to adapt children to their ideology: "Eine Jugend von klein zu blindem Glauben erzogen, von klein auf in Uniform gesteckt und zu militärischem Gehorsam gedrillt, das war das Ideal der nationalsozialistischen Erziehung (Ideal Nazi education envisaged a youth that from infancy onwards wore a uniform, was uncritical in their beliefs, and exercised military obedience)" (Huber & Müller, 1964, p. 168).

The NSDAP's near unlimited access to the children—even while still voluntary in 1934, over half of all eligible youngsters had joined the HJ, giving it a membership of three and a half million (Tofahrn, 2003)—and their success in manipulating them became an important feature of the evacuation. When the decision to evacuate was reached in September 1940, its operation was naturally entrusted to the HJ rather than the suspiciously autonomous and unmanageable teachers.

Both England and Germany subscribed early to the idea of professional administration by the state apparatus. Political and economic life had become more complex and differentiated in the early 20th century, and bureaucratic administration became more crucial. In both societies, interwar Britain and Nazi Germany, citizens had increased demands upon the state: "Not only were the newly enfranchised asking more of the state in areas such as education and health, but they were also asking for uniformity of treatment between persons with similar categories of need" (Held, 2006, p. 132). This policy study has to consider both the civil services' new and changing roles as well as the public acceptance of their providence. Both societies experienced bureaucratic intrusion on an unprecedented level in the period under investigation here. An interesting comparison from the field of economics might shed more light on differing attitudes to state provision. A recent commentary on Paul Einzig's seminal 1939 book *Economic Problems of the Next War* (Imlay, 2007) draws attention to his claim that totalitarian systems like the German Reich had the advantage over democratic systems like Britain when it came to disciplined war preparations. While Germans at that point were already conditioned to accept interventionist policies into their lives, British (and French) people would be more resistant to overburdening government influence. According to Talbot Imlay, Einzig's view was widely shared at the time, especially in England, where it added to the fear of being inadequately prepared for war.

This is mainly a local study, with clearly defined boundaries: the city borders of London and Berlin. The next sections briefly introduce the state of the cities at the outbreak of war, concepts of evacuation that were used by the cities' (or in Berlin's case, party's) planners and—because of the unique German competition over children by different agents—an overview of state schooling in the Third Reich.

The Cities

London Before the War

> *London—the world's most unmissable target, so densely packed with people at its core*
> —White, 2001, p. 38

That London's evacuation was a state-run operation is symptomatic of the changes in administration of the interwar and war years—times of transition and reform initiated by the experiences of WWI, worldwide economic turmoil, and Britain's changing role as a world power. During the late Victorian and Edwardian period, governments started to gain knowledge of their populous by ways of census data, surveys, mass schooling, and the newly developed child study movement, which during the first decade of the new century led to government acts on school feeding, school medical inspections, and education (Hendrick, 2007). There was a move away from individualist towards collectivist solutions of social problems. In the interwar years, the government aimed to control and influence the habits of its citizens—and found that it could gain access to families via their children.

Political stability was the main benefit of this new, nurturing attitude. At a time of radicalization and political turmoil in most of Europe, the civil society in the United Kingdom did not break down and successfully shunned extremism. Children—while not being the major focus of government policies—gradually became the objects of social welfare intervention, and the evacuation can be seen as the result and proof of the state's increased level of care.

Children and parents did not necessarily appreciate the government's increased attention during the interwar years, though. Middle-class mothers might have on the whole already adopted the new loving, permissive, child-focused approach, but among the working classes, strict, traditional child-rearing persisted well into the 1940s (Hendrick, 1997). Some working-class children did not understand the attempts to delay their access to adulthood (like compulsory schooling or working restrictions); they looked forward to adult life and to contributing to the family income, "for by the start of the Second World War, childhood had not yet been firmly defined as a period in which children are first and foremost learners, in schools" (Mayall & Morrow, 2011, pp. 2–3). Truancy was especially high in London, where the *school board men* (attendance officers—the term was officially abandoned in 1904, but lived on in the vernacular) had to use threats and court summons to get the children into the schools (Hendrick, 1997).

Between 1890 and the outbreak of the Second World War, London's population grew from 5,638,000 to 8,700,000 (Porter, 1994), ensuring that London remained the biggest city on Earth—even though other metropolises like Berlin, Paris, Tokyo, and New York grew substantially in the same period. London was not only the seat of government and focal point of the British Isles, but also of the vast British Empire. The companies in the City guaranteed that more than half the world's international trade was financed through London (Ziegler, 1995). Unlike previous growths in its population, though, this time London spread out into the suburbs. The first decades of the 20th century saw a major population move from urban slums to suburbia. Between 1911 and 1939, growth happened entirely outside the LCC boundaries (Porter, 1994). This expansion was only possible due to planned public transport for the longer commute. Underground railways had been around since 1863 (the Metropolitan railway from Paddington to Farringdon), but the new power sources—electricity and petrol—accelerated the building of a dense underground network that by 1932 already resembled the current tube map. In 1933, the various local train providers were organized as the London Passenger Transport Board (L.P.T.B.). The port of London and the growing number of manufacturing businesses provided a lot of the employment, while the West End established itself as the location for London's nightlife. Politically, the 1930s saw the rise of fascism in the metropolis, epitomized by Sir Oswald Mosley's rallies and the Cable Street incident in London's East End in 1936. When the prospect of war became more real for Londoners and its government, the political agenda shifted: "London in 1939 was not merely the greatest city in the world; its rulers believed it to be the most threatened and the most vulnerable" (Ziegler, 1995, p. 8).

It was the historical precedents that raised the fear level in London. Most politicians and civil servants would still remember the (comparatively tame) Zeppelin and Gotha raids on London 1915–1918, but more recent events from around the world brought the dangers of air raids home to the Londoners via the daily press: the 1935–1936 Italian poison gas attacks on Abyssinia, the 1937–1938 Japanese bombing of Shanghai, and the 1937 German bombing of Guernica. In panic, the government grossly overestimated the casualties of the next war, predicting that 4,000 would die in London within the first 48 hours of war (in reality there were "only" 30,000 London casualties in five years of war; Inwood, 1998). More outrageous predictions calculated 58,000 dead after the first Luftwaffe strike (White, 2001). Fire— London's old nemesis—was the top concern among Air Raid Precaution (A.R.P.) planners. Thousands were recruited for the fire brigade and the auxiliaries, but that did not solve the planners' biggest problem: the shortage of water. Another main issue was the expected mass hysteria and public disorder. To tackle this, crowd control experts were brought in from India, and troops drafted for riot control (Inwood, 1998).

The LCC and its charismatic chairman, the Labour politician Herbert Morrison, ruled the city. Established in 1889, the LCC succeeded the Metropolitan Board of Works with the aim to reform local government. By 1939, the LCC gained a reputation as a "smooth-running bureaucratic machine of limitless capacity" (Saint, 1989, p. ix). Its councillors ran the LCC in line with respective party politics. After WWI, the London Labour Party rapidly gained influence, becoming the main opposition to the Conservatives, before coming to power in 1934 and increasing their majority again in the elections in 1937. In those years, Labour pursued an ambitious agenda, using the income from ratepayers to increase financial assistance for education, health, and social welfare—while at the same time improving the transport for the city. The demolition and rebuilding of Waterloo Bridge became a symbol for the determination and decisiveness of Labour and Herbert Morrison (Saint, 1989).

It has been argued that London in 1938 was Morrison's city more than anything. He branded the LCC and London with his governance, his desire for tidiness, and administrative efficiency. Throughout his time at County

Hall, he was under pressure to show that Labour was fit to govern while being confronted with a Conservative central government for which he had only contempt and which he considered unable to cooperate on issues concerning the metropolis (Donoughue & Jones, 1973). Furthermore, there was the constant threat of a vacuum created by the confusing power sharing between Whitehall and County Hall, elected politicians and civil servants, between governmental departments and ad hoc advisory committees. It was Morrison who relentlessly pushed the capital's A.R.P. and evacuation plans up on the national agenda, trying to expose the Air Ministry's hunger for resources and power as obstacles to more sensible measures (Lowndes, 1969). As a representative of local authorities, he fought the Home Office on the issue of financing the A.R.P. measures from 1935 to 1937, eventually emerging successful in persuading the government to pay up to 85% of the total costs. By mid-1938, Morrison was again frustrated by the Home Office's inability to decide on evacuation plans and its refusal to make use of the advanced planning by the LCC and its ready and willing staff (Donoughue & Jones, 1973).

Schooling in London had already undergone substantial reforms when Labour came to power in 1934. When the LCC took over from the London School Board in 1904, it recognized that education differed in many ways from other municipal services. As a result, the role of Education Officer was created, "thus doing away with the artificial separation of administration from professional advice" (Maclure, 1990, p. 82). The first holder of the post, Robert Blair, was crucial in fashioning the role of the Education Officer as a major player within the LCC. Working in the shadow of an (often conservative) national government, the interwar years were used to improve rather than to fundamentally change the existing system of confusingly varied—and occasionally seriously overcrowded and under-resourced—elementary, senior elementary, trade, municipal secondary, and grammar schools. It was a time when multilateralism and comprehensive schooling was considered and advanced in London, but the efforts of its promoters were blocked by the Education Officer (Blair's protégée) Edmund M. Rich's own conservative belief in the tiered system (Maclure, 1990). While other cities already viewed the provision of education "as a mechanism for social justice, as a means for the creation of wealth and opportunity and, ultimately . . . a source of civic pride" (Grosvenor & Myers, 2006, p. 244), Rich promoted an education system that should provide schooling on the base of the children's likely future role in society. A slight, if somewhat unimpressive, increase in secondary education in London was recorded (Maclure, 1990), but real reform was not attempted for fear of opposition from central government, financial constraints during the depression, and ultimately the outbreak of war. Eighty-eight percent of children were catered to by the elementary schools in 1938 and would leave school with or without examination success at age 14—and with little knowledge beyond basic numeracy and literacy (Simon, 1991). Within the existing system of schooling, the London Labour Party attempted to improve the most pressing issues like school-leaving age, class sizes, resources, and fees, but had to acknowledge that equality in education "was defined in meritocratic terms, rather than in . . . more egalitarian forms" (Saint, 1989, p. 165). With regard to the later plans for the evacuation, though, it is noteworthy that all schoolchildren were treated equally irrespective of their and their school's location or situation.

Berlin Before the War

Undoubtedly, Berlin was an impressive metropolis, but it never matched London in importance or size. Even under Nazi rule, Germany maintained its traditional geographic and political federalism, with Hamburg, Dresden, Munich, Stuttgart, and the cities along the Rhine being capitals in their own rights. By the 1920s, Berlin had become a cultural hotbed for architecture, literature, drama, and film. The capital attracted artists and academics alike—W.H. Auden wrote about Berlin, Carl Jung developed analytical psychology there, and Albert Einstein served as director of the Kaiser Wilhelm Society. Berlin during the Roaring Twenties was famous for its nightlife—but also an easy target for philistine critics like the Nazis who labeled it decadent and *undeutsch* (not German). Criticism eagerly constructed connections between the morally reprehensible cultural life and the large Jewish community. A third of the German Jews, approximately 170,000, had settled in Berlin and became the subject of increasing anti-Semitism (DHM, 2011).

It is important to note that Berlin was not the original Nazi stronghold. The party had grown mainly in rural areas, especially in Bavaria. Until 1933, Berlin was dismissed as either too bourgeois or too communist—but after Hitler's ascent to power, the Nazis tried to make the capital their own. By 1940, Berlin's allure of the Roaring Twenties had been replaced by Hitler's megalomaniac plans for Berlin as the administrative nerve center of the Reich. WWII interrupted his and Albert Speer's plans to completely transform multifaceted Berlin into the uniform *Welthauptstadt Germania*. Cultural Gleichschaltung led to conformist mass entertainments—and for the Nazis these included marches, parades, and political rallies. The 1936 Olympic Games had showcased Berlin's new role: big, clean, Aryan, and well organized. Whatever was left of the vibrant, anarchic nightlife had moved underground or into private homes.

In Berlin, the *petit bourgeoisie* had replaced the *Bürgertum* (middle class) as the dominant cultural force. "The NSDAP was a lower-middle-class phenomenon and hence a kind of petit bourgeois revolution" (Rempel, 1989, p. 5). The Weimar Republic stood for the shame of Versailles, indecisive democrats, libertine excesses and economic turmoil and, as such, did not possess the mass appeal of the NSDAP, a party that fitted their policies to prevailing public opinion, made ludicrous promises (on the back of an unsustainable war economy), and ruthlessly silenced political opposition with any means necessary. The NSDAP provided the infrastructure for daily and cultural life: Its various organizations and their members dominated life in Berlin in much the same way they would later dominate the evacuation. This study is therefore less concerned with the official administration of the city, but rather with the party organizations that wielded—by the grace of their near omnipotent Führer—the real power. After all, there was still a mayor of Berlin, but by 1940 his role was almost purely ceremonial. The party's Gauleiter (district executive) Dr. Joseph Goebbels and his deputy Artur Görlitzer were in charge of political and administrative decisions (Hartl & Knopp, 1999).

Before the Evacuations

Origins of Evacuation in England and Wales

During the 1930s, the rise of Hitler was not the only geopolitical event that triggered the British perception of an impending war. News coverage of the Spanish Civil War and the arrival of Spanish evacuees in Britain from 1936 onwards (see also Myers, 1999) illustrated that future wars with their blanket bombings would have a much bigger, devastating impact on the civilian population than previous ones—and that the government's preparation and alertness would be vital for the protection of the most vulnerable members of society (for an elaboration on the changes of the new warfare for civilians see Süß, 2011). The people expected their government to make arrangements for their safety in those unstable times. Whatever the government's real motives for evacuation might have been—Titmuss suggested that it was a mere military expedient, a counter weapon to the air raid's intention of demoralizing the population and thus part of the ideas of modern warfare (Titmuss, 1950, p. 23)—there were also suggestions that evacuation was necessary to prevent a situation where "after bombing the poor would flock to the wealthier areas and loot them wholesale" (Brown, 2005, p. 2). In public statements, the emphasis would be on humanitarian aspects and concerns about the army's transport networks becoming unusable during private flights from London.

Origins of evacuation plans can be traced back to 1803. During the Napoleonic wars, the threat of invasion led to the development of emergency protocols for the coastal towns on the Channel with detailed plans for the register, transport, and accommodation of inhabitants "not desired by Government Service" drawn up by some parishes (*Times*, 21.03.1939). Following WWI, the fear of invasion by boat was replaced by the threat of air raids, which made London particularly vulnerable. Already in 1923, the government entrusted the *Committee of Imperial Defence*, an advisory body founded in 1904, with the design of the country's A.R.P. From 1924 to 1935, the A.R.P. committee worked on the development of auxiliary fire brigades, barrage balloons, and inner city trenches. For this study, the work of the committee becomes relevant on July 9 1935, when a circular drawn up by the committee and published by the Home Office invited suggestions from local authorities for their wartime measures. This circular had a major impact, as it was the first public admission of the government's hitherto secret preparations for the event of war (Crosby, 1986)—and was subsequently hotly debated in parliament and the press, with the main accusation being that it intentionally "has been issued to the civilian population to prepare them for war" (Manchester *Guardian*, 17.07.1935). No political party was in favor of war; liberal and socialist forces were still shell-shocked by the sudden rise of populist, aggressive, and authoritarian movements on the continent, while the conservatives "may not have been concerned with fighting Fascism, but they were very much concerned with the problem of fighting Germany, and in view of the appalling disparity of air power they felt in no condition to do so yet" (Howard, 1981, p. 103).

Nevertheless, over the next three years, various A.R.P. measures were published and discussed, notably the Air Raid Precautions Act from December 1937 that initiated the Board of Education's circular 1461 from January 1938, which dealt with the protection of children in the event of war and suggested that local authorities should consider the evacuation of children from particularly vulnerable areas to safer districts. It is then that "London's part in the story begins in 1938. Before that year the Council had no occasion to think about evacuation" (L.C.C., 1943, I 2).

Schools Under the Nazis

There had not been major changes in education and schooling in the transition from the Prussia-led Kaiserreich to the Weimar Republic. Humboldt's concept of compulsory, tiered and comprehensive schools had been well established by 1900, and for new governments, education was not a priority. The vast majority of students attended state schools, where they studied a varied curriculum with a strong emphasis on the sciences. However, dramatic changes to the construction and experience of childhood and schooling came with the change of political power in 1933—although not to all. Those schools that had preserved their traditional, nationalistic stance during revolutionary Weimar and got shunned then by the officials were not of immediate interest to the NSDAP since they were already ideologically close (Goldberg, 1994, p. 256). Hitler's NSDAP understood itself to be the party of youth, made propaganda and education their priority, and pursued explicitly anti-intellectual and anti-science policies (Bracher, 1969). Schools were suddenly forced to provide less academic and more vocational curricula, with a return to mainly physical activities for boys and home economics for girls.

The NS regime regarded schools and academic instruction as anachronistic and dangerous. To them it was a liberal and bourgeois legacy of a bygone era (Kock, 1997)—and they had not been really successful in penetrating the institution anyway. Wolfgang Benz argued that mainstream schools (but not the Nazi elite boarding schools *Napolas* and *Adolf Hitler Schulen*) were not places of systematic indoctrination (Benz, 2000). Teachers, who had themselves been educated under the Kaiser or in Weimar Germany, were reluctant to accept the Nazi anti-intellectualism and to implement the new curricula. Major changes were prescribed for history (the glorification of Germany's Aryan past) and biology (*Rassenkunde*—race education), but there is evidence that the inhumanity and irrationality of Nazi ideology did not reach the children in the same intensity at school as it did in the HJ. In reaction, the official education policy was built less on offensive strategies and more on slow habituation. After all, while *Rassenkunde* might have been a genuinely new subject, there were already ample nationalistic and racial tendencies left over from Weimar Germany—the NS education ministry just needed to adjust them to the new demands. Additionally, it provided a space for collective rituals (assemblies, flag salutes) in schools. The party thus provided symbols and public acknowledgement to the grateful adolescents at an age when their search for meaning was at its most desperate—and ensured their lasting loyalty (Franck & Asmus, 1983). Indoctrination was emotional rather than intellectual: Children should experience the new ideology, not understand it. Collective rituals like singing, shouting, saluting were all tools for the near religious experience of Nazism (Goldberg, 1994).

Long before the evacuation, Berlin's schoolchildren felt the impact of war. From September 1939 onwards, sports halls were no longer available for PE, but commandeered for use as grain sheds. From January 1940, almost all schools closed for a few weeks due to coal shortage, and at the same time it became apparent that, despite a surplus in financial funding, it became almost impossible to get books and exercise books (Giles, 1992). The war entered the curriculum as well: quickly run-off pamphlets (replacing textbooks) painted a picture of an aggressive England responsible for war. The propaganda claimed that the English would not accept the Germans' right to live and wanted to monopolize riches and power. Germany was only defending itself by conquering foreign countries (Franck & Asmus, 1983).

The competition between schools and HJ was never between equals. The HJ got all the support from the government, while the Ministry of Education was sidelined. Schoolchildren and teachers were thus subject to a confusing duality: While the education ministry was officially in charge, it became very obvious that the power shifted towards the party's HJ and NSLB. In order to understand the NSDAP's access to children, one has to therefore look beyond the schools to the branches of the party.

Origins of the Kinderlandverschickung—HJ, NSLB, and NSV

When looking at the origins of Berlin's evacuation, it is important to acknowledge where the real executive power lay. The city's local administration had to accept a supporting role in the evacuation, whereas the party's organizations ran it. So complete was the Nazi grip on Berlin's governance that the local clerks and politicians uncritically followed the NSDAP's lead. This chapter will therefore look at these Nazi organizations rather than the city's civil service or elected officials. Nevertheless, it must be understood that what follows is only the briefest of introductions; either organization's history is complex enough to fill this volume.

Hitlerjugend and Bund deutscher Mädel

> The Hitler Youth is not a Boy Scout or Girl Guide organization. It is in no respect comparable to any organization for young people known to the Western World. It is a compulsory Nazi formation, which has consciously sought to breed hate, treachery and cruelty into the mind and soul of every German child. It is, in the true sense of the word, "education for death". Under no circumstances should the Hitler Youth be taken lightly or be considered a negligible factor from an operational or occupation point of view. (from the Allied Expeditionary Force Handbook. MIRS London Branch, 1944, p. 6)

The NSDAP's most prominent organization, the HJ, became the largest youth organization ever created in Germany. Founded in 1926, the HJ started as one of many youth organizations, most of them substantially larger and older (church, workers', or scouting associations). A key HJ principle was *Jugend führt Jugend* (youth leads youth), which led to boys and girls only a few years older than the participants running the meetings, drills, and activities. Many aspects of the organization had military origins: Members of the HJ wore uniform (everywhere), swore allegiance and loyalty to the Führer during flag salutes, learned to march, played sports very competitively, were part of a strict hierarchy, and demonstrated their sense of belonging by snubbing non-members. By the beginning of 1933, the HJ had 100,000 members, but after Hitler seized power there was a large increase in membership due to propaganda, incorporation of other groups, and the wholesale ban of all competing organizations. Like the NSDAP monopolized politics, the HJ monopolized youth. Since the 1936 introduction of the *Jugenddienstpflicht*, there was a quasi-compulsion to join, and by 1939, the HJ had over seven million members. Virtually every German child would be organised in one of the HJ's branches: the actual Hitlerjugend, Jungvolk, Bund deutscher Mädel and Jungmädelbund (motto: *Wir helfen!*— we're helping!). In 1939, membership in the Hitlerjugend (for boys aged 14–18) was 1.7 million, with an additional 2.1 million in the Jungvolk (DJ— for boys aged 10-14); 1.5 million girls aged 14 to 17 were members in the Bund deutscher Mädel, with another 1.9 million younger members in the Jungmädelbund (JM—for girls aged 10–14) (Kinz, 1991).

The Bund deutscher Mädel, the League of German Girls (BdM), founded in 1930, was the female version of the HJ. Both groups recruited their members from their junior partners: boys aged 10–14 would join the Deutsches Jungvolk (DJ), doing activities similar to boy scouts today, and girls the same age would join the Jungmädelbund (JM). Even younger children were already participating in *Kindergruppen der NS-Frauenschaft* (Nazi women's associations' groups for children). Ideally—from the point of the regime—there would be a supervised succession from childhood to adulthood, with every step monitored by an NSDAP organization. Transition points (entry into HJ at 14 and NSDAP at 18) would be celebratory, public events.

Less outwardly military, the BdM's focus was on useful and fun group activities like arts, crafts, sports, and excursions. Overall, the organization seemed to have offered a sense of belonging without the pressure that the boys were exposed to in the HJ (Klaus, 1985). Nevertheless, the BdM did not disguise its ulterior military ambitions: Already in 1932, pamphlets were entitled *Fight with Us!* They promoted joining the Nazi organization as an alternative to becoming a superficial fashion dummy that only cared about cinema, dances, and pulp fiction. Despite all its useful activities, though, the BdM supported the Nazi view of motherhood as any woman's ultimate ambition—but simultaneously offered the girls a greater level of independence than their families would (Goldberg, 1994).

Third Reich ideology constituted a major setback from the Weimar Republic in terms of gender equality. Nazi Germany was a *Männergesellschaft* (male-dominated society) that promoted marriage and motherhood. This dogma became increasingly hard to uphold when the war began to demand working women. By necessity, the NS' image of womanhood had to be flexible—for example, in the early 1930s, women were discouraged from attending universities to avoid overcrowding, but when the dismissal of Jewish staff and students as well as reduced birth rates led to empty lecture halls, the propaganda went into full swing in favor of academic women (Goldberg, 1994). The BdM was involved in the war effort in many arenas and prepared girls to fill the vacancies in the factories or trained them for nursing duty (Goldberg, 1994). There were hardly any women in high positions within the regime; the highest-ranking female official was fanatic Nazi Gertrud Scholtz-Klink, the leader of the Nazi woman's association (Benz, 2000). BdM leader and psychologist Dr Jutta Rüdiger was one of the few women in power, but still hierarchically positioned well beneath the men governing the Hitlerjugend.

Despite its popularity (and its actual greater involvement in the evacuation), the BdM never emancipated itself from the HJ. In the male-dominated, sexist Third Reich (Kinz, 1991), the BdM had to mirror the paramilitary HJ structure, while the men of the Reichsjugendführung made all the key decisions—and took all the credit. Publicly the HJ was the executive body of the KLV, whereas in reality only a minority of children were in camps. The majority—especially children too young for the KLV camps—were under the supervision of NSV and BdM in billets. The BdM (despite a membership of 1.5 million, plus the 2 million affiliated in the JM) continuously struggled with "reale Bedeutungslosigkeit" (real insignificance—Klaus, 1985, p. 114) within the NS regime—and the historiography's emphasis on the boy's HJ might have further promoted a distorted view of the organizations' importance (Buddrus, 2003, p. 887).

As with the adults, the NSDAP targeted children of lower middle and working class backgrounds most successfully. The uniforms and merit-based paramilitary activities acted as social levellers; success within the HJ hierarchy could be achieved by anyone regardless of background, provided they belonged to the *gesunder Volkskörper* (literally: healthy body of the people). Furthermore, the HJ sponsored trips and excursions, which for many working-class children who grew up during the recession meant the first opportunity of a holiday. More pragmatic reasons to voluntarily join the HJ would be considerations for their own future career or their parents' current one. Even despite the later compulsion, the youth organization and its activities were popular. Apart from the attractive breadth of activities offered, the HJ's main attraction was its structure. Unlike schools, where children always were subordinated to authoritarian teachers, the HJ offered its young members attainable positions of authority. "Unlike family, church and school, the HJ was not weighed down by tradition and taboos and seemed to offer an exciting opportunity for young people to be respected and responsible" (Kater, 2004, p. 1).

Within a few years, the HJ managed to become the third authority over young people in Germany, competing with parents and school for their time and minds (Noakes, 1998, p. 397). Academic education was not an HJ priority, though. Instead, it subjected their members to a variety of communal—and charitable—tasks like helping with the harvest, collection of medicinal herbs, and raising money for the *Winterhilfswerk* (winter aid). Physical exercise, preferably outdoors, was an important part of the after-school activities. After September 1939, the tasks were closer linked to the war effort, like collecting recyclables (bones, scrap metal, conkers, pumpkin seeds, glass), knitting for the soldiers, or combat training for the boys' future in the army.

> Anti-Nazi parents might fear the Hitler Youth for its ideological indoctrination of the young, and both parents and teachers might resent its challenge to their authority, but precisely these things often appealed to the young themselves. With their dichotomy between good and evil, their appeal to feeling and their demand for moral commitment, Nazi values could have been designed for adolescents, and it was among this group of the German population that their purchase would last longest during the Second World War. (Stargardt, 2005, p. 33)

The HJ had long been preparing their members for war, but the outbreak still took them by surprise. Buddrus summarizes that a "zielgerichtet und planlos" (purposeful but desultory) HJ might have been ready for war in 1939, but not for a war actually starting in 1939 (Buddrus, 2003, p. 2). Thus the HJ, like most of the regime and officials, improvised along an unfolding war: There were no detailed plans or concepts. Just before the evacuation's initiation, the organization faced a twofold leadership crisis. At the very top, Arthur Axmann succeeded Baldur von Schirach on August 3, 1940 as Reichsjugendführer, a change that came as a surprise at the time, since Schirach was not only the HJ's public face, but also its architect. That he wished to leave the position in favor of the less prestigious post of governor of Vienna has never been fully explained, but his departure left the HJ

rudderless (especially since Schirach took with him competent deputy Hartmann Lauterbacher). Axmann was Schirach's choice of successor, a good
organizer and strong candidate for the post, but no real competitor for Schirach's legacy. Historians judged him as a mere administrator of Schirach's estate (Buddrus, 2003). The second aspect of the leadership crisis arose from
the HJ principle of youth leading youth. Ninety-five percent of instructors,
who were only a little older than their charges, had been drafted for army
service by mid-1940 (Buddrus, 2003). At grass-roots level, the organization
was handed to younger and younger leaders, who neither had the experience nor authority to cope (an aspect that will become important for the
evacuation's forced relationship of teachers and HJ leaders in camps).

Within the regime, the HJ was a priority and never short of funding.
Its key functions, to naturalize young people to the NS-state and neutralize
their parents' influence, served the party and the war effort simultaneously.
For a long time, the HJ had instilled a mentality of *Opferbereitschaft* (self-
sacrifice) into the young that during the war would produce loyal soldiers
who valued honor and honorable death above anything. It was against the
background of a very organized youth constantly exposed to Nazi ideology
and propaganda that the evacuation's organizers decided their marketing
strategy. Unlike London, where appeals were made to responsible parents,
Berlin would target the young people directly. The KLV was to be their big
adventure and not a cowardly flight from the city.

The German evacuation experience was inextricably linked to the HJ,
and no similar organization existed (or exists) in England. There had been
youth groups for a long time (YMCA 1844, YWCA 1855, Boy Scouts 1907,
Girl Guides 1910), but none monopolized childhood in the way the HJ
did. However, there were attempts in England to copy the successful youth
movements from totalitarian states. The 1937 Physical Training and Recreation Act ordered LEAs to introduce activities for the 14–20 year olds.
Compulsory registration was considered in 1941 and introduced with little
opposition soon after. The program, under the auspice of the Ministry of
Labor, never left the ground, though, since the war caused a shortage of
supervisors for the activities (Gosden, 1976).

Nationalsozialistischer Lehrerbund

Compared to the youthful appeal of the HJ, state schools became to be
seen as an anachronism. The Nazi regime never managed to fully reform
or even control state schooling, but not for lack of trying. Already in 1929,
the NSDAP founded the Nazi teachers' association Nationalsozialistischer
Lehrerbund (NSLB) that 97% of teachers of all types of schools had joined

by 1936. Through the NSLB, the party exercised power and pressure on staffing and curriculum.

Teacher shortages became a major issue during the 1930s. The Nazi regime—and especially the HJ—had reduced a profession that once commanded highest public esteem in Prussia to mouthpieces of its ideology—and publicly dismissed schools as obsolete (Buddrus, 2003). Teachers began to feel the "heaping derision" and that they no longer were the role models they used to be (Giles, 1992, p. 19). The loss in social standing paired with the increasing demand for a literate commercial workforce during the post-recession boom years led to many teachers leaving the profession for higher-paid office jobs. In 1938, there was a shortage of 3,000 teachers in Prussia's territory alone (Franck & Asmus, 1983). Those still working in schools had arranged themselves with the regime (or had been long replaced with party loyals). The NSLB organized workshops to (re)educate teachers about new subjects and desirable content. These workshops were blatantly military, with teachers donning uniform and doing group- and character-building exercises outdoors for weeks. Foreign languages were no longer taught in the Volksschule. Still, resistant schools and teachers got some backing by industry and commerce in the late 1930s. Their representatives publicly complained about the lowering of standards, academic inadequacies in school graduates, and the time pressures on the children imposed by the HJ (Franck & Asmus, 1983).

The Bayreuth-based NSLB gained influence, because the regime—especially the admiralty—thought it to be more efficient in accessing and changing teaching in schools than the responsible ministry: the Reichserziehungsministerium. Bernhard Rust, the education minister for the whole of the NS period, was a loyal Nazi, but regarded as weak and incompetent by his fellows. Goebbels and others in the Reichsleitung increasingly challenged his authority by deciding education issues over his head. In contrast, the NSLB, headed by Fritz Wächtler, who was also the party's chief educationalist, was seen as the future of school politics (Kock, 1997). Nevertheless, the association managed to marginalize itself in the course of the war. The NSLB struggled to maintain a grip on its administration and finances but failed. In 1943, the NSDAP treasury effectively—and amid little protest—shut the association down (Schäffer, 2010).

Within the evacuation the NSLB became responsible for the assignment, support, and supervision of teachers. The association oversaw the staffing of the camps, but also the teaching content. Although locked in a permanent rivalry with the HJ about supremacy over the running of the camps, both party organizations together succeeded in taking away from the state a large part of the control over state education—which for Germany was a historic precedent (Kock, 1997).

Nationalsozialistische Volkswohlfahrt and the Original Kinderlandverschickung

Started as a self-help group in Berlin in 1932, the Nationalsozialistische Volkswohlfahrt (NSV) became the regime's social welfare organization, growing to 17 million members by 1943. The NSV aimed to centralize all charitable work and was a direct competition to the churches and the Red Cross, whose influence it curtailed and reduced. The NSV gained unique access to the population by its all-encompassing activities, including *Winterhilfswerk*, medical care, kindergartens, nursing, shelter for air raid victims, and the provision and distribution of food (DHM, 2010b). Especially the *Winterhilfswerk*'s ability to raise money through door-to-door runs, street collections and the access to lottery grants and corporate donations made it a major financier of the NSV and thus the evacuation. The NSV's biggest branch, the *Hilfswerk Mutter und Kind*, offered recreational stays in the country to mothers and children. By 1942, five million urban children had been sent for short stays to rural areas by the NSV. The infrastructure put in place for that (local staff and offices everywhere) would become a backbone of the government's evacuation scheme.

However, the NSV—as a Nazi brainchild—offered its charity only to a select group. German (read: Aryan) families whose members were healthy enough to still contribute to society were cared for; alcoholics, ex-prisoners, delinquents, and of course Jewish people were not. As a welfare organization affiliated with the NSDAP, it closely followed the socio-Darwinist Nazi ideology. Nevertheless, Kock (1997) claims that the NSV never became as powerful and influential as its size and money would have suggested, since the Nazi rulers remained ideologically ambivalent to the concept of charity.

The evacuation's spontaneous and rushed set-up in October 1940 was only possible because the NSV's extensive transport, staffing, and accommodation infrastructure for the peacetime Kinderlandverschickung (KLV) had already been in place for nearly a decade. Georg Braumann's (2004) comprehensive introduction to the original KLV sheds light on its roots and developments. Already in 1872, a charitable school society, the *Wohltätiger Schulverein*, started to organize free, recreational stays in the country for deprived urban children. The sickly children were housed with private billets or in camps—and exposed to a routine of community service, personal hygiene, and exercise and games in fresh air by supervising teachers. Proud reports note that during the three- to six-weeks-long stay (in subsequent years up to five months), children gained up to three kilos in weight.

By the beginning of the 20th century, various churches, councils, or philanthropist societies ran similar programs, some focusing more on the holiday, some more on the medical aspect. Political parties later established their own schemes and during WWI, fuelled by the dwindling food supplies in the cities, the KLV booked record numbers of over half a million children for stays in rural areas. From 1917 onwards, attempts were made to centralize the KLV in the hand of the central agency *Reichszentrale Landaufenthalt für Stadtkinder e.V.* In 1934, the NSV division *Mutter und Kind* took over the Reichszentrale and forbid or marginalized all other operators (including major organizations like the Red Cross and Caritas), thus effectively creating a monopoly on the KLV. In the same year the NSV published the ambitious aim to create KLV places for 500,000 children from big cities, industrial centers, and depressed areas. In subsequent years, participation numbers far exceeded that benchmark: each year approximately 650,000 children aged six to 15 were sent, with 875,000 going in 1938 (Kock, 1997).

Catering to these large numbers meant that the NSV had to set up permanent links to the rail authorities, organize medical staff in the cities and reception areas, staff offices all across the Reich, negotiate appropriate insurance policies, and have a large roster of potential host families on their files. Potential billets were carefully vetted for suitability and infestations, children were carefully checked and labeled, and weeks ahead of the actual move the urban parents would know their child's destination. A lot of effort went into welcoming the children with celebrations at the train stations, communal breakfasts, music, and so on. The cooperation between NSV and HJ was also long established before the war, since the HJ ran the KLV camps for their members. These were short-term holiday programs, but there were even precedents for a longer lasting stay in camps. The education ministry had a long-established program for delinquent teenagers, who would be taken out of their families and into camps in the countryside in order to work on farms. The HJ had attempted to take over responsibility for this *Landjahr* since 1934 (Kock, 1997). Neither KLV nor *Landjahr* was short of financial support, since Goebbels immediately recognized the program's potential for propaganda and indoctrination. For the evacuation's organizers, the institution and terminology of the older KLV was a stroke of luck. "Der Vorgang der Kinderlandverschickung stellte also bis ins Jahr 1940...im Bewußtsein der Bevölkerung ein within bekanntes, völlig normales, eher positiv besetztes Geschehen dar (Up until 1940, the public viewed KLV operations as common, normal, and rather positive features of life)" (Buddrus, 2003, p. 886).

Braumann (2004) concludes that long before the outbreak of war an "evacuation scheme" already existed that included the following operational aspects: age group and racially based selection, use of charter trains, escorts and catering on board of trains, welcome reception at destination, accommodation in camps and families, focus on physical exercise and discipline, importance of community spirit and camaraderie, strict routines including assemblies and flag salutes, visits by party functionaries, and media representation. Also already firmly established were elements of peer pressure and pester power, as well as the concealment of homesickness, incidents of bullying, and the problem of missed schooling (Braumann, 2004). Not only did the original KLV precede the war and continue throughout, it also survived it. In the post-war years, the British Red Cross assisted the re-establishment of recreational visits into summer camps, the *Sommererholungslager.*

Chapter Conclusion

London and Berlin organized their evacuations in very different political and social environments. In London, the interwar years (a period of small changes and reassuring continuity) had been used to make plans for the protection of civilians in case of war. For fifteen years government branches—first secretly then publicly—contemplated A.R.P. measures for a war they did not want or could not afford, but considered inevitable. London, the overcrowded metropolis and world's hub for politics and finance, was well advised to anticipate the devastating consequences of a war that would affect city life more than any previous one. The LCC—the city's executive—was not only a capable agent to introduce and realise war measures, but also much more determined to do so than the national government that clung to its appeasement policy. Thus, evacuation did not come as a surprise to London, but as a measured response based on historic precedent and the new paternal role of government.

There is an inherent irony that Berlin started the war but did not prepare itself for it. The heart of centralistic and growing Nazi Germany, a once vibrant multicultural metropolis that succumbed to Nazi uniformity, anticipated the war to be fought elsewhere, and its officials had no evacuation plans until British bombers actually reached Berlin. They had something else though: an organized youth and the infrastructure to move thousands of people at short notice, because they had been doing just that for a long time. Whereas state interference was still relatively new to the British, the NS regime could rely on organizations that had long established close links with their parts of the population and a high level of intrusion into their lives. Utilizing these for an evacuation scheme could be done on short notice.

Arrival of London Evacuees at Stevenage, September 1, 1939
Imperial War Museum Photograph Collection HU 69028

2

Plans and Preparations

At some point evacuation had to become more than just a rumor. For London this point came in May 1938, when the LCC education officer's staff anticipated the Anderson Committee's appeal for A.R.P. suggestions with the unofficial circulation of a short memo for a possible evacuation scheme. It started extensive and careful bureaucratic planning in City Hall for the exodus of the city's children in case of war. In this chapter, a few crucial and lesser known sources like the aforementioned memo, minutes from a meeting of headmasters, and the correspondence from the Chelsea rehearsal will be discussed to show the evolution of what was to become Operation Pied Piper.

The German evacuation was neither planned nor prepared well—and what little planning there was hardly left a paper trail. On the streets of Berlin, evacuation became a rumor after the first devastating RAF air raid on September 25, 1940. Hitler, always one to swiftly react to shifting public opinion, demanded an evacuation scheme the next day. The massive operation that was initiated not a fortnight later seems to have had only a two-day planning phase. There are only a few surviving sources that show how a

Operation Pied Piper, pages 25–52
Copyright © 2012 by Information Age Publishing
All rights of reproduction in any form reserved.

long-established charitable holiday organization became the wartime evacuation program. This chapter will foreground Schirach's first draft of the KLV and the Education Ministry's translation of it, but also has to concede that there are still gaps that cannot be filled after the wilful destruction of the NS regime's archives near the end of the war.

This chapter's purpose is to provide answers to research questions surrounding agency and bureaucracy by following the schemes' evolution from mere notion to concrete plans. Please note that Chapters 2 to 6 treat the cities and their evacuations separately (with very few exceptions, i.e., isolated cross-references that cropped up in the source analyses and needed to be treated immediately). A systematic and contextualized comparison is the subject of Chapter 7.

London

A First Plan for London

> In retrospect an inexplicable psychological phenomenon of the years between the rise of Hitler in 1931 and the outbreak of the Second World War in September 1939 is the ostrich-like attitude of large numbers of ordinary people in Britain, who brushed aside the notion that another war was inevitable. This attitude was not held by those in Whitehall whose concern it was to keep the nation's 'War Book' up to date. (Lowndes, 1969, p. 190)

London's planning started with a short working paper entitled *Evacuation of the Child Population of London—An Appreciation* (source I). It mainly appreciates the scale of the task of evacuating up to a million children and later gained substantial authority by the inclusion of its recommendations in the Anderson Report. At the time when organized evacuation became a likely option for London, it was already in circulation for some time before being submitted to the Anderson Committee on June 2, 1938. George A. N. Lowndes, then an Assistant Education Officer under E. M. Rich, later claimed authorship and suggested that his policy recommendations were influenced by an impromptu billeting survey done by coastal towns for naval battle casualties during WWI, his own experience of billeting and boarding difficult children for the LCC (Lowndes, 1969), and the previous movements of children on festive occasions like the 100,000 children who visited Crystal Palace in 1911 (to attend the Festival of Empire in celebration of the coronation of George V), 70,000 schoolchildren travelling to Constitution Hill in 1935 (George V's Silver Jubilee celebrations), and the 37,000 schoolchildren who attended the coronation of George VI at the Embankment. The education officer later agreed that the evacuation, "although it would probably be the biggest piece of organisation ever carried out in peace time," would differ in size but not in nature from the previous logistical challenges (Rich, 1938).

The calculation was that evacuation procedures would have to cater to approximately 500,000 schoolchildren in the area covered by the LCC and—if they wanted to be included—another 270,000 children from the adjoining counties. The paper also already determines that trains are the only viable option for transport and estimates the need for 700 special trains. Regardless of the scale of the operation, the memorandum is optimistic about the logistics, but appreciates that "the real difficulty would lie in educating both those who would have to part with their children and those whom one would hope to persuade to receive those children." The role of the teachers, which became so crucial in the success of the scheme (Crosby, 1986), was already highlighted here as a major contributor to the cooperation of parents in London and billeting households in the reception areas.

Three alternate policies were considered with regards to accommodation: the creation of a ring of camps at some distance from London, the occupation of the whole of the boarding house accommodation in the reception areas, or billeting the unaccompanied children with foster parents. Only the third option was regarded as viable, though. The arguments against camps—coincidently the method favored in Germany later on and a favorite amongst letter writers to the *Times,* including one G. R. Lowndes (!) who used that platform to urge "that the camp scheme should be undertaken at once and on a national basis" (*Times,* 02.02.1939)—were the cost of erecting the camps, especially in view of the cost of the re-armament program, as well as the difficulties with catering, supervision, and medical services. It was also feared that the National Union of Teachers (NUT) might oppose from the outset a scheme that put teachers in a permanent supervisory role, acting *in loco parentis* for large groups of children around the clock—a concern that was raised with regards to the second option as well. The Ministry of Health later made some concessions to public opinion by providing camps for difficult billets via the specially founded National Camps Corporation Ltd. that, endowed with £1,200,000, was in charge of building and operating 50 camps with a capacity of 300 evacuees each. Those camps were, however, not ready for the evacuation of 1939, but later hosted *difficult* billets (a term with precious little specification in the documents), homeless refugees, and children with disabilities (Titmuss, 1950).

For the *Appreciation,* though, boarding the children with foster parents remained the only feasible option. Lowndes later justified this option rather emotionally: it is every child's right to be the sole object of someone's affection (Lowndes, 1969). The questions of financial incentives for the foster parents and how to raise the money—that is, if the parents of the evacuees should, at least partly, contribute to the cost of their children's lodging— were also already under consideration. In determining the amount of the boarding-out fee the *Appreciation* mentions the then-current government rate for public assistance children at 10s/6d per week, but recommends a higher per-person payment for the evacuees of 13s to 15s "to attract a sufficient and early response," since their stay is likely to be shorter and more ad hoc. The paper further argues in favor of the government shouldering the full cost of the evacuation for three reasons: (1) a fee would act as a deterrent for parents to part with their children, (2) the organization of the recovery of the outstanding payments would be enormous, and (3) a free evacuation service would help the morale of the adult population during enemy action.

An action plan completes the *Appreciation*. Its most urgent recommendations are:

- Reliable numbers of schools and children in London and their proximity to one of the mainland railway stations needed to be obtained via school administration and teaching staff.
- According to those figures, billets would need to be found in the reception areas in rural England and Wales. An assessment would need to be made on the willingness of the population to receive children, for how long, and at what cost.
- Arrangements would have to be in place for the special schools, "i.e., the blind, deaf, physically defective, tubercular and mentally defective children." Their transport would have to be arranged with a fleet of seventy ambulance buses.

Although not explicitly spelled out, there is another important assumption in this paper that would be the topic of hot debate later on: Evacuation was to be voluntary; ultimately the parents would have to make the decision to send their children away. The government's role was to provide the infrastructure, give incentives, and educate parents. Compulsion was neither proposed nor discussed in this paper—an absence that might be seen as a legacy of the liberal tradition in the face of the new *big* government.

With this paper, and over a year before its operation, the evacuation scheme already existed as a skeleton. Subsequent plans and official reports were really just amendments to this original plan. The key points of the government's evacuation scheme—keeping evacuation voluntary (although there will have to be discussion of the parents' freedom of choice in a situation where all schools closed and moved away—see Chapter 7), financing it publicly, billeting the evacuees with foster parents, traveling in school groups by train, and children staying under the supervision of their teachers—were already spelled out. This document also already established the Education Officer's office as the most suitable government branch to oversee London's evacuation.

The timing of the document is also noteworthy; its circulation coincided with the evidence gathering by the Anderson Committee. Named after its chairman Lord Privy Seal and later Home Secretary Sir John Anderson, the committee was set up on May 24, 1938 and has since been critically reviewed as a civil service device to put the controversial issue of evacuation into "cold storage" (Lowndes, 1969, p. 197). Nevertheless, members of the committee began interviewing representatives of women's volunteer organizations, teachers' unions, police, train companies, and so on, to determine the shape of a possible government evacuation scheme. The Anderson Report later became the evacuation's most authoritative document, mainly because it provided its legislative and legal framework. It does not feature here as a source, though, since historians have already extensively covered this document for policy studies. Suffice to say that on July 26, 1938 the committee submitted their report to the Home Secretary, where its publication was stalled for two months. Regardless of political delays in Whitehall, the preparation work in London went on.

A Conference with the Heads of London Schools

By mid-September 1938, the perceived threat of an imminent war, triggered by the Munich Crisis, led to a rush to finalize plans for an ad hoc evacuation. On September 15, 1938 the Education Officer's Department—by then the unofficial nerve center for the exodus from London—held a *Conference with Heads of Secondary Schools and Junior Technical Schools* (sources IIa-b). Later on the same day, Rich also met with the heads of elementary schools, and the minutes of these two meetings reveal both the actual stage of the planning as well as the cooperation that could be expected from the teachers—whose support, after all, was crucial for the scheme's operation. It needs to be understood that at that time, evacuation was not yet an uncontested solution. Dispersal strategies—the de-cluttering of densely crowded quarters or buildings (like schools)—were popular with politicians, as was the notion of not doing anything at all. Extreme opinion was that London's population was legitimate bait to lure the Luftwaffe into RAF traps (Lowndes, 1969). During the meetings, Rich made it a point to discredit alternatives with the help of a WWI incident where fourteen children were killed by one bomb in a council school in Poplar (for more on the incident see: Ziegler, 1995, p. 9). The minutes of both meetings are particularly interesting sources since the Education Officer seemed overall less guarded than in official communications—and more willing to admit weaknesses of the plans as well as to criticize the central government for their inactivity.

There is a sense of urgency evident in the headmasters' questions and the answers from the LCC staff. The heads agreed to every resolution the Education Officer proposed for the operation, and some even urged Rich to stop waiting for the national government, but to roll out the LCC evacuation plans immediately and without official consent. From the questions asked, it is apparent that the head teachers agreed with the evacuation scheme in general, were willing to cooperate, but were also frustrated that they could not go ahead and confer with parents and set the wheels in motion straight away, since they perceived the political situation to be such that a state of emergency could arise any day. The issue of informing parents early—even without government approval if necessary—was especially important to the heads. Their stance seemed to have been that open communication would help avoid panic and improve predictions of participation rates and that, generally, to parents the major concern would not be the unknown destination of their children's travels, but how well they would be treated wherever they would end up. One of the Education Officer's remarks neatly sums up the agreed priorities:

> I shan't know how many are going to turn up, but just think for a moment; the first thing we have got to do is to get these children away out of danger. When we have got them out of danger and we have a chance to look round, we may be able to make all kind of adjustments. (Source IIa, p. 8)

There is crucial knowledge about the state of the evacuation plans to be gained from what was said at these conferences—and especially from what had *not* been said. After all, the head teachers were arguing technicalities, not principles. There was already mutual agreement on the necessity of the schoolchildren's evacuation and the subsequent closure and move of the schools; there was consent that teachers—rather than parents—should be in charge of the pupils and that children should be the first to leave London. For Rich, the heads' reaction must have come as a great relief. The meetings showed that most of the heads were not only extraordinarily supportive to the proposed scheme, but also anticipated the same operating problems as the civil servants.

The government-prescribed secrecy towards the parents remained the dominant issue. At that time it was considered politically desirable to keep evacuation plans secret in order to avoid panic among the British population and misinterpretation by the foreign press. This secrecy left the planners with the dilemma of the numbers. On the one hand, there was agreement that evacuation should be voluntary, but on the other hand it was not possible to consult parents about letting their children go to an unspecified destination. The school headmasters made it clear that they regarded the secrecy as damaging to the whole scheme, stating "that the ignorance, the mystery of it, is psychologically very bad" (p. 4). Since parents had already been asking them about plans for a national emergency anyway, the heads demanded permission to consult with them. There was optimism that once the plan was laid open, a large proportion of parents would be willing to entrust their children to the schools, even if they were going to an unknown destination. Only a few days after those meetings, the Munich Crisis put an end to the secrecy, and the heads' prediction would be proven right in the later course of events.

The Emergency Evacuation Memorandum

In the run-up to the Munich Agreement, all branches of government prepared for war, albeit as secretly as possible so as not to fuel the political situation. The national government still did not commit to an evacuation scheme; quite the contrary, its leaflet *The Protection of Your Home Against Air Raids* recommended private evacuation, regardless of its logistical nightmare and obvious social inequality (Padley, 1940). In the absence of clear guidelines, Morrison and Rich at County Hall prepared the evacuation according to their own design and hoped that the Home Office under Sir Samuel Hoare would fall in line eventually. The *Emergency Evacuation Memorandum* (source III) testifies to the end of the stalemate between central and local government. This document—discussed and agreed upon in one single night—also marks a shift in political power play, with the MoH, BoE and LCC taking over the evacuation's responsibility from the Home Office.

On Thursday September 22, 1938, only seven days after the Education Officer consulted with the head teachers, the Home Office informed the LCC that owing to the urgent situation, heads had to stay in schools over the weekend, ready to evacuate their pupils at short notice. In that night the Education Committee approved the memorandum that specified transport issues, labeling the children, billeting allowances, and signals for the wireless ("Pied Piper Tomorrow").

For the evacuation's logistics—and the resolution of the question of agency—this all-night meeting of the Education Committee and the memorandum itself are of major importance. The local authority's fears that the Home Office was too slow, too underfunded, too understaffed, and too secretive in light of the dire political situation were now confirmed (Lowndes, 1969). When the impossible request finally came to arrange London's evacuation overnight, the LCC—which had anticipated the emergency—got what they needed: authorization for the plans they had already drawn up in previous months. The time pressure put an end to budget discussions and enabled the publication of measures that had been deemed necessary all along. A previously unresolved issue like the billeting allowance was now set at 10/6d per child per week for a single child in a school party—the exact same rate mentioned in the *Appreciation*.

The memorandum organized the exodus from London. Heads in schools were now able to inform parents, anticipate the size of the school parties, assign assembly points, instruct on clothes and luggage—and eventually take the pupils to their assigned train stations. However, what would happen once 500,000 schoolchildren left the mainline railway stations was still largely unresolved. The memorandum only states that local authorities at the unspecified destination within the specified distance range—from Kent to Peterborough—were in charge of the billeting, that no attempt of private billet search should be made, and that the government would pay the billeting cost. The reception areas' individual plans for the evacuees had not yet been synchronized. Prompts provided to the heads for addressing assembled parents recommended frankness about these structural planning weaknesses. In anticipation of parents' questions of the whereabouts of the evacuated children the script recommended the following answer: "that we could not tell you until later..., but we would know that it would be in a safer area, twenty or thirty, perhaps fifty miles outside London" (p. 3). The distance mentioned was a result of the train companies' assessment of their rolling stock's ability to run shuttle services. It would later become apparent that the "safer" areas promised to parents were occasionally school buildings already abandoned by schools who deemed the proximity to London as enough of a reason to evacuate themselves, as in the case of the private King's School in Canterbury (Titmuss, 1950). The LCC and head teachers had agreed on a level-headed approach: schools in London would be closed in the event of war and, despite the improvised nature of the organization, letting the children go with their schools was the only sensible thing to do.

Things then moved very fast—the evacuation of the school population of London had been scheduled for Friday, September 30. Priority within the evacuation had always been given to "handicapped" and nursery children who were to travel by bus to allocated schools in the country or, in the case of "physically defective children" to a holiday camp in Dymchurch, Kent. On 26 September the Home Office authorized the evacuation of the priority groups (later known as Plan I). On September 27, 2,000 physically defective children moved to Dymchurch; two days later the other priority groups—1,200 nursery children and 1,000 "blind, deaf and mentally defective" children—were dispatched to their reception areas and billets (I 22, L.C.C., 1943).

However, the general evacuation did not follow, as the Munich Agreement was signed on its scheduled date. The immediate crisis passed and the evacuation was called off. All of the priority class evacuees were back home by October 6 (please note that the *special parties* outside the mainstream schemes are not part of this investigation, but that there is currently research done on the evacuation of deaf children by John Hay at Wolverhampton). Nevertheless, the crisis forced Hoare, Anderson (by then as Lord Privy Seal officially in charge of Home Security), and other members of the central government into action. Concessions made during this time were impossible to take back. For London this was crucial: The situation after the Munich crisis enabled Morrison—who considered Chamberlain's appeasement policy a national betrayal—to publicly point out that London's protocol was a "triumph of emergency organization" while the central government had no evacuation strategy at all (Donoughue & Jones, 1973, p. 266). All in all, the cancellation of the evacuation at the last minute came "much to everyone's relief, for the scheme was nothing if not rudimentary" (Brown, 2005, p. 6).

Accelerated Planning

Once secrecy was no longer an issue, open dialogue with parents could be established and the support of the public utilized. The planners could now estimate the number of schoolchildren for whom evacuation was desired with some—but still not total—accuracy.

> To build an evacuation plan on this voluntary principle was an immeasurably harder task than if a measure of compulsion had been put behind the scheme. It meant that concrete plans, worked out to the smallest details, had to be created on the basis of a number of unknown and variable factors. Assumptions had to be made about the probable mental reactions of over 10,000,000 individuals living in, and conditioned by, widely differing environments who, historically, had shown a marked affection for individuality. (Titmuss, 1950, p. 34)

During the Munich Crisis, many things happened: there was the unstructured flight of the middle classes in private cars from London; the distribution of gas masks stirred up panic among those staying behind; and the absence of any public announcements regarding the evacuation added to the civilians' worries. Even though the public was initially very supportive of A.R.P., the schemes opened themselves up to unnecessary criticism. The Home Office—although officially still in charge—lost their momentum with the publication of increasingly impracticable ideas like drafting in troops for ground control in London. At the same time, the LCC was eager to capitalize on its success and presented a joint report with the MoH, successfully arguing that the Home Office was not the appropriate government department to organize the evacuation (but even favoring the understaffed MoH over the BoE has retrospectively been criticized: Gosden, 1976). In November 1938 the Evacuation Planning Division (EPD) was set up at the MoH with staff drafted from the Board of Education and later the LCC to organize England's evacuation scheme. In January it was decided that the exodus from Greater London should be organized by one central authority. E. M. Rich, a member of the EPD, set up the Evacuation Branch that—by MoH invitation—oversaw all aspects of the exodus of the 1,250,000 Londoners in the scheme's priority classes. Responsibilities in spring 1939 were then distributed as shown in Figure 2.1.

In addition to the administrative County of London, the Evacuation Branch would also organize the evacuation of the adjoining boroughs of Acton, Willesden, Hornsey, Tottenham, Edmonton, East Ham, West Ham, Barking, Ilford, Leyton, and Walthamstow—collectively known as the MEA, the Metropolitan Evacuation Area (L.C.C., 1943, II 6). Most of the reception areas for the metropolis lay south and comprised nearly all of the area from Bristol to the Wash, with the exception of the areas in the vicinity of the major port towns. From the experience with Plan I, the LCC had no illusions about the limitations of their operation and the promises they could make to parents and head teachers. All aspects of the evacuation had to subordinate to the transport logistic.

> The rest of the organization had to be built on the transport possibilities, because such questions as the retention of school identity, special destinations for particular parties, the allocation of special reception areas to whole boroughs...all depended for their answers on the limit of the numbers which should be housed in the reception areas, the maximum amount of time which could be given to the evacuation operations before the declaration of a national emergency, the amount of rolling stock available, and the capacity of the railways to convey the evacuees to the reception area within the time available. (L.C.C., 1943, II 8)

For the transport planners, a further complication was the socioeconomic layout of London. Initially, there was no match between the capacity

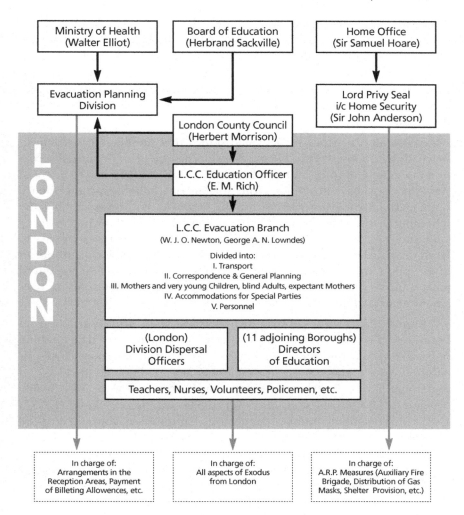

Figure 2.1   Responsibilities for London's evacuation in Spring 1939.

of the mainline train stations and the number of evacuees in their vicinity, which led to the involvement of the L.P.T.B. and their tube trains. It would fall to the underground to bring the evacuees from the North and East—where most of the children had to rely on the government's provision for their evacuation—to the entraining stations in the south and west of the metropolis: to Waterloo for trains to Dorset and Devon, to St. Pancras for trains to Bedfordshire, to Marylebone for Buckinghamshire, and to Paddington for all trains on the Great Western route to Cornwall (Crosby, 1986). Unlike mainline trains, though, the tube system had to work on very tight schedules that did not allow trains to wait for delayed school parties at one of the stations—which in turn endangered those parties' arrival at their designated destination. It was apparent for everyone involved that, even though there was close co-operation between the LCC, the L.P.T.B., and the mainline railway companies, the sole fact that the close-knit operation involved 600,000 children meant that chaos could and would ensue despite the best-laid plans.

Above all, the Munich Crisis had shown that the biggest problem in evacuating London was not the exodus, but the lack of an organized reception in the neighboring counties. The winter of 1938–1939 had to be spent surveying possible accommodation, sorting out billeting arrangements, setting up a local infrastructure for the evacuees, and ensuring that the schooling of the children would continue. By January, the whole of England and Wales was divided into evacuation, neutral, or reception areas. However, the decisions did not stay uncontested; over 200 local authorities of reception areas requested to be reclassified as neutral, while 60 neutral areas wanted to be evacuation areas. Unsurprisingly, no local authority of a neutral area volunteered to be listed as a reception area (Titmuss, 1950).

By mid-1939, it was clear that the evacuation of the priority groups from London would take longer than previously anticipated: three days on some railways, but four on others. This interfered with the aim to evacuate just before the declaration of war, leading to new tension between the LCC and the Home Office. By then the Evacuation Branch had to oversee 20,000 teachers, 1,000 official staff, and over 20,000 voluntary helpers (L.C.C., 1943, II 11) —and the number was growing continuously, since the LCC invited private schools to join the scheme. The private schools in London responded in four different ways: they either joined the scheme unconditionally, attached their pupils (if it was a very small school) to a local elementary school, requested transport but looked after themselves in the reception areas, or made entirely private arrangements (L.C.C., 1943, II 15).

It should be mentioned again that the school parties that are the focus of this study only constituted a part of the evacuable population the Evacuation Branch needed to consider. "Special parties" was the term given to groups of blind, deaf, mentally or physically defective (sic) as well as nursery children. From February 1939 the term also included orphans and inmates of public institutions. Special parties were to travel together and be accommodated in a vacant building in the reception areas or camps. By July 1939 accommodation for 17,000 children in 300 parties was secured and transport by coach arranged. In addition to the teaching staff traveling with the special parties, 36 LCC nurses were drafted to stay with them (L.C.C., 1943, II 29-34). The other priority classes (mothers with children under school age, expectant mothers, and blind adults) proved to be equally difficult to organize.

The Chelsea Test Evacuation

The *Chelsea Test Evacuation* (sources IVa-c) was simultaneously a dress rehearsal for the A.R.P. planners in London and a showcase to drum up public support for the wartime measures drafted in County Hall. By then all of Britain was in preparation for war—and the evacuation of schoolchildren was only a minor part of the major work going on. All LCC branches were somehow involved in the distribution of gas masks, the digging of graves, the mapping of evacuation routes from the city, the potential move of civil service branches into rural England and the building and maintenance of shelters. The Civil Defence Committee, overseeing all the preparation work, was eager to test their measures and eventually initiated a rehearsal in Chelsea (while never fully explaining the choice of borough). The plan was that on June 19, 1939, nearly the whole borough would come to a standstill between 12:30 and 12:45 PM. Air raid warnings would sound, followed eight minutes later by RAF bombers flying over Chelsea, and the whole of the daytime population—an estimated 65,000 people—would make their way to designated shelters, directed there by 400 air raid wardens. Several incidents (fake bomb explosions) were planned as part of the exercise, and it was hoped that the exercise would provide valuable data on crowd movements, the timeframe for reaching and filling shelters, traffic disruption, and so on. This *Experiment in Civil Defence,* as the Chelsea Borough Council labeled it, was the first of its kind and attracted a lot of attention. Invitations to watch the proceedings from viewing stands and balconies all over Chelsea were sent out to politicians, the press, and colleagues in other boroughs.

Considerations for the role of the schoolchildren in this rehearsal cropped up comparatively late. A letter dated May 31, 1939 from the town clerk of Chelsea to Rich mentions three possible provisions for the children. Since the rehearsal would happen during lunch hour, the schoolchildren could just join the spectators on the streets (deemed undesirable, though, as it would distort the outcome; since during a real air raid the schoolchildren would have been already evacuated from Chelsea). Alternatively, the children could be kept in school until after the test, or they could be included by means of a test evacuation. The Education Officer, who had previously contemplated a rehearsal run, but was denied it on grounds of possible alarm caused by the sight of evacuation proceedings in public, instantly endorsed the latter proposal and mapped out movement details for the children of Chelsea. On June 12, a proposal was circulated that set out the trial evacuation in great detail. Children from schools within the Borough of Chelsea would walk to Earl's Court, South Kensington and Walham Green stations or—in the case of very small children—be taken there by bus. All schools who were assigned Sloane Square as their entraining station in the evacuation scheme would also participate in the exercise, irrespective of whether they were actually in Chelsea or not. A detailed schedule was drawn up that ensured that all children would be back in schools at noon and before the actual air raid rehearsal began. Headmasters received their instructions and all teachers were to be included in the trial. Staffing was crucial since documentation was as important as the operation itself. Official and volunteer helpers were equipped with detailed timing and feedback sheets so as to provide the LCC with data on movement and dispatch speeds. Parents were instructed to equip children with luggage and gas masks, while the school staff provided the identification labels.

Even though there is evidence to suggest that the A.R.P. test run in Chelsea was not entirely taken seriously by the locals, some of whom might have thought that fleeing from imaginary bombs into imaginary shelters was little more than good fun (Ziegler, 1995), there was a great feeling of achievement after the trial evacuation by its executioners. Five thousand children had been moved to their fictitious train departures within three hours, and there was universal praise for the orderly manner in which the whole operation unfolded. However, the test also flagged up some of the problems that would still have to be overcome in order to smoothly run the evacuation logistics on a larger scale. Most of them concerned inadequate preparation by the parents—children arrived at schools without overcoats, proper shoes, or rucksacks. For the organizers, finding small flaws like the identification labels' vulnerability to rain was as much the object of this trial as the big logistical challenges like the turnaround time and stacking of buses. Overall, though, the test evacuation was deemed a great success, prompting a confident press statement by Rich that "if the arrangements in Chelsea can be taken as any indication of the state of affairs in all the twenty-three dispersal divisions of the metropolitan evacuable area, and I think they may be, I am satisfied that, from the London end, the Government's evacuation scheme could be effectively carried through if the need ever arose" (Press Statement reproduced in: L.C.C., 1939).

In addition to the valuable observations for the logistics of a large-scale evacuation, the Chelsea rehearsal had a two-way positive effect on the government's evacuation scheme. Firstly, it provided much-needed positive press coverage. Photos published by the *Evening News* showed well behaved, good-humored middle- and working-class children under the supervision of policemen and teachers—which was exactly what the government needed to restore trust in their scheme after parents became increasingly critical of the idea to part with their children for an indefinite length of time. Secondly, the success of the test evacuation, especially after such short preparation time, firmly established the Education Officer's authority over London's schoolchildren. The previous power struggle over the responsibility of the evacuation was now finally resolved and the scheme's collective supervision by the MoH, BoE, and LCC would remain uncontested until the end of the war.

Impressed by the example set in Chelsea, other cities followed with their own evacuation rehearsals. In Manchester, this involved the whole school population of their 80,000 children (*Manchester Guardian*, 29.08.1939). Henry Buckton recounts a rehearsal run in Wigston, where 800 local schoolchildren pretended to arrive at the train station and were efficiently dispatched to their billets (Buckton, 2009). Back in London, the Evacuation Branch awaited the inevitable war in the safe knowledge that they had done what they could.

Berlin

Precipitate Planning in Berlin

The Kinderlandverschickung went from the Führer's ad hoc decision to operation in only a few days. There is no evidence to suggest that evacuation plans for children existed before the first RAF air raids in late August 1940, and Martin Parsons' contradictory dating to early 1938 is confirmed neither by the documents nor German historiography (Parsons, 2008). It was arrogance that greatly delayed the government's evacuation scheme in Berlin. Hermann Goering's—now proverbial—claim that people could call him "Meier" if the enemies would bomb a single German city became a symbol of the Nazi government's smugness and delusions about the war. The swift victories of the first year, the absence of British air strikes, and the fact that the war was fought outside Germany all added to a false sense of security in Berlin. If there ever had been early plans to evacuate schoolchildren, they were swiftly shelved after the victory over Poland (Kock, 1997). Up until August 1940, there were widespread expectations of an early peace. However, even after the German victory in France, a British peace offer was not forthcoming and Hitler announced on August 1, 1940 that air raids against England would be intensified ("verschärfter Luftkrieg"), possibly as an overture for Operation Sea Lion, the German invasion of the British Isles. Air strikes against London commenced on August 24, 1940, with the Royal Air Force's retaliation following immediately after. On September 24 and 25, 1940, Berlin was subjected to a devastating British air raid, closely followed by the Führer's demand for an evacuation scheme. The ad hoc provision for children was thus closely linked to military developments: The evacuation's establishment coincided with the insight that Britain would neither capitulate nor be defeated in the near future (Kock, 1997, p. 82).

On September 26, 1940, Hitler met with Baldur von Schirach (governor of Vienna, but more crucially, inventor, figurehead, and former supremo of the HJ) and NSV leader Erich Hilgenfeldt to discuss voluntary evacuation for the children of Berlin and Hamburg. Overnight, Schirach drafted plans for a government scheme with close colleague Helmut Möckel—probably relying on earlier drafts (Kressel, 1996) —and presented them to Hitler in a second meeting on September 27 (incidentally, a very busy day for the Nazi regime as the Tri-Power Treaty between Germany, Italy, and Japan became public knowledge then).

The two invitees at the meeting with Hitler were key figures within the NS regime. Erich Hilgenfeldt joined the NSDAP in 1929 and became a major figure in its Berlin administration. From 1933 onwards, he headed the supposedly charitable NSV, but publicly maintained the attitude that charity should be only for those who can still contribute to society: the strong and the healthy. Hilgenfeldt remained a key Nazi administrator and committed suicide in 1945 (Klee, 2008). It was Baldur von Schirach, though, who would officially be in charge of Germany's evacuation scheme. Hitler assigned him the task despite Schirach's time-consuming other task of governing Vienna for the NSDAP. The Führer's reasoning might have been that no-one appealed to the target group—the potential evacuees—more than the HJ's former leader. Schirach, an outstanding organizer and propagandist, joined the party early and became a close ally of Hitler, who put the loyal youngster in charge of all the party's youth organizations: HJ, BDM, Jungvolk and NS-Schülerbund. Legendary CBS correspondent William Shirer portrayed the popular Nazi critically in his memoirs: "Despite his banality and a certain appearance of softness, Schirach was possessed of a great driving force, a flair for organizing and a brutality shared by all who got ahead in the jungle world of the brownshirts" (Shirer, 1984, p. 186).

In 1945, Schirach was arrested, put on trial at Nuremberg and spent 20 years in prison at Berlin-Spandau—but not for his work for the HJ or the evacuation, but the atrocities against the Jewish population of Vienna. In 1967, he published his memoirs: *Ich glaubte an Hitler* (I believed in Hitler), and in 1974 he died in Kröv (Klee, 2008; Lang, 1991).

There seems to be little doubt that Schirach's role in the evacuation's operation was largely ceremonial. During his Nuremberg trial and in his memoirs, he not only overplayed the humanitarian aspects of the operation, but also made easily refutable claims (like inventing the original KLV movement that dates back 30 years before his birth) while displaying a general lack of detailed knowledge. His former colleague, head of BdM Dr. Jutta Rüdiger, rightly pointed out that the real work had probably been done by others (Lang, 1991).

It is not clear why Joseph Goebbels was not at that meeting; after all, any plan involving Berlin was likely to include his input or at least acknowledgement. The "master propagandist of the Nazi regime and dictator of its cultural life" (Wistrich, 1995, p. 76) was the executive ruler of Berlin as well as the head of the propaganda machine that would support the KLV (see Chapter 1). It seems that no-one knew the sentiment on the streets like Goebbels, who suspected that the people of Berlin would regard an evacuation program as evidence of two things: the regime's expectation that war would last longer than propaganda suggested, and that Berlin's air defense was weaker than propaganda suggested (see below). Thus, Hitler's request for an evacuation scheme was bound to be controversial.

The plan submitted to Hitler on September 27, 1940 (source V) has obvious similarities to London's *Appreciation*: They are both very concise but detailed, they have the same confident tone of authority, and they both actually became the authoritative documents of their cities' evacuations. Section I of the memo opens with the division of children into two distinct groups. The first group are the 6- to 10-year-olds who would be evacuated into billets by the NSV. Very similar to the English scheme, these evacuees would stay with foster families and join the local schools for their lessons. The second group is made up of 10- to 14-year-olds who would travel with the HJ and be accommodated in communal camps. It is very important to note here that *camp* was a social concept more than a spatial one; it denoted the set group of people that would travel and stay together. Camps could then be accommodated in youth hostels, monasteries, school buildings, rural mansions, tourist hostels, and hotels. Reception areas designated were the Bavarian Ostmark, Mark Brandenburg, Upper Danube (in today's Austria), Silesia (in today's Poland), Sudetenland (in today's Czech Republic), Thuringia, Wartheland (in today's Poland), and Ostland (territory of today's Estonia, Lithuania, and Latvia). Despite the spread and distances, the paper is optimistic about parental cooperation and recommends voluntary evacuation:

> Auch bei Wahrung der Freiwilligkeit ist anzunehmen, dass die Eltern zum großen Teil der Verschickung der Jugendlichen begrüßen werden, da diesen hierdurch eine ungestörte Nachtruhe gesichert wird und sie auch vor sonstigen Gefahren bewahrt bleiben. (Even within a voluntary scheme one

can assume widespread approval from the parents for the dispatch of their adolescents, since it guarantees them undisturbed nights and safety from miscellaneous dangers.) (Source V, I)

Disturbances from sirens and lack of sleep caused by moving in and out of air raid shelters were the official justification for the whole operation—not the mortal danger from the enemy's bombing (although the memo vaguely admits "miscellaneous dangers"). In 1940, the regime was not yet ready to admit that the RAF could pose a serious threat to the safety of Germany's urban population (see Schirach, 1967). Accordingly, the term "Evakuie*rung*" was not to be used—in this memo that was only a recommendation, but later it became an official guideline (even in an earlier 1939 evacuation of children from the vulnerable industrial West the term used was "*Freimachung,*" which translates as "vacation" —as in "to vacate a room"). The paper's first section closes with an estimate of numbers within a voluntary evacuation: in group two, 50,000 and 30,000 children from Berlin and Hamburg respectively. In his memoirs, Schirach remembered the numbers differently: 200,000 schoolchildren with their teachers and 50,000 infants with their mothers would leave Berlin and Hamburg by free rail transport to be accommodated in 3,600 seized buildings at a cost of two million Reichsmark per day. He haughtily added that Hitler okayed it all (Schirach, 1967).

Section II lists various aspects of the operation for consideration. Propaganda for the scheme is the first item on the list, even though recommendations do not go beyond a vague "will be decided by local authorities in line with nationwide uniform ('*reichseinheitlich*') propaganda guidelines." Transport arrangements—which were such a big issue in London—seem simple, straightforward, and worth only one paragraph. The Reichsverkehrsministerium (transport ministry) was to provide five to seven charter trains per day (each holding up to 1,000 evacuees), with the HJ and NSV sharing the task to organize medical support, provisions and station guides. Due to the long-established holiday KLV, the NSV already had a lot of experience and staff on hand that Schirach could rely on here. Another thing he could rely on was the overwhelming and powerful bureaucracy that could requisition, confiscate, and withhold anything at time of war.

Catering in the reception areas was very straightforward for group two: the local rationing and supply authorities would provide their groceries and cooks. Group one's catering needs are only mentioned in passing: the host family would provide the meals. There is no mention yet of reimbursement or payment. Local authorities in the reception areas were also enlisted for medical care and the provision of equipment and clothing. The party's subdivisions, on the other hand, would provide the camp leaders who were in charge of the operation, the daily routine, and the provision with sport activities and cultural activities (music evenings, film screenings). Education was to be overseen by the NSLB, and teachers for the camps were allowed three days of preparation time ahead of the arrival of their charges.

Section III recommends that any child or young person with relatives or friends in the country should seek private evacuation. Their individual transport would be provided by the NSV, and they would join the local school and HJ group. Section IV closes the document with a list of ministries that need to be informed in order to organize their contribution to the scheme. After discussing the scheme with Hitler, Schirach added a note with some details from that conversation. The last handwritten remark has great significance for later controversies about the scheme that will be picked up in Chapters 4 and 5: "Lehrer sollen bei Transporten nicht mitreden" (Teachers shall have no say about the move.) (Source V, 2 Aktenvermerk).

A major distinguishing feature of this document to London's *Appreciation* is the level of the author's authority. While Lowndes had to advertise his ideas to others higher up in the London hierarchy, Schirach knew well that he was close enough to the Führer's ear to demand and order instead of asking. The choice of words shows this clearly: there is no potential for discussion or contemplation, these are orders—there is not a conditional phrase in the document. Another difference from the London plans concerns the inclusion of charitable organizations and churches. Whereas the London organizers welcomed their contribution, the Berlin planners deliberately reduced the involvement to the three Nazi organization mentioned, despite offers from churches and charities to support the evacuation (Buddrus, 2003).

Not explicitly spelled out, but prevalent in most NSDAP measures, is the KLV's target group: the lower middle- and working-class families. While the rich could look after themselves, the upstanding German worker deserved the party's assistance. In England the concept was similar, but of course never publicly admitted. Propaganda in Berlin was designed for those families who lived on their allotments and had no cellar. Evacuation was not to be an obligation, but evidence that the party cared for the little people (Kock, 1997, p. 82).

It is also worth noting again that at this point parents would already been used to state intrusion with regards to their children. Nazi ideology praised the family as *Keimzelle des Volkes* (people's germ cell—somewhat lost in translation), but the resulting children would be transferred early to the supervision of the party. JH and BdM helped to keep children and parents in line—after all, the jurisdiction allowed the state to remove children from their families and to place them with (more conformist) foster parents or in a boarding school (Fürstenberg, 1996, p. 27).

As Kock (1997) points out, there were some minor alterations made to this initial plan before it was distributed and published within the administration. The directive to the government departments issued on October 2, for example, no longer recommends but demands non-compulsion to participants; there must be no pressure exercised on the parents. Transport capacities had been reduced to two or three trains a day (probably a concession to the transport ministry rather than lowered expectations of participation numbers), equipment and clothing fell into the responsibility of parents not the NSV, and the NSLB succeeded in making teachers, not HJ leaders, heads of the evacuee camps (Kock, 1997).

The sources available do not allow for an elaborate discussion of motives for Berlin's evacuation, and the collaborators' accounts are too unreliable for an assessment of the government's ambitions. While afterwards some key personnel organized itself in the *KLV e.V.* society in order to whitewash the scheme as singularly concerned with the safety and welfare of children, at the time it was very likely seen as a military expedient—similar to concerns in London—and a good platform to show the caring side of the NS regime. Kock further posits that the KLV's planning and timing allows for the conclusion that those in charge were not guided by real concern about the children's lives, but by concerns about their parents' reaction to real or imaginary danger (Kock, 1997). After all, the NS regime worked in a dichotomy of simultaneously craving public support and executing measures that showed a general disregard for human life. Noakes suggested an additional motive:

> Schirach had seized the opportunity of securing the responsibility for setting up the KLV programme in the hope of realising a long-standing goal of establishing for the HJ the dominant role in German education.... The HJ was indeed successful in marginalizing the NSLB and, at least until the last phase, virtually excluding the state authorities (Reich Education Ministry) altogether. (Noakes, 1998, p. 435)

However, while this presciently reflects later developments, it is hard to believe that Schirach was provident enough to anticipate them during those turbulent few days of planning.

To appreciate fully the questions of agency within the complexity of the NS regime's bureaucracy it is sensible to look at one other document from the evacuation's early stages. The Reich's Education Ministry—which had been deliberately excluded from the planning despite their authority over the schoolchildren—could naturally not openly rebel against a Führer-approved plan but included some very subtle criticism when rewording Schirach's orders for the headmasters in schools.

The Education Ministry's Orders

On October 2, 1940, Bernhard Rust announced the evacuation to headmasters and local education authorities (source VI). The declaration largely follows the blueprint given in Martin Bormann's circulars. However, Rust sets his own emphases—for example, voluntary cooperation is mentioned much earlier and spelled out more explicitly ("auf Grund freier Entschliessung der Erziehungsberechtigten"—on the basis of the parents' free decision). It also contains considerations that possibly were of no interest to Schirach—for example, that not just any teacher should be drafted for the KLV, but preferably those who were unmarried or had children that they wished to evacuate with them.

The silences are more interesting than the words, though: The NSLB— after all the organization put in charge for all educational matters arising from the KLV—is only mentioned once. The prominent role assigned to the ministry's rival not only remains largely unacknowledged, but is contradicted by the announcement:

> Die Festsetzung der Unterrichtszeiten und des Stundenplans für den im Aufnahmeort zu erteilenden zusätzlichen Unterricht ist Sache der Schulaufsichtsbehörde. Über etwa auftretende Schwierigkeiten ist mir zu berichten. (The education authority is in charge of timetable and curriculum in the reception areas. Any problems that might arise from this have to be brought to my attention.) (Source VI, p. 2)

With regard to the camps, though, the ministry had to admit defeat. The camps were a party-run operation and any educational issues as well as staffing left in the hands of NSDAP branches. Nevertheless, attempts to hold on to at least some authority are evident everywhere in the text: the ministry grants leave to the students signing up for the KLV, education authorities in the reception areas have the final word on admissions of evacuees into their schools, the choice of teachers for the camps is made in cooperation between NSLB and ministry (although Schirach's memo explicitly assigns this to the NSLB alone), and teachers in camps are still subject to their civil servants' status and regulation by their education authority at home.

Even within the restricted format of an official proclamation, the controversy shines through. The unresolved dualism of party and state that governed the whole NS regime was to be a part of the KLV as well as the competition between HJ and schools for access to the children. Unlike in London, where the power struggles were prominent in the planning stages but resolved by the time of operation, Berlin children and parents would find themselves exposed to conflicting interests throughout the lifespan of the KLV.

The KLV Takes Shape

Within a few days, the KLV infrastructure had to be in place. Dabel claims that there had been consultations with suitable organizations like the Youth Hostel Association under Johannes Rodatz, who theoretically could have run the operation (Dabel, 1981). Schirach's decision, though, was to establish a new office at the Reichsjugendführung at Kurfüstenstrasse in Berlin: the Dienststelle KLV in charge of all matters relating to the children's evacuation and headed by Helmut Möckel who had previously been in charge of the peacetime KLV. Möckel, then aged 31, also deputized for HJ leader Axmann (Buddrus, 2003).

Only a handful of clerks organized the nationwide operation, and roles in the office were assigned to divisions: Möckel became head of operations (Büroleiter), with Eberhard Grüttner managing the office, Horst Hechler in charge of transport and accommodation, and Gerhard Dabel overseeing the camps' conduct und ideology (Führung und Ausrichtung). Other departments oversaw medical care, schooling in camps, administration and business management. The strange power accumulation and distribution—so typical of the Third Reich—can be beautifully illustrated here: Schirach was officially in charge, but in reality far away in Vienna. So Schirach put Möckel in charge, but he was really too busy looking after all of Schirach's positions in Berlin. Thus, it seems that Eberhard Grüttner, the merchant who during the 1930s displayed a flair for organizing large events like the HJ summer camps, supervised the actual work of the KLV. A visual display of the distribution of responsibilities for the evacuation of Berlin and Hamburg in October 1940 (following Dabel's documents and Kock's research) can be found in Figure 2.2.

Since all aspects of the evacuation were in the hands of NSDAP subdivisions, responsibilities could be clear cut and assigned without discussion and argument. The NSDAP paid for everything (with the HJ paying for accommodation, catering, and equipment; the NSV paying for transport, medical care, and insurance; and the NSLB paying for the cost of teachers and lesson

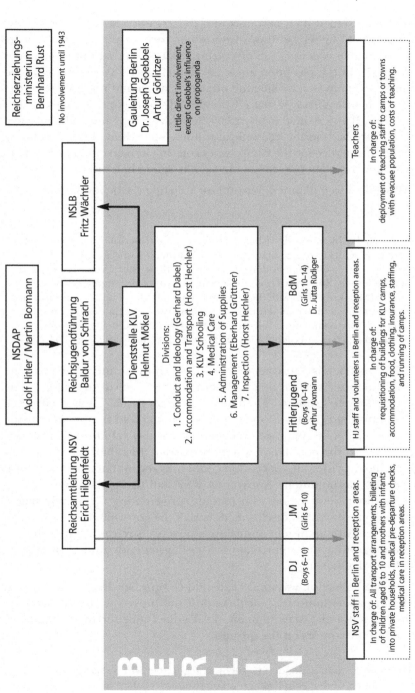

Figure 2.2   Responsibilities for Berlin's evacuation in October 1940.

material) and settled their accounts with the Treasury. Staff needed for the operation would either be drawn from other party or public offices, or indeed seconded or ordered from private businesses under wartime regulations (Kock, 1997). In the reception areas, existing HJ and NSV personnel would be utilized as camp staff or billeting officers. One should not underestimate the infrastructure already in place from the HJ's peacetime activities. Before the war, the HJ entertained nearly 2,000 "holiday" camps and had access to a further 35,000 beds in the 288 official youth hostels (Kinz, 1991). Even requisition of properties for the camps was easier in Germany than in England, since wartime regulations enabled the party to seize whatever they needed.

All seemed well planned, but still on 1 October, Goebbels noted in his diary:

> Schweres Problem mit der Kinderverschickung aus Berlin. Da ist der N.S.V. sehr ungeschickt vorgegangen und hat enorme Unruhe geschaffen.... Da haben zu viele durcheinanderregiert, darum diese Meckereien. Aber nun nehme ich die Zügel wieder in die Hand und führe die Angelegenheit klar durch. (Major problem with the evacuation from Berlin. The NSV's approach was very clumsy and created unrest.... Too many people messed around with this, thus the complaints. But from now on I will take matters in my own hands and give clear guidance on the matter.) (Fröhlich, 1998, pp. 354–355)

What Goebbels is referring to here is less a shortcoming in the planning than a PR disaster created by overambitious NSV staff in the capital. The SS security service's reports "Meldungen aus dem Reich" (Boberach, 1984, p. 1622) informed Goebbels on September 30 that wild rumors were flying around Berlin about a planned evacuation of the city's children. The consequence was that the population was more worried then than at any previous stage of the war. After all, evacuation could only mean that a major English air offensive was imminent. Apparently, NSV staff had gone from house to house to discuss evacuation with parents, pre-empting a carefully staged public announcement by disclosing details of the government scheme. The report closed with an urgent appeal to issue a press release with corrective and calming official announcements ("richtigstellende und beruhigende amtliche Verlautbarung").

Goebbel's reaction was immediate and comprehensive. On October 1, the Berlin papers uniformly (at this point the press was already "*gleichgeschaltet*") published a statement by the Berlin Gauleiter that directly responded to the rumors on the ground:

> Hier und da auftauchenden Gerüchten gegenüber wird erklärt, dass selbstverständlich weder eine Zwangsevakuierung noch überhaupt eine Evakui-

erung von Kindern aus der Reichshauptstadt geplant ist. Es handelt sich lediglich darum, solchen Eltern, denen für ihre Kinder keine genügenden Luftschutzräume zur Verfügung stehen, oder die befürchten müssen, dass der Gesundheitszustand ihrer Kinder durch häufigere Luftalarme gefährdet wird, die Möglichkeit zu geben, diese Kinder durch Hilfe der NSDAP bzw. der NSV in Gebiete zu verschicken, die weniger oder gar nicht luftgefährdet sind. Diese Verschickung ist eine durchaus freiwillige und widerrufbare.... Die Aktion soll bestimmt sein vom nationalsozialistischen Gemeinschafts-gedanken. Sie stellt ein zusätzliches Hilfsmittel im Kampf des deutschen Volkes gegen die englische Luftpiraterie dar und hat nicht das geringste mit Zwang zu tun. (This is to announce that, contrary to occasional rumors, there naturally are no plans whatsoever for a compulsory evacuation or any evacuation at all for the capital's children. The actual plan is that NSDAP and NSV are offering parents who have insufficient access to air raid shelters or worry that their children's health suffers from the frequent sleep inter-ruptions by sirens the opportunity to send their children into areas with lesser or no danger from air raids. This dispatch is completely voluntary and revocable.... The operation is governed by national socialist commu-nity spirit. It constitutes just another resource for the German people's fight against the British air pirates and has nothing whatsoever to do with coer-cion.) (*Berliner Lokal Anzeiger*, 01.10.1940)

Only two days later, the first evacuees left Berlin by charter train. Goeb-bel's ability to steer the press is evident from the enthusiastic newspaper articles that covered the event. The *12 Uhr Blatt* was even more compliant than others. Their headline for 9 October reads "Children on their way to Paradise," with smaller captions exclaiming: "a luxury train rolls afield," "no costs—no worries," and "now they're off for some relaxation in the Gi-ant Mountains" (Das 12 Uhr Blatt, 09.10.1940).

Whereas the British evacuation played its part in a larger transformation of society (Beaven & Griffiths, 2008), the KLV would become an integral part of the Fascist regime's attempt to actually create a new society. The party elite propagated itself as thoroughly modern and ruled with little considera-tion for the past. Unlike the English 19th-century laissez-faire tradition that worked well within newly democratic societies, Germany chose a different path: democratic and liberal notions had to succumb to a totalitarian state that had—often successfully—evoked an emotional bond between people and nation (i.e., regime) that superseded former family or community ties. A large and efficient bureaucracy was a necessary tool for ambitious NSDAP agendas like the KLV—whose planning wholly relied on children accustomed to state interference and a state apparatus that could be positioned for the new task on short notice. At this point in the planning, the regime accepted some level of discord among its offices and officials but assumed that the NS government still had a strong emotional bond with the German people.

The Train Companies

Both regimes relied on trains as the main mode of transport for their evacuees. Rail transport was the backbone of the evacuations' logistics, and it is therefore necessary to briefly introduce the companies and their situation at the outbreak of war.

In September 1938, the Ministry of Transport took over control of the English railways with the Defence of the Realm Act. Without the public noticing, the government effectively nationalized all rail companies and formed the Railway Executive Committee that drafted defense regulations in September 1939 (including evacuation, troop dispatch, and war economy supply chains). At war, the trains had to carry army horses and alien internees, they evacuated the civil service and the port of London, and they brought food and goods to the evacuees (Crump, 1947). As such, he government had direct access to whatever capacities they needed for London's evacuation, and the London and North Eastern Railway officers were responsible for matching district population, trainloads, and destinations (although there is a competing claim that this planning was done by Charles Hart at the LCC—Lowndes, 1969). Thus, they were partly responsible for the confusion on September 1–3. They did their best, but with a shortfall in numbers from the 203,484 passengers (203 trains) scheduled for evacuation to the actual number of 101,540 (82 trains), chaos was inevitable (Crump, 1947). Still, from the point of view of the railway companies, the evacuation "rates as one of the smoothest and most efficient movements of passengers ever carried out by the railways of this country" (Bryan, 1995, p. 16). Contemporary and later commentators will disagree.

The train companies' nationalization happened earlier in Germany than in Britain. The various regional and local train operators merged into the Deutsche Reichsbahn as early as 1920. It was then an independent company owned by the state (it still is). In WWI, the Reichsbahn's predecessors had been important contributors to Germany's military success, but in the 1930s the company was underfunded and under chaotic leadership. Hitler preferred cars and systematically neglected the trains' potential in the preparation for war (Schueler, 1987). "The DRB [Deutsche Reichsbahn] prepared evacuation plans well in advance, but the German civilian authorities frequently delayed using them until the last moment for fear of spreading panic among the population" (Mierzejewski, 2000, p. 159).

Still, the regime had unlimited access to trains during the war. Restrictions to their use for the KLV were only imposed by the simultaneous need for trains for the invasion of Russia. There did not seem to be a conflict, though, despite the 17,000 trains required for the Eastern attack. Optimistic planners calculated that the Reichsbahn would only be needed for the initial attack; the occupation could be achieved with captured Russian trains (Mierzejewski, 2000).

In Dabel's heavily edited KLV reader, the former PE teacher and KLV transport organizer Horst Hechler recalls the cooperation with the train companies. If registrations from an evacuation area would justify the dispatch of a charter train (between 600 and 800 evacuees) and matching accommodation in a reception area was found, he and local KLV officials would meet with the Reichsbahn representatives at Fahrplankonferenzen (timetabling conferences) that were hosted in different cities. The first—and only one in 1940—was held in Leipzig; afterwards the meetings would happen every two to three months at different locations. At the conferences, the KLV staff would patiently wait while the Reichsbahn staff minutely sketched out every charter train's progress through regions, cities, and stations. Return journeys were not subject to the same detailed preparation, mainly because of differing regional policies about minimum and maximum lengths of stays in the camps. The Reichsbahn operated returns mainly by blocking compartments on regular trains or just adding a few carriages to regularly timetabled trains (Dabel, 1981).

Chapter Conclusion

The documents discussed in this chapter show the turning points on the long way to a practical scheme for the evacuation of London—and the spontaneous setup of the one in Berlin. In London, the *Appreciation* marks the beginning of a period full of consultations, discussions, and decisions that shaped—but also delayed—the London scheme. The minutes from the Headmasters' Conference are testimony of the difficult relationship between LCC and central government. While London's planning advanced quickly, Whitehall only followed suit under the pressure of the Munich Crisis. The Emergency Memorandum proves that the LCC was indeed the political powerhouse of contemporary perception: the scheme approved in that all night session was an LCC brainchild. The subsequent takeover by the MoH, BoE, and LCC of the evacuation's responsibility away from the Home Office only further enabled Morrison, Rich, and his officers to press ahead with the preparations deemed necessary for the metropolis. Finally, the Chelsea practice showed the planners' growing confidence with the measures designed and discussed behind closed doors for years. The rehearsal clearly demonstrated that those responsible had finally put aside vanity and competition in favor of a joint, unified scheme. After years of discussions and numerous shifts of responsibilities, the evacuation scheme was unveiled to the expectant public.

In Berlin there was no need—or space—for discussions. The regime's iron grip on all administrative branches allowed the organizers of the evacuation scheme to get away with nearly no preparation at all. The Führer had demanded a scheme, and the apparatus instantaneously fell in line. Schirach's first draft reveals the nature of NS hierarchy: There were to be no consultations; instead, all executive branches were informed of the scheme and its requirements from them. This was particularly easy for the KLV planners, since they did not have to invent a scheme but only to modify a well-established holiday program to the new circumstances. Stepping on someone's toes in the process—in this case the ones of education minister Rust—was seen as almost necessary by ruthless party officials who were constantly trying to increase the NSDAP's power over state institutions. Thus, the planning stages already show each evacuation scheme to be victim of the complex and sometimes volatile state–society relationship in its country. Discussions about the schemes' designs were invariably discussions about class, power, and state organization.

Girls cheering with Swastika flags from train carriage
Bundesarchiv Berlin Photograph Collection 146-1978-013-14

3

Operation

When evacuation finally came to London, it did not come as a surprise. By then, the scheme had been subjected to years of controversial discussion and careful communication. When the order came, the LCC felt well prepared for an operation that, after all, would involve a substantial part of London's population, either as the objects of the government's providence or as the army of helpers—professional and volunteer—enlisted as traffic wardens, assembly point checks, platform supervisors, first aid nurses, messengers, drivers, and so on. It was time to test whether the local bureaucracy's assumptions about citizen's behavior and social communities were accurate enough to successfully execute the evacuation scheme. This chapter will review how the LCC's theoretical planning translated into action through two key sources containing the council's account of the operation—and a collation of them with accounts from other vantage points, such as the sociological researchers surveying evacuees in the reception areas.

In Berlin, the short time between the idea of an evacuation scheme and its operation must have been filled with the feverish synchronisation

Operation Pied Piper, pages 55–76
Copyright © 2012 by Information Age Publishing

of different government and party branches that had all done something vaguely similar before (like summer camps, army transport, placement of foster children, etc.), but now had to quickly adapt to the new challenge. Luckily for the Dienststelle KLV, the challenge was on a much smaller scale than that facing London. There was never a plan to evacuate all of Berlin's children in one go, but rather to have a continuous flow of trainloads into the reception areas. The story of this operation will be told through an NSV order that summarizes the provisions put in place and a letter from the HJ to members embarking on their *adventurous* evacuation. The review of the operation will be on a much smaller scale here for the obvious absence of recorded criticism—the citizens' concerns will only become apparent later through the adjustments to the scheme made by a bureaucracy torn between autocratic rule and need for public validation. Within the analytical framework, this chapter thus fits into research aspects concerning executive power, administrative competence, and public acceptance of government provision.

London

Plan II: The Biggest Exodus from London

The Munich Crisis was a turning point for the attitude of the Londoners towards war. Both Ziegler and Lowndes suggest that up until then the civilians in London were not politically minded and displayed a public apathy that was fed by sheer disbelief at the possibility of a war so soon after the last one and helplessness since they had no influence in the decision. In 1939, "little by little Londoners reluctantly accepted that something had to be done and even—though this was harder—that they might have to be the ones to do it" (Ziegler, 1995, p. 13). It was widely anticipated that German air raids of London would immediately follow the declaration of war. During that summer, preparations were evident all over London: houses were made ready for blackouts, sandbags were piled outside municipal buildings, and Anderson shelters were delivered and set up. Extra trenches were dug in the cemeteries to cope with the corpses that would be buried without coffins due to wood shortages. Forty barrage balloons, the blimps, became a permanent feature in the London sky. From August onwards, the television went off air (for fear of its signal somehow helping German piloting), hospital wards were cleared of all but the most critical patients, and the House of Commons and the House of Lords got ready to move to Stratford-upon-Avon (Ziegler, 1995). On the radio, Herbert Morrison urged the parents of London to register their children for the evacuation scheme (Donoughue & Jones, 1973), and teachers mentally prepared their children for life in the country before spending the evenings running from house to house convincing reluctant parents (Arthur, 2004).

In the Evacuation Branch in London, preparations were going ahead as planned, while the clerks there noted that surprisingly few requests for information came from the reception areas (L.C.C., 1943, II 58). During August, tension in London increased when the international political situation went from bad to worse. On August 24, 1939, schools were ordered to recall their staff from the summer holidays and to reassemble one day later. The official "get ready" signal was issued on August 26, and on August 29 there were test runs of the assembly procedures, with children already coming to school in evacuation order—that is, younger siblings going to the schools of their older brothers and sisters. The days of standby were particularly difficult for the teachers who had to entertain their pupils while acting as registrars for latecomers to the evacuation scheme. On Thursday, August 31, the LCC received the evacuation order for September 1, and it was quickly ascertained that the transport providers were fully prepared— or at least as prepared as anyone can be when dealing with 1,589 assembly points, 160 entraining stations, eleven transfer stations for mainland services, 271 arrival points in the reception areas, and an estimated 1.5 million children (L.C.C., 1943, II 60). On the morning itself, *The Times* announced *Evacuation to-day* while reassuring readers that this was no sign that war was inevitable, that peaceful France had already taken similar steps and that the best way to cooperate with the evacuation was to refrain from using the trains, underground, or roads. The article closes with a persuasive quote by Herbert Morrison, who spent September 1 touring train stations and schools wishing the evacuees good luck and a safe return, where he expressed confidence that Londoners would accept the change "in the calm, cheerful and friendly spirit which has never flagged throughout the period of tension" (Donoughue & Jones, 1973, p. 267; *Times*, 01.09.1939).

This study will deviate from classic source analysis here. There seems to be little merit in evaluating how these Evacuation Branch bulletins compare to other contemporary and subsequent accounts of the evacuation, since they *all* rely on them. One has to cautiously acknowledge that the LCC had the most accurate overview of an operation that was too massive in size for other observers (including individual evacuees) to truly grasp. These two bulletins were sent from the Evacuation Branch to senior officers within the LCC and other ministries, Education Officers in the adjoining boroughs and officers on duty in the reception areas. Although not, strictly speaking, documents intended for publication, it is safe to assume that the reports of the operation were not sensitive or confidential. Indeed, the press coverage relied on the exact numbers given in these documents—

making the branch's accounts the original fact-sheets for the public debate on the evacuation. At the same time, one has to acknowledge the potential unreliability of documents published by the agency that had pushed its agenda against political opposition and gambled their reputation on the evacuation's success. Thus, the bulletins' role in this study is twofold: As the most authoritative documents on the operation, they will guide the narrative—while simultaneously revealing the attitudes and sensitivities within the LCC through this self-portrayal of its achievements.

Two LCC Bulletins

Bulletin No. 25 was the first one to be published after the execution of Plan II and summarizes the proceedings (source VII). The evacuation began on Monday morning, September 1, 1939, with the assembly of the school parties in their schools. The first to leave the capital were 300 parties with a total of 17,000 "handicapped" and nursery children who left by coach and safely arrived at their designated destinations. At the assembly of the primary and secondary schoolchildren scheduled to leave by train, it became immediately apparent that numbers were substantially lower than anticipated. This, together with increased time pressure on the operation due to the worsening political situation, led to major logistical problems at the entraining stations, where station masters had to abandon their carefully worked out train capacity measurements, which in turn led to unexpected destinations for a lot of school parties (Lowndes, 1969; Samways, 1995). Since this was probably considered a problem for the reception areas rather than the LCC, the bulletin makes a very positive assessment of the first day, reporting high numbers of volunteers and helpers, smooth operation throughout, no casualties or serious incident, and a total of 286,918 evacuated children.

While the first day was devoted to school parties, and school parties alone, the second day's challenge was to see off a much more diverse crowd of evacuees. On September 2, the following priority groups were evacuated: remainder of school parties (57,144); children under five with their mothers and occasional siblings (128,777); expectant mothers (last month of pregnancy) (2,935); Blind people (3,200). The last two groups left London by bus, while the first two were entrained. As on the previous day, the actual number of evacuees was much lower than anticipated. The total of 192,056 represented only two-thirds of the estimated 300,000 enlisted in these priority classes. The Evacuation Branch offers two reasons for this behavior, but does not conceal their surprise about the poor showing. One reason given concerns the refusal of wives to leave their husbands in London—an issue that had been recognized early by the organizers, but never sufficiently resolved. The other is that simultaneously to the official evacuation "there has been *unofficial evacuation* on a considerable scale. Many people who registered . . . have *gone off under their own steam*" (Source VII, p. 5).

The bulletin mentions two more reasons that, although the Evacuation Branch firmly dismisses their credibility, deserve mentioning. One is the apathy of the Londoners, the "general belief that by talking about war one made it more likely to come about" (Ziegler, 1995, p. 12). This might have been true for the time of the Munich Crisis, but Newton—the author of the bulletins—rightly assumes that, with all the other war preparations going on in the capital, no Londoner could have been in doubt about the seriousness of the situation—so much so that people who originally declined to sign up for the scheme joined their friends and neighbors spontaneously on the day for fear of missing a real opportunity (Buckton, 2009). Equally true for earlier times might have been the accusation that the Evacuation Scheme was badly publicized and not enough advertising had been done in advance, but by August, publicity was no longer an issue "as Hitler has done the propaganda" for them (Source VII, p. 4).

While the lower turnout on the first day of the evacuation messed up transportation arrangements and confused the entraining procedures, the bulletin claims that on the second day the low numbers actually made the management easier and only caused more comfort on the trains. Cooperation by the train companies, especially their provision of porters to deal with an unorthodox high volume of luggage, is noted enthusiastically and discipline within the groups worth commendation. The LCC even provided for latecomers, or *stragglers*, with a fleet of privately chauffeured cars. Beside the optimism, though, there are first signs of the problems the evacuation caused in the reception areas. Londoners left without a billet in the country reported back to the LCC, prompting them to manifest the limits of their responsibilities. Since the Evacuation Branch provided numbers in advance—and actually sent fewer people than anticipated—a shortage of billets must have been caused either by poor planning on the part of the authorities in the reception areas or the high volume of unofficial evacuation. In any case, it was not deemed a problem for the LCC:

> We have no responsibility for this state of affairs in the Reception Area and I have no means of judging if whether the calls we had betoken an unsatisfactory state of affairs generally or not. I hope no judgment will be made yet at all for we have no means whatever of sizing up the general situation, and of course we heard the grumbles and nothing much of the satisfactory work which was no doubt done in many places. (Source VII, p. 4)

It is difficult to judge if it is the Evacuation Branch's arrogance that triggered this comment—the patronizing behavior of an office that is proud of the implementation of a mammoth task—or if it is self-defense against accusations of shortcomings well beyond the responsibilities of the LCC. It seems certain, though, that the occasionally chaotic entraining at the London mainland stations caused a lot of the confusion in the reception areas. It is also understandable that Londoners held *their* government responsible for whatever happened to them—and this clash of attitudes turned out to be a major problem for the subsequent evacuations during the Blitz.

The third day of evacuation, Sunday, September 3, proved uneventful, despite it being the day when Britain went to war. The great majority of the 106,321 evacuated on that day were mothers with their own children. Again, numbers were lower than anticipated, with "unofficial evacuation" mentioned as the chief reason for the absence of previously registered Londoners. On the Monday after, the scheduled fourth day of evacuation, only 22,340 more registered evacuees turned up as part of a mopping-up operation. This left train capacities in extent of 30,000 seats unused, which the LCC immediately wanted to utilize by opening up evacuation to the whole London population. The bulletin reports the ensuing clash of opinions between the Evacuation Branch, whose chief concern was the safety of the Londoners, and the Ministry of Health, who opposed the impromptu extension of the evacuation on grounds that the reception areas were already overburdened with official and unofficial evacuees as well as military billets. The LCC grudgingly had to cancel the extra facilities and closed their evacuation operation on Monday in the late afternoon. Within those four days, 607,635 evacuees made use of the evacuation scheme, the operation had no casualties to report, and the Evacuation Branch staff congratulated themselves on a job well done, with E. M. Rich publicly announcing that they "have earned the gratitude of the people of London" (Bulletin 25, p. 7). Even in recent assessments, there is no doubt about the smoothness of the dispatch—the problems started in the reception areas (e.g., Mellegard, 2005).

Bulletin No. 27 (source VIII—undated, but incorporating events up to the 16 September 1939) testifies to the surprising and swift deterioration in the relationship between state officials and citizens that began immediately after the evacuation's launch. The document is de facto a universal reply to the "avalanche of inquiries which gathered strength as the days and weeks passed" (L.C.C., 1943, II 65) and an instruction manual for the officers in the reception areas. From this document one can infer the gravity of operational problems that had not been foreseen during the planning stages. The bulletin was issued in an attempt to reduce the correspondence to the Evacuation Branch—by now relocated with the County Council to emergency headquarters in Englefield Green in Surrey—and gives clear guidelines on matters that had reached County Hall either from parents in London or evacuees in the reception areas.

The bulletin might have additionally been used to influence or discredit the evacuation's press coverage (already a feature of Bulletin No. 25: "A Man was killed at Enfield Station. His death had nothing to do with evacuation. The children did not witness it or hear of it. If the press says the LCC or the Evacuation Scheme killed him the press will be wrong"). In the end, though, the positive reports of the evacuation in the press prompted a flood of further requests from parents in London who did not previously register their children for evacuation. Additionally, requests for evacuation seem to have come from Londoners who, even though not included in the priority classes, could have been considered vulnerable as well as expendable in the metropolis: the aged, infirm, elderly, and crippled (Source VIII, p. 3). To all of them the message was unambiguous: the evacuation is closed for the time being; there had been an additional registration on September 11 and 12, and those who did not register then would have to wait until further notice—and a redefinition of the priority classes by the government (Source VIII). It is naturally not documented if this harsh reply was intended as a snub to those who initially had not put their trust in the evacuation scheme.

Parents in London wishing to establish the whereabouts of their evacuated children were advised to contact the caretaker of their children's school. This could be regarded as evidence that the postcards that children should use to give their address to parents were not printed and distributed or that the post office was not able to deliver them within the fortnight following the evacuation. Bulletin No. 27 also indicates that the private returns of children to London had begun—the LCC denied public money to assist with train fares home. Public funds were also denied to those who evacuated themselves or their children privately.

For dealings with the reception areas, it seems to be an explicit aim of this and the previous bulletin to establish the local billeting officers, the education officer's staff, and the local authorities in general as the first point of contact for the evacuees. For most inquiries, the reply was that "all matters connected with the well-being of evacuees in the reception area are the concern of the local authority in the country and not of the London County Council" (Source VIII, p. 3). Nevertheless, some principal advice was given on some major concerns like that of families who had been evacuated into different parts of the country (i.e, older children wh their schools, younger siblings with their mothers) and wished to reunite. In thosite cases, local authorities were asked—subject to available accommodation—to grant the request, but no financial assistance was given towards the travel costs. However, most issues—including the one of evacuees entering paid or voluntary employment—were directed to the staff on the ground.

It must have been frustrating for the organizers to realize that no amount of planning could overcome the human aspect of the evacuation. First they had to improvise all travel arrangements due to the shortfall in numbers of children showing up—leading to unpredicted destinations for the school parties and subsequent complaints by the public—and then, days after the evacuation, when parents finally came around to desire evacuation for their children they had to deny them, with complaints by the public again being the consequence. Since the official documents remain silent on these issues (a weakness of official records, no doubt) there is little value in dwelling on it. It is clear, though, from the nature of the matters with which the Evacuation Branch had to concern itself after the execution of Plan II that the operation was in many ways successful. After all, mastering problems arising from an increased demand in the scheme must have been seen as preferable to dealing with dead, injured or lost children or a collapse of the transport system (Brown, 2005).

The Aftermath of Plan II

Having given the LCC viewpoint a lot of space, it is now necessary to contrast the organizers' view with that of the evacuation's beneficiaries in order to grasp changes to society–state relationships. The evacuation that started in September 1939 and continued for most of the war was arguably "after bombing, the most crucial life-event experienced by the civilian population" (Macnicol, 1986, p. 7), which explains why there are so many accounts, studies, and retrospective analyses of it. Logistical issues were not necessarily appreciated by the evacuees, who only perceived "that exact destinations were kept secret, and rail journeys long and slow—with the result that many of the children, already traumatised by separation from their families, arrived at their destinations tired, frightened and lonely" (Macnicol, 1986, p. 6). The transport strategy's complete disarray after the serious shortfall in participants and the haste prescribed by the government only amplified what would have been a difficult enterprise in the best of circumstances. Even though the planners of the evacuation in London were aware of the "popular dislike of evacuation" (*Times*, 12.07.1939), an issue they tried to tackle with various publicity measures, they never fully grasped the extent of it. Even on the actual day of the exodus, Herbert Morrison was disappointed that, after his extensive publicity measures for the scheme, only about half of the 1.5 million children originally enlisted in London turned up at the assembly points (Donoughue & Jones, 1973). Retrospectively, this seems all the more surprising since there is evidence that parts of the target population did not view the evacuation as voluntary or optional. A former evacuee was not evacuated in 1939, and it seems that he was at the receiving end of the chaos with transportation timetables created by the overestimate of participants for September 1. While his mother had duly sent him to school all packed and equipped, he returned home later that day because the coach for their particular party did not arrive (the rest of the school went, though). He recollects:

> As far as I know there was no attempt to send us another coach. However, I am certain that my family would have thought it God's will (or fate) that the coach did not arrive. "He was not meant to go" would have been their philosophy. I do not think there was any decision made by parents to keep or send away a child, all went without a fuss. I know of no coercion, or refusal by parents—it just happened. Difficult to comprehend in 2010!... There is another aspect. My family were working class and poor. They were not inclined to fight authority, at least not for this reason. (Dan Regan in an email to the author)

One reason for the shortfall in numbers seems to be that the scale of private evacuation was substantially higher than anticipated. Since the organizers in London were dependent on the cooperation of the reception areas, their information to parents had always been unsatisfactory. This prompted affluent Londoners to send their children away independently, to "buy or hire safety for themselves and their dependants" (Titmuss, 1950, p. 102). There is no sufficient explanation yet how the people in charge of the evacuation missed the private exodus of an estimated two million from the vulnerable areas and did not allow for this in their planning (Brown, 2005).

It has also been argued that the situation of the poorer urban parents without links to the country—for whom the official evacuation scheme was mainly designed—had not been sufficiently acknowledged by the civil service. Optimism to reach this target group with the scheme was high, since that part of the population was traditionally more open to public provision. The planners were aware of some reluctance to register children in the East End who were contributing to the household income by working before or after school—or enabled parents to work by looking after siblings or elderly family members (Titmuss, 1950). Still, civil servants with privileged middle-class (boarding school) backgrounds found it difficult to "understand fully some of the issues involved in separating children from the closely-knit working class families" (Crosby, 1986, p. 7)—as is evident from the contemporary surveys reviewed below.

The true origin for the widespread criticism of the government's evacuation scheme, though, might be found with more cynical reasoning. The scheme was always designed to be an emergency measure, but the emergency—the immediate bombing of London by German aircrafts following the declaration of war—did not arise, yet. England was entering the so-called "Phoney War" (an American label; the British press called it *Sitzkrieg* and Churchill later wrote about the period as the "Twilight War"), and enemy bombs would not hit the capital for nearly another year. In a real emergency, criticism of the evacuation scheme might have been scarce, but "as it was, there was plenty of time for everyone to dwell on the shortcomings of the scheme" (Ziegler, 1995, p. 35) —or as Maclure sums up:

> The whole complicated operation was carried through with remarkable efficiency. But this efficiency—aided, of course, by the absence of the air raids on account of which the evacuation programme was being put in hand—was soon forgotten in the face of the chorus of complaints which began to come in from the reception areas about the hygiene and conduct of the children (Maclure, 1990, pp. 135–136)

Actually, the popular complaint in rural communities about the invasion of dirty and unhealthy Londoners seemed all the more surprising as London had a well-established School Medical Service dating back to the 1900s. Pre-war, the main duties of its inspectors were the recognition and treatment of skin diseases, defective vision, swollen tonsils, dental problems, and the like. The Medical Service worked with the LCC before and during the evacuation by inspecting the evacuees prior to their departure and by providing paperwork on potential medical problems during the evacuation procedure (Gosden, 1976). Nevertheless, the culture shock in rural England became the defining evacuation moment and an elementary part of its legacy; as Ben Wicks poignantly put it: "The poor may have seen the countryside for the first time, but the countryside also saw the poor of the cities. It was a shock for both" (Wicks, 1988, p. 196).

Reviews of the Evacuation in Contemporary Surveys

Following the theoretical foundations laid by Marx and Weber, there was substantial interest in the relationship of state organization, class, and power in the 1930s and 1940s (Held, 1989). It is not surprising then, that the evacuation was used as exemplar for the study of state–society relationships. The Fabian Society, who commissioned a survey in 1939, provided instant feedback on the evacuation. It is a sharp, thorough, and comprehensive document. Its weakness is its early publication, since it predates the Blitz and only covers the problematic Phoney War period. Margaret Cole, one of the editors, shows awareness of this by opening with a defense of the scheme as a military expedient. However, she also offers harsh criticism: A scheme that "turns out to appeal to less than half of its supposed beneficiaries, can hardly be described as a resounding success.... It is quite obvious that psychologically the scheme failed to appeal, partly, I suggest, because it was drawn up by minds that were military, male and middle-class" (Cole & Padley, 1940, p. 4).

The survey's criticism goes further: Both key problems—low numbers in the government scheme and high numbers in private evacuation—could have been anticipated. Richard Padley draws comparisons to the Spanish Civil War, where the administration in Madrid struggled with similar parental reluctance to send children to safety. The MoH actually estimated that a quarter of the evacuation would be private and thus could have been aware that billeting figures were unreliable, but "there is ample evidence that the Government's attitude at the outbreak of war was close to panic" (Padley, 1940, p. 36). It was not only panic, though, but also unresolved power struggles leading to administrative incompetency.

> Of the departments concerned with administering the scheme, the only one which showed sufficient imagination, the Board of Education, was lacking in initiative, and allowed itself to be refused any major share of control. The Ministry of Home Security was obsessed with Wellsian visions of destruction, and was in any case too busy with other aspects of civil defence; the Ministry of Transport saw the whole business purely as a technical problem; and the Ministry of Health, which was responsible for the scheme, was far too timid to produce any serious policy. (Padley, 1940, p. 37)

Padley actually goes further and terms the scheme's ability to persuade parents and children "a demonstrable failure." He also laments the neglect of properly organizing the reception, an issue outside this study's reach. His colleague Joan Clarke will have made LCC officials very happy with her recommendation to transfer more power over the evacuation to London's local authority (Clarke, 1940, p. 209). In her contemporaneous report, Monica Cosens supports the claim of incompetency. According to a head-teacher questioned in the survey, there was "no co-ordination between the different bodies. The transport people transported, the reception people received, the billeting officers billeted. And then we all began to live...." Pleas to keep schools together were ignored despite obvious mismanagement where half of two schools' populations were billeted in the same village. Another mistake was that the male organizers, besides the attributes Cole noted, were simply ignorant of the fact that taking care of children was hard work (Cosens, 1940).

London children were also evacuated to Cambridge, prompting a group of social workers and child psychologists under the auspice of Susan Isaacs to conduct a similar study there in 1939. The published report draws largely similar conclusions to the Fabian Society's, but allows much more space for the condemnation of the evacuation planners' ignorance of psychological considerations. If the civil servants had considered the working class mind "with a tithe of the labour and intelligence which we put into questions of transport, if human nature had been taken into equal account with geography and railway time tables," (Isaacs, Brown, & Thouless, 1941, p. 4) the planners could have avoided the damaging drift back to London.

> Among the simple and the poor, where there is no wealth, no pride of status or of possession, love for the members of one's own family and joy in their bodily presence alone make life worth living. So deeply rooted is this need that it has defied even the law of self-preservation, as well as urgent public appeals and the wishes of authority. (Isaacs et al., 1941, p. 9)

Despite the patronizing tone, a slightly romanticized view of the working-class family, and the privileged hindsight position, the Cambridge Evacuation Survey offers a very coherent argument for the high numbers of returnees. With the absence of bombs, it argues, the real question should not be *why did some children return to London,* but *why did so many stay in the reception areas* (Isaacs, et al., 1941)? After all, at the time of the survey the threat was abstract and theoretical; the bombing only existed in propaganda. Titmuss later tried to defend the scheme against these accusations voiced from the privileged Phoney War vantage point. He argues that the scheme was foremost a military expedient: "Inevitably, the effect on the sensitive mechanism of the child's mind took second place.... This was no social experiment; it was a surgical rent only to be contemplated as a last resort" (Titmuss, 1950, p. 109).

Based on their findings, the team at Cambridge closes with a list of recommendations for the evacuation scheme's organizers, including the obtainment of better information about the evacuees before their departure, a better availability of social workers in the reception areas, the introduction of cheap train travel for visiting parents, and a neutral, communal meeting place for London parents and their children. Chapter 5 will show how the LCC and the authorities in the reception areas attempted to regain some of their credibility with the people by implementing these recommendations and improving the evacuation scheme.

Berlin

Kommt mit in die Kinderlandverschickung!

The earlier outline of London's evacuation could have been a blueprint for the NSV's provision for younger children. The similarities are striking and probably not accidental, since press and security services were well informed of events across the channel. This remains speculative, though, since too little is known of the German evacuation's genesis. Here as there, local authorities in the reception areas were advised to compile lists of available places with host families. The hosts' incentive for volunteering was the child's rationing card and the NSV payment of 2 Reichsmark per child and day. Only in emergencies would the local authorities make use of the law (Reichsleistungsgesetz) to force householders into cooperation, but knowledge of this option probably aided the decision to volunteer in the first place. Families might also have volunteered knowing that ostentatious compliance put them in the regime's good books. On rare occasions, households—mostly owners of B & Bs and small hotels—paid their way out of their billeting obligation. When only a few evacuees would join a community they would be sent to join classes in the local school, but for larger groups the schools developed a shift system with teachers drafted in from Berlin (Kock, 1997).

Unlike London parents, the families in Berlin had to sign their children up for a minimum duration of six months (a measure contemplated in London but dismissed as achieving nothing more than an immediate mass return—Gosden, 1976) and to agree that on reaching the age of ten they would be transferred into the charge of the HJ. Thus, once the billeting officer had placed the child and made arrangements with the closest school, the NSV's work was done, apart from paying the billeting fee and the occasional troubleshooting (Kock, 1997). Actually, later assessments showed the evacuation of children below the HJ age to be the most successful. During the war, the NSV oversaw the dispatch of over two million children (with or without mothers) into billets. Neither in Berlin nor the reception areas did this evacuation create logistical problems since the infrastructure was already in place from the holiday KLV that, after all, had "evacuated" well over 500,000 German children each year since 1933 (see Chapter 1).

The NSV's KLV Directive

Documents about the evacuation do not become more authoritative than this one. This is the directive issued to the NSV offices and staff in the evacuation and reception areas (Source IX); it is the operation's official framework as communicated to those who most urgently needed clear guidelines about the impromptu evacuation. "Arbeitsanweisungen" like this one issued on October 15, 1940 were to civilians what orders still are in the army: They had to be obeyed to the letter. Like orders, the language is unambiguous and straightforward, leaving no room for common courtesy. There are no subjunctive clauses in this document, no modal verbs and no "please." Instead, the operational issues are manifested in a manner already establishing the desirable as reality—for example, there will be live music at the assembly point and on the platform during the children's departure ("Auf dem Sammelplatz und auf dem Bahnsteig hat je eine Kapelle zu spielen"). It falls to the recipients of these instructions to make that true. Unfortunately, most of these linguistic peculiarities are somewhat lost in translation, but would merit further sociolinguistic analysis in a different context.

The directive opens with a section on the scheme's promotion that follows the familiar lines laid down by Schirach. The voluntary nature of the scheme is mentioned, as is the mandatory commitment to a minimum duration away from home. The section "general remarks" lists the reception areas and distinguishes the groups and qualifying criteria (see below). Whereas Schirach's focus was on schoolchildren alone, the NSV—as the Reich's universal charity—defined the evacuable population more broadly. In addition to groups I and II (unaccompanied children), the directive includes mothers with children up until the age of 14 staying with friends or relatives (group III—Verwandtenkinderverschickung), mothers with young children going into billets (group IV—see below), and mothers with infants or pregnant women going into communal homes (group V). Predeparture medical checks are detailed and seem to have been executed with great bureaucratic effort. Questions of clothing take up some room in the document: The NSV offers to supply clothes in cases where parents cannot afford to provide the items listed in this directive, and thorough checks should be made before departure that every child has a complete set. Considering the wave of complaints organizers in London had to face after the dispatch of ill-clothed and ill-equipped children from the East End, this measure shows some foresight and the NSV's more intimate knowledge of their evacuation's clientele. The NSV seemed to know its officers very well, too. In anticipation of over-eagerness on part of the cloth checker the directive clearly states: no child must be left behind because of clothing issues ("Keinesfalls darf aber die Verschickung wegen Nichtvorhandenseins von irgendwelchen Kleidungsstücken scheitern"—p. 3).

Departure arrangements differed from London in so far as the children assembled under NSV or HJ supervision rather than in schools. Once a NSV section (town or district) had registered enough children to justify a charter train, transport arrangements would be put in place by different party branches and the Reichsbahn. The directive distributes responsibilities down to the level of music, sweets, and volunteers in uniform. Probably to avoid emotional scenes, mothers of children leaving Berlin were not to be used as volunteer helpers at their children's departure, but could and should be used on any other. Bureaucracy again dominates this section: Various labels, certificates, health insurance documents, rationing cards, and the like have to be properly displayed or stored. This section closes with a remark that private evacuation still remains desirable (probably because of the scheme's high cost) and parents are, if not encouraged, than at least permitted to make their own arrangements at their own costs.

The remainder of the directive deals with the groups individually, and for the purpose of this study, only the first two are of interest. Unaccompanied evacuation into billet was offered to children from the age of three. Primary schoolchildren would join the local infrastructure (nursery, school) in the billet's area. Host parents were to be vetted by the local NSV staff in line with health and moral standards and to ensure that each evacuee has his or her own bed (actually termed: Schlafstätte—a place to sleep). Siblings from different age groups are not to be split up, and all children of school age are subject to compulsory schooling. Group II does not get a lot of mention since their evacuation is—with the exception of transport arrangements—run by the HJ and NSLB. The directive confirms the NSLB's leadership status over the teachers who will travel to the KLV camps three days ahead of their students, and only once they too have been thoroughly medically inspected and found to be free of TB or other infectious diseases.

Some of the instructions given in this document perfectly illustrate the humanitarian attitude as well as the inhumanity of the NS regime. As mentioned before, charity was a big feature of the regime's provision (and popularity), but only extended to those deemed worthy within NS ideology. While there was undoubtedly an egalitarian attempt of inclusion, there were also exclusion clauses for the undesirables. The Arbeitsanweisung is quite specific about eligibility:

Da die Verschickung sich nicht nach Bedürftigkeit richtet, ist die Angabe des Einkommens unwesentlich. Die Entsendung der Kinder und Mütter erfolgt grundsätzlich kostenlos. Soweit Eltern jedoch wirtschaftlich in der Lage sind, ist es ihnen anheimzustellen, einen entsprechenden Beitrag zu leisten. Desgleichen ist die Entsendung nicht an die Erholungsbedürftigkeit gebunden. Bei der Erfassung von Kindern ist soweit wie möglich die Würdigkeit und haltungsmäßige Eignung der Kinder zu prüfen, um nach Betragen und Haltung ungeeignete Kinder gegebenenfalls in festen Einrichtungen zu erfassen. Zu bevorzugen sind in erster Linie Kinder

a) aus Häusern mit ungenügendem Schutz durch unzureichende Luftschutzräume,

b) aus Wohngebieten, die durch Bombenabwurf in besonderer Weise gefährdet sind. (Source IX, p. 2)

(Since there is no means testing, documentation of parental income will be unnecessary. Principally, mothers and children are evacuated free of charge. However, if parents are in a position to contribute to the cost they are encouraged to do so. There is to be no testing of the evacuees' actual need for recreation, but of their worthiness and attitude in order to bundle unsuitable children together in designated camps if necessary. Priority should be given to children who live in houses without appropriate air raid shelters or in areas that are particularly exposed to air raids.)

The Arbeitsanweisung is a very thorough and concise document that defines and prescribes a lot of operational aspects of Berlin's evacuation. It is also true to the cliché of German efficiency: after all, it was circulated not three weeks after Schirach's and Hitler's initial meeting—at a time when the first trains had already left Berlin. The document also shows the operational advantages and moral hazards of a centralized, uniform, and ruthless civil service. The operation was up and running (and running smoothly) —at least for those conforming to the physical and psychological demands of the NSDAP.

As mentioned in the Arbeitsanweisung, the NSV was also in charge of the Mutter-Kind-Verschickung offered to mothers with infants under the age of three (later raised to six). Very much like London's priority group two, mothers would be billeted into host families and expected to help out there. The government's initial ambition was to calm the nerves of husbands and fathers fighting abroad, but there was another incentive for Berlin's rulers: Under war regulations it could command the vacated city home, offering it to those who had been bombed out of theirs, but had to stay in Berlin as part of the war effort (Kock, 1997). Nonetheless, Mutter-Kind-Verschickung became a popular and widely accepted form of evacuation, not least because mothers were allowed to take older children with them, provided they had one in the appropriate age bracket. It thus proved to be a real alternative for mothers reluctant to send their children into the unknown. In the course of events, demand substantially exceeded supply, and local authorities had to limit the duration of evacuees' stays in the country. Meanwhile, the NSV's own peacetime recreational homes for mothers and children (Mutter-Kind-Heime) were reserved for expectant mothers and mothers with nurslings.

Sending Older Children into HJ Camps

While the experiences of younger children from London and Berlin were strikingly similar, the second group of German evacuees had a very different war than their British counterparts. Under the auspice of the HJ, hundreds of thousands of adolescents were dispatched into camps where they would be under a party-approved teacher's supervision in the morning and obeying the orders of a HJ leader (only marginally older than the evacuees themselves) in the afternoon and evening. Life in KLV camps—usually located at the fringe of the Reich—continues to be a popular research topic and not much about it will feature here, unless the experiences of Berlin children have a direct impact on their hometown.

The KLV began at schools. Even though the party ousted the Education Ministry from the operation and allowed no interference by the teachers, it still needed their support. The party's own NSLB thus proclaimed: "Die Ehre der deutschen Erzieherschaft heißt, für die Durchführung dieser großen herrlichen Aufgabe die Anerkennung des Führers zu erringen. (It is the honor of German teachers is to fulfil this glorious, magnificent task in order to gain the Führer's recognition.) (NSLB Circular 51/40 in: BBF/DIPF GUT SAMML 191).

Information evenings were held in Berlin schools to advertise the "Erweiterte Kinderlandverschickung." Afterwards parents would sign registration slips confirming their commitment to send away their children for a minimum of six months. Although voluntary, it was the aim of organizers and schools to send whole classes or year groups away. Pester power became vital for the success of the evacuation, and "peer pressure made it virtually impossible for a single child to stay behind" (Kater, 2004, p. 45). Parents signing up would have to confirm that no one in their household had had a contagious illness in the last two years and that the child did not wet the bed. Furthermore, they received a Rüstzettel (packing list) that itemized necessary clothing and equipment. The NSV would compensate wherever parents were unable to equip their children properly. Three days ahead of the departure a vague announcement of the destination—usually just an area, like *Ostmark*—would be given. Transportation would be mainly by train, even though from 1942 a large fleet of cruise ships and excursion boats—unused during the war—would ease the strain on the transport networks by shipping evacuees to their reception areas. Berlin children would travel on the rivers Havel, Spree, Oder, and the Hohenzollern canal (Dabel, 1981, p. 27ff).

As has been mentioned earlier, numbers for the operation are notoriously hard to come by, since the Reichsjugendführung refused to publish them. Their dilemma was that low numbers could be seen as a public refusal of party provision, while high numbers could be considered an indication of growing panic. Both were undesirable. Industrious researcher Kock cites a note from Schirach stating that by November 4, 1940, 66,273 children were evacuated from Berlin, with 15,776 sent into KLV camps and the rest billeted with the NSV. A later memorandum from the Dienststelle notes that in March 1941, 412,908 children from Berlin, Hamburg, and the industrial West were evacuated in government schemes, of whom 136,061 stayed in KLV camps (Kock, 1997). These numbers provide only an incomplete picture, though, since administrators in Berlin seemed to have been thankful for any child privately evacuated or not returning from the summer holidays—so much so that the Schulpflicht was relaxed and schools advised by Rust to grant leave to those students absent. Even without those private evacuees (or Gastschüler), the operational costs were high. Retrospectively the KLV did cost the state one million Reichsmark per day (Buddrus, 2003; the Bundesarchiv's total for the operation is 1.25 billion RM—Naasner & Schmidt, 1995).

As a consequence of the Nazi regime's construction of citizenship, the KLV organizers preferred to address the children rather than the parents. *Youth leads youth* meant that the evacuees would volunteer rather than being signed up. This was an important aspect of HJ culture and part of its overwhelming appeal during the 1930s. The KLV e.V. has in their collection a letter dated May 9, 1941 from Bremen's local NSDAP official Karl Behrens, instructing young evacuees on their impending departure into billets (source X). The tone, especially at the end of the letter, is noteworthy since it clearly demonstrates how the HJ bypassed parents and communicated with the youth directly.

> Danke es dem Führer durch tadelloses Betragen und Gehorsam! Schreibe sofort nach Deinem Eintreffen an Deine Eltern, damit sie wissen, daß Du gut angekommen bist und Deine Anschrift wissen. Schreibe dann hinterher auch dem Jungbann bzw. Untergau und auch mir einmal, wir alle würden uns sehr freuen! Ich wünsche Dir nun eine schöne Reise und herrliche,

ereignisreiche Tage im Heim und bitte Dich, Deinen lieben Eltern einen recht herzlichen Gruß zu bestellen. Sei auch Du herzlich gegrüßt mit Heil Hitler! (Source X)

(Show gratefulness to the Führer with immaculate behavior and obedience! Write to your parents immediately upon arrival, so that they know your new address and that you had a safe journey. Afterwards, write a letter to your HJ group at home and maybe even one to me, we do look forward to hearing from you. Have a very good journey and wonderful and exciting days in camp. Please give my regards to your dear parents. All the best to you: Heil Hitler!)

Even when allowing for legitimate concerns about the author's sincerity, it is still evident that the German promotion of the evacuation scheme differed greatly from the British. This source demonstrates that the two governments had different views on childhood, different expectations of children in war, and different agendas when it came to public provision. The evacuation schemes were similar to some extent, but especially in their organizers' attitude towards older children they had nothing in common. This letter from Bremen shows why older boys and girls wanted to be part of the scheme, despite (or because of) their parents' scepticism. It also shows how much of the scheme already existed long before the war, since the relationship between youth and HJ was already well established. "Wonderful and exciting days" was the promise and to many youngster probably the raison d'être of the evacuation—which meant that the NS regime successfully detached the evacuation scheme from the war. Both aspects—the differing attitudes towards childhood and the link between evacuation and war—are vital for a successful comparison of the schemes and will be picked up in Chapter 7.

Familiar Problems

Nearly instantaneously, the German organizers faced challenges similar to those of the British evacuation. Berlin-based Dienststelle KLV had to deal with a myriad of issues from both evacuation and reception areas: mothers were evacuated with children who were too old and should be with the HJ, school groups were split by reception authorities, buildings assigned to the KLV were already occupied by the army, children had to sleep on dance floors because there was not enough room at the inn, there were too few teachers sent with the children, and so on. Furthermore, evacuees found out that the facilities in the camps were unusable, or that the local staff had already sold the food rations and equipment on the black market (Lang, 1991). Like in English reception areas, there were concerns from both sides in Germany: The urban parents and headmasters feared the detachment from homes and schools, whereas rural communities felt threatened by the newcomers, even ones as tiny as child evacuees. Over the years the concerns grew more serious, such as the local authorities' fear that the influx of evacuees would create a parallel society in their community (Fürstenberg, 1996; Kressel, 1996).

The culture shock at the meeting of urban and rural populations was not exclusively English either. The urban poor invading the countryside caused complaints: Already in November 1940 demands reached Berlin to better match the evacuee families to the milieu of the host family (Kock, 1997). The SS security service report from December 9, 1940 was particularly disturbing. It mentions children stealing from their host families, the destruction of furniture, and a substantial lack of discipline. The culture shock took a new twist, though, in Silesia, an area populated by poor farmers who had problems adjusting to the visitors from the city:

> In solchen Gegenden, die an sich selbst Notstandsgebiete sind, bringen Volksgenossen ein ganz besonderes Opfer wenn sie sich bereit erklärt haben, Kinder aufzunehmen. Umso verheerender müsse es sich hier stimmungsmäßig auswirken, wenn die Kinder sich dort vollkommen disziplinlos benähmen, große Ansprüche stellten und in ihren Ansichten sogar von ihren Eltern unterstützt würden.... Ein großer Teil der Kinder sei sehr verwöhnt hinsichtlich des Essens usw. und in keiner Weise bereit, auch nur die geringste Arbeit im Haushalt zu leisten. (In poor and war-torn areas it is a very special sacrifice by fellow citizens to accept children into their homes. It must be all the more devastating for their spirits when these children run completely wild, demand the world, and receive support for that attitude by their parents.... A large amount of children are very spoiled in terms of food, etc. They are not the least bit prepared to help their hosts with even little chores around the house.) (Boberach, 1984, p. 1865ff)

It is important to keep several things in mind for a successful comparison with London. While seemingly similar to the British plans, even the NSV evacuation of smaller children into private homes had two crucial differences. Firstly, the children were younger. So far, we have no reliable data from London on the age structure of the returnees, but it seems sensible to assume that those children who left their billets, returned autonomously to the city and discredited the government's scheme would have been at least ten years old, an age at which their German counterparts were already under the all encompassing control of the HJ in camps. Secondly, homesickness might have been less of an issue on the German side, since the Nazi youth organizations idealized detachment from parents. Children often aspired to join the Pimpfe (Jungvolk) or Jungmädel as soon as they turned ten. Additionally, children might have had already some experience in separation when they participated in the peacetime KLV for health reasons.

Another crucial difference from London's evacuation—and probably the key to its comparative initial success—was that the German organizers never attempted to evacuate Berlin all at once. Like the later "trickle" evacuations from London, the number of evacuees leaving per day was limited and manageable. Berlin was already at war and subject to air raids when evacuation started, so the panic rush of London (to get all children out before a declaration of war) would not be duplicated there.

Chapter Conclusion

In London, a short moment of celebration over a logistical challenge well executed was swiftly followed by a sobering period of dealing with complaints from the evacuees, their parents, and their host families. The exodus itself was carried out with great efficiency—and the historiography up until this day has nothing but unequivocal praise for the actual logistics. Nonetheless, successful logistics—especially if it stops at the county's borders—did not automatically make for a successful evacuation. Contemporary critics convincingly argued that the LCC plans suffered from unresolved issues that should have been contemplated instead of timetables: the social relations of working class families, the scale of private evacuation, or the state of planning in the reception areas. Londoners did not stop being Londoners just because they were evacuated to Surrey, Sussex, or Kent—and they held *their* LCC responsible for whatever happened to them in the country. Initial bad reports of troubles, magnified by the absence of a real national emergency, quickly eclipsed the initial success of the four days in September.

In Berlin, the KLV planners, too, nearly lost control over public opinion when citizens had been confused by differing rumors about the evacuation that—as the propaganda ministry explicitly pointed out—was not an evacuation at all. Once the scheme was operational, it relied on peacetime work previously done by NSV and HJ. Thus, the infrastructure both in Berlin and the reception areas was quickly put in place—and since the scheme did not attempt an immediate wholesale evacuation of all children, its reputation did not suffer the same blows as its British counterpart. The operation was executed with rigor and thoroughness. Still, with nearly no planning time, the first weeks of operation in Berlin and Hamburg were the testing ground for a continuous flow of evacuees into the far corners of the Reich throughout the war. As in London, though, the success of the evacuation with children and parents would not so much rely on the logistics, but on the public trust extended to government provision and the party's ability to detach the KLV from the war in the evacuees' minds. While the London planners were probably neglectful of psychological considerations, the Nazi leaders in Berlin were well aware of the traps, but also of the potential of exclusive access to the schoolchildren.

Not to pre-empt the formal comparison in Chapter 7, but already at this early stage in the evacuations' operations there are promising angles for assessment. One is the way the schemes reflect the political landscape and state of democracy. London had a professional and efficient bureaucracy, but the public did not accept its provision uncritically. After all, Weber's prediction of a spread of rationalism through professional public service did not just rely on civil servants knowing their trade, but also knowing the recipients of their provisions. The Evacuation Branch's surprise at the *irrational* decision by families not to evacuate is evidence of the civil service's failure to understand their clientele. Londoners, especially from the newly confident working classes, were exercising their democratic right not to engage with a voluntary scheme—and the civil servants had to learn fast that asking for support was different from ordering it. At the same time, democratic concerns were no longer an issue for the safely established NS regime; as early as 1933, Goebbels declared a difference between the "new authoritative Germany and the democratic world surrounding it. The nation and the government are one thing" (speech at the League of Nations, 30 September 1933, National Archives FO 371/16728). Thus, it was not democratic concerns that kept the evacuation voluntary—and vulnerable—but Hitler's craving for public support at a time when the "competitive elitism" (Held, 2006, p. 134), characteristic of liberal democracies in the early 20th century, only happened internally within the combined party/state system. In both countries, evacuation participation became a question of trust. In 1939 London, government provision was relatively new, but generally welcome. Low participation here would most likely stem from mistrust in an inexperienced apparatus (thus the high level of private evacuation). In 1940 Berlin, the population was convinced of the government's abilities, but increasingly suspicious of its motives.

Crowded London departure with Routemasters, schoolchildren and helpers
Imperial War Museum Photograph Collection IWM 552-127 (1939)

4

The Cities Left Behind

The children had left, and their stories of life among strangers have already been extensively documented elsewhere. Histories of the evacuation have usually gone with the evacuees and focused on their experiences in the reception areas (not surprisingly, since the majority of the publications are based on former evacuees' biographical testimonies), but what happened in the cities they left behind has not generated the same level of interest. This chapter looks at both cities after the departure of the first wave of evacuees: at the children left behind, the children returning, schools being closed or only offering curtailed provision, and the councils struggling to maintain control over their schemes in the face of widespread noncompliance from *their* citizens. The public reaction to the bureaucracies' efforts should provide evidence about the state of citizenship, acceptance of public provision, and flexibility of the state apparatus. This chapter will provide general accounts of life in wartime London and Berlin, but at its core are the analyses of sources from the evacuations' executives: In London those are the LCC's universal reply to criticism of the scheme and Morrison's press conference transcript defending the scheme and present-

Operation Pied Piper, pages 79–104

ing its modifications; in Berlin the key source is the minutes of a meeting of KLV executives in June 1941 that reveals a lot about attitudes and concerns after a good eight months of the evacuation's operation.

In England, the state of the nation during the Phoney War—the absence of battles on British soil paired with the constant psychological threat of invasion or bombing—seriously impaired London's evacuation scheme from the moment it was put in motion (Gosden, 1976). A constant drift back into the metropolis immediately followed the successful dispatch of children and other priority groups. No poster campaign, radio broadcast, or amount of urging by politicians could prevent that 80% of evacuated mothers and their infants had returned home by Christmas 1939, convinced that being strangers, unwanted and unoccupied in the country was worse than the bomb threats in the metropolis (Lowndes, 1969). About 40% of schoolchildren drifted back to London at that time, creating a real problem for the LCC, since nearly 100% of the teachers were still evacuated and the schools were closed and used for wartime purposes (Brown, 2005; Lowndes, 1969).

Berlin's evacuation and subsequent problems were more subtle than London's in the beginning. Unlike the mass exodus from English towns in September 1939, Berlin was only gradually thinning out—first by the disappearance of men drafted to the front and then by the successive departures of children into the KLV. During the war's first year, Berlin did not suffer, but people worried about the deterioration of discipline among children—brought on by the lack of supervision following the absence of male authority figures and partial closures of schools. The administrators in Berlin were as surprised as their London counterparts about parental reactions to their efforts (low participation rate and immediate demands to return the children). Despite paperwork to the contrary, parents insisted on having their children back before the agreed duration and even at times of acute bombing. While the city had to cope with stray children, the KLV organizers had to rethink their approach to parents in order to get more children out of town and, more importantly, successfully keep them there.

London

"They Went Away. They Came Back. They Are Running Wild."

> *Mum said that after we left it was like a cathedral, it was so quiet, the whole area, she said it was unbelievable. They didn't realise 'til then the noise of children playing. The streets had been our playground.*

—former London child Ronald McGill, in Arthur, 2004, p. 12

The impression did not last. In September 1939, 241,000 of the 490,000 eligible schoolchildren had been evacuated, but by January 1940, 78,888 had returned to London. Only 34% of London schoolchildren were still in reception areas (Titmuss, 1950). People soon realized that instead of empty streets and playgrounds, the city was full of idle and unorganized children. After all, the usual adult supervisors were all in the countryside. With the teachers gone and two-thirds of school buildings used for civil defense, the LCC had to weigh its options for the large number of stray children. Reopening the schools was politically unwise and a public admission of the evacuation scheme's difficulties, but keeping them closed meant denying schooling (and supervision) to up to half a million children. Conservative estimates based on LCC figures claim a child population back or still in London of 200,000, of which 69,000 did not receive any schooling at this point (Gosden, 1976; Maclure, 1990). Stephen Inwood estimates an even higher population of 520,000 schoolchildren for September 1940, a time when further evacuations should have reduced the number closer to 81,000 (Inwood, 1998; L.C.C., 1943, VIII, 8.). It seems that unreliability in numbers stems from unrecorded children in private evacuation, varying definitions of London (county vs. Metropolitan area), and the willful distortion for political reasons.

The loss of schooling for the children in London (and other major industrial towns) became a serious issue for national and local government, not only for the actual loss of education, but also for a lack of supervision, social control, and medical inspection. The immediate reaction was a home schooling scheme: teachers (or parents) would supervise small groups of children in private or rented rooms. At its height, the improvised home tuition scheme reached 100,000 children. Up to 2,000 teachers made long journeys and climbed a lot of stairs, but they also gained new insight into their students' home environment and could test new teaching strategies in the informal settings (Clarke, 1940). There was unofficial provision as well: Churches and settlement workers offered group activities on church floors and in disused halls (Cosens, 1940).

Already on November 1, 1939 the national government permitted the reopening of some schools in the evacuation areas, but the LCC took a stronger stance and resisted. After all, the London administration was in a real dilemma: "Compulsory evacuation was politically impossible, yet the other extreme to reopen the schools in the evacuation areas would be to kill the government evacuation scheme" (Gosden, 1976, p. 21).

Faced with an increasing number of stray children on the streets, the LCC could not avoid intervention for long. Still, in 1939, the LCC opened 12 emergency secondary schools for 250 students each, and by January

20, 1940, 78 schools were open and 23,360 students attended in a double shift system. Official guidelines only allowed as many students in a school building as there was bomb shelter space on the premise, but since everyone had expected the children to be out of London, no one had built any (Gosden, 1976).

The BoE was strongly in favor of reopening schools in London, but their recommendations suffered from their lack of authority. Padley's point about the BoE losing the internal government power struggle over the evacuation (see Chapter 3) seems to be confirmed here. The circulars sent out by the BoE were clear on content, but feeble in terms of assertive language. While the long documents show great understanding for the local problems of individual authorities, they do not set deadlines or goals. Rather than ordering the continuation of schooling for up to half a million children in London, the BoE recommends, asks and requests: "the Board take the view, therefore, that all Authorities should set themselves the goal of providing full-time education for all children," because the government (as deferred authority) is "anxious that the law of school attendance should again be enforced" (from BoE Circular 1498—NA: ED 138/48—476). The BoE not only failed children in London, though. After all, the loss of education in reception areas "was not alleviated by the shocking weakness of the Board of Education and its failure to press the legitimate claims of the children upon the War Cabinet" (Cole & Padley, 1940, p. 6).

By April 1940, there were 85,000 places in 275 emergency schools. Attending school was voluntary at that stage and for over 11s only. The Fabian Society found that students appreciated the return to school—at least those from homes where parents valued education themselves: "General opinion seems to be that children were definitely working in excess of the prescribed hours, especially in districts where short-term considerations of earning capacity outweighed with the parents the possible careerist value of continued education" (Clarke, 1940, p. 203).

Nearly immediately after it recovered from the first evacuation, schooling in London was disrupted again by news of the fall of the Low Countries and France, as well as the later onset of the Blitz. In November 1940, only 20,000 students of an estimated population of 100,000 schoolchildren attended classes regularly (Crosby, 1986; Maclure, 1990). Examinations were taken in reception areas and in London, but the evacuated children had the clear advantage of uninterrupted, longer schooling with a familiar teacher. Plus, going to school in London remained dangerous. Among LCC schools, the worst bombing incident of the war happened on January 21, 1943, when a single bomb penetrated all floors of Sandhurst Road junior and mixed secondary school in Lewisham, killing 36 pupils and six teachers (Crosby, 1986). Taking exams in London was also confusing, since students still notionally belonged to *their* evacuated grammar schools. Emergency schools were thus just hosting students from a variety of schools for the exams, and some students were even expected to travel to their schools in the reception areas for the exams (Maclure, 1990). Attempts have been made to actually measure the loss of education for those children of war, but results must be classified as speculative, since no convincing measuring technique exists that accounts for other influences of war outside the lack of schooling.

Despite best efforts by some, "the whole educational system in the county of London suddenly disintegrated" when child welfare support structures collapsed (Clarke, 1940, p. 200). In October 1940, there were still nearly 5,000 teachers in London, but only 2,000 of them were actually teaching. The others were running rest centers, helping with emergency meal services, administering the evacuation. or being on sick leave (Gosden, 1976). In November, the *Guardian* voiced the disappointment and judged the current state to be detrimental not only for the evacuation but also for the relatively new institution of compulsory schooling. It suggested: "The first point about having an educational system is that it should follow the children; wherever they are they should be getting the best teaching we can organise" (*Manchester Guardian*, 28.11.1940).

Parents were concerned about the loss of education and the stray children in London, but they also contributed to the situation by allowing a certain wartime slackness and by using sons and daughters to hold places in the shelter queues or earning money for the family (Gosden, 1976). Those children who actually made it to school were harder to teach since they had enjoyed their absence, were in poor physical shape, more restless and noisy, and displayed a lack of personal hygiene (Gosden, 1976). The continuous lack of schooling accelerated problems brought on by other war measures. The blackouts and the opportunities to earn extra money in the war industries were made responsible for the rise in juvenile crime as teenagers now had the opportunity and money to secretly drink and gamble (Gardiner, 2005a).

For this policy study it is important to look at how the Council coped with and reacted to the criticism laid at its door—and how much it wanted to recover trust in an evacuation scheme that during the Phoney War had created many more problems than it had solved. The two documents discussed here cover the extremes: the LCC's early and stubborn defensiveness and the later reconciliatory acceptance of necessary changes.

An LCC Response to Criticism

It is in war conditions that the Londoners will have to live as strangers in a strange land. It is in war conditions that the good country folk have billeted upon them many strangers accustomed to a very different way of life from their own. A reflective person would be surprised that the operation worked so smoothly and that the volume of complaint has not been larger than in fact it has been.

—Source XI, p. 1

The war conditions, though, were not fully appreciated by Londoners since there was no war yet. Already in October 1939, the LCC composed a single communiqué that attempted to universally reply to a myriad of requests, criticism, and insults—but also to retaliate against partial reporting in the press (source XI). One aspect of this document is that it tries, like the ones discussed in Chapter 3, to outline the limits of the LCC's responsibilities and capabilities within the evacuation scheme. For some aspects the LCC had to face liability, but their officials were obviously loathe to take the blame for anything outside their area of authority. The language reveals some of the annoyance felt by the organizers, who were well aware that the scheme was universally talked down and on the brink of collapse at the time.

The document opens with a reply to complaints that London evacuees "were dirty, verminous and had bad habits" (Source XI, p.1). It acknowledges that concerns arose from the ignorance of country people about the extent of poverty and overcrowded housing in London, but still suggests that a few extreme cases dominated public discussion. The LCC also immediately ascertained that it "had no means of controlling uncleanliness amongst the adult population." Its influence was limited to schoolchildren, and here the defense follows along three different lines: It would be unjust to deny evacuation to a child based on his or her personal nit infection status, that evacuation coincided with the end of the summer holidays when children "are more neglected, and their personal hygiene is at its worst" (Source XI, appendix), and that inspections and data collection had taken place but the council's data had not been used by reception areas' authorities. The first point shows consideration and sound moral judgement, especially if contrasted against travel restrictions for verminous children introduced in 1942 (L.C.C., 1943, VIII, 11.) or the stringent participation criteria applied in Germany, but the other two points seem to be attempts to shift the blame, be it to parents in the former or the billeting staff in the latter. Bedwetting seems to have been a particular cause for concern by rural hosts. The LCC gallantly defends its children, claiming that above average instances of bedwetting were not habitual but caused by the stressful situation of adapting to a new home. Some complaints directed at the LCC must be seen as outside the council's sphere of influence—and the communiqué is quick to point this out. Poor accommodation provided for evacuees and the potential dangers in some reception areas ("proximity of military formations, aerodromes and anti-aircraft guns and in one case of a circus of wild animals") were issues for local authorities or national government.

The council then gives a somewhat surprising lecture as reply to another area of criticism: excessive visits to the reception areas by London parents. Due to the absence of war, more parents and other relatives traveled to the countryside than "has been desirable or convenient." In their reply, the civil servants demonstrate hitherto hidden class sensitivities:

> What has to be borne in mind at the same time is this: Middle-class parents who send their children to boarding schools realise that thy are not expected to visit the children until half-term and that it is in fact unsettling to the children to be visited too often by their relatives, but the poor people of London—and the majority of people whose children have been evacuated are poor people—are not accustomed to being parted from their children. They know nothing of boarding schools and the traditions attaching to them. (Source XI, p. 6)

Despite the patronizing attitude towards parents from a class below that of the civil servants, this statement actually shows a steep learning curve on the part of the administration. While the men of the Evacuation Branch had obviously been oblivious to behavior patterns outside their own class when designing the whole scheme, they now managed to pinpoint the reason why they failed to persuade a lot of parents to sign up for the evacuation scheme in the first place—if they just extended their valuable observation about parental visits. There is no evidence that they did, though, but if they did they would have pre-empted Margaret Cole's not so gentle reminder of their ignorance.

The tone of this document is one of disappointment. The authors maintain that "the London planning beforehand was imaginative and thorough" and the task intimidating. The LCC had to oversee 600,000 evacuated Londoners spread over 470 reception areas overseen by 73 local education authorities. Instead of the gratitude they so clearly expected, the planners faced complaints they had not anticipated and did not feel responsible for. Still, the communiqué is more diplomatic than the previous ones. The disappointment is slightly better concealed:

> It would be easy to balance the complaints from the country . . . with a series of complaints from Londoners as to the conditions in the country; but that

will not be done. The heavy burden imposed upon the countryside is recognised, just as it is recognised that as time goes on the Londoners will be made more comfortable. It must be stated, however, that dissatisfaction with conditions in the country has been one of the most fruitful causes of the considerable return to London. (Source XI, p. 4)

Blaming the reception areas was one thing, but it must have dawned on the evacuation planners that some of their own earlier decisions were close to naïve, like the wholesale closure of schools despite the known fact that large numbers of children had never been registered for evacuation. Something had gone wrong, and it got worse: Many of the efficiently evacuated children were rushing back to London.

Reasons for Returning to London

The returns to London were only partly caused by the evacuees' negative experiences in the country: the perceived hostility towards the urban dwellers, the strangeness of the new living conditions, and the feeling of being away from the family without reason. Another reason was London's pull. Peter Ackroyd describes, with some pathos, that London was too large, too complex, and too momentous to be destroyed—and that Londoners were largely comforted by that and defiant of the bombings. There was a sense of unreality about the situation as the city exerted its "curious magnetism" that explained the low participation numbers in the evacuation scheme and the high numbers of immediate returnees. Ackroyd calls it the "strongest, perhaps most melancholy, instinct—the need to get back to the city, even if it becomes a city of fire and death" (Ackroyd, 2000, p. 742). The academics at Oxford's Barnett House study group expressed the city's appeal and returnee children's attitude more poignantly:

> London to them was not only a place of noise and bustle, glittering shops and markets, and fascinating amusements, but a world peopled by loved relatives, and the familiar figures of the streets, the rag-and-bone man, the old-iron-man, and many others. In contrast, Oxford seemed full of old ladies who were inclined to forbid everything, and the country was swarming with farmers whose only concern was to kept the children from damaging their crops. (Adams & Emden, 1947)

Social class was a major factor in the decision to return. Titmuss identified East End children as far more likely to return than those from the rich Western parts of London. He blamed economic and educational poverty, but also stronger family ties and a higher likelihood of rejection by rural householders (Titmuss, 1950). Cosens posited that particular mothers were to blame: "the girls who have gone back are the daughters of fearful, undecided or grumbling mothers at home" (Cosens, 1940, p. 13). She explains that children will always behave true to type. Naughty children in London would be naughty children in the reception areas, but suddenly had more options to misbehave—that is, to return to London under their own steam.

Another reason for returning to the city was that older children actually feared for the safety of their parents and thought they could help keep them safe. This was not only true for evacuees, but also for some boarding school students, who deserted their school to return to London (often on bike—Brendon, 2009). Their attitude received academic credibility when child psychologist Anna Freud's study of wartime effects on children was published. For many children, according to Freud, the benefits of evacuation (safety, hygiene, occupation, food) did not outweigh the trauma of separation from the family. Children are emotionally tied even to negligent, unaffectionate, or violent parents. These ties proved so strong that "London children, therefore, were on the whole much less upset by bombing than by evacuation to the country as a protection against it" (Freud & Burlingham, 1943, p. 37; but see also Macnicol, 1986).

Parents in London might have additionally sabotaged the scheme by urging their children to come back in order to provide a raison d'être for women abandoned by husbands (military service) and children (evacuation). After all, "mothers not only love their children, they also need them" (Holman, 1995, p. 29). London parents could be either dissatisfied with their children's foster homes, or indeed jealous of them (Isaacs et al., 1941). Returns were particularly high among the second priority class: mothers with very young children. Mothers were pulled back to the city where they at least had support networks of friends and relatives as well as a working social service infrastructure (poor-law medical services, clothing clubs, dental repair shops) that often beat the provision in remote rural areas (Titmuss, 1950). "The life of the working-class mother begins, ends and has its being in the setting of husband, children, home.... They understood Mr Churchill and the Luftwaffe among their own people, and in their own homes, not in somebody else's. And so they went home" (Titmuss, 1950, p. 182). Largely for that reason, subsequent evacuation schemes would not include adult evacuees—and neither does the focus of this study.

The strong family ties that held some London families together were also evident in Berlin, where a similar attitude of better dying together than be separated was a main reason not to evacuate (Noakes, 1998). Another observation that seems to be true for both cities is that, on the whole, children seem to have been more resilient to war than adults. They formed street gangs and had adventures, but also helped with fire fighting and attending the wounded (Ackroyd, 2000). The fear of war and bombing was unreal, and children only learned it from their parents during the nights in the shelter. In both cities, there was a strange disparity between the terrifying nights below ground and the peaceful, quiet days above.

The Evacuation Branch anticipated some emotional responses, but the absence of war took away their only convincing argument for the hardship evacuees and parents endured. The administrators knew that keeping open channels of communication between parents in London and their evacuated children was important. Letters proved to be a great source of comfort for both sides (Cosens, 1940). In the end, though, that was not enough. It became apparent that Christmas was going to be the crucial moment for the survival of the scheme. It was feared that the holidays would trigger a bigger drift back, so the organizers provided presents for the evacuees, initiated parties (including pantomimes and film screenings) in the reception areas, and cancelled all transport opportunities (Crosby, 1986). Similarly in Germany, the NSV tried to prevent a major drift back to Berlin over the holiday period by providing Christmas presents to all evacuated children and mothers, as well as Führerbilder (greeting cards with Hitler's image on the front) to the hosts (Kock, 1997).

The story of departure and drift back is not the same for all evacuees, though. Barnett House's survey showed that return journeys were made in the opposite direction as well. London children returned to Oxford because they preferred being evacuated, or because they struggled to re-adapt to family life in London (Adams & Emden, 1947). Quantification is difficult, since there are no reliable numbers to show how many children smoothly settled with their foster parents for longer periods (Lowndes, 1969). Barnett House collected evidence from evacuee children through essay-writing tasks like "where would you like to live when you grow up?" or "what's the difference between Oxford and London people?" (Adams & Emden, 1947) Their pre-conclusion was that evacuation must be seen as "a social experiment of the first magnitude" rather than the transfer of some children from day schooling to boarding schools. They described the evacuation as the "prelude to a continuous wave of internal migration necessitated by the war" (Adams & Emden, 1947, p. 11).

After six months of operation, the evacuation scheme was unpopular and widely regarded as unsuccessful. The situation had not changed in London; the threat to the population only existed in newspapers and government leaflets. At the same time, the accounts of horrible evacuation experiences from neighbors and their children who had returned to London were very real—so much so that an extensive canvassing of London households in spring 1940 bore nearly no result. A lot of people simply refused to discuss evacuation. The LCC reacted by going public and facing the criticism head on. On Wednesday March 6, 1940 (when invasion and bombing was a real but not immediate threat), Herbert Morrison gave a press conference at County Hall to familiarize the press with the modified provisions offered by the Evacuation Branch.

"What About Your Child? Have You Decided?"

The documents from the press conference show the considerations of a city government in a dilemma (sources XIIa-b). Without the actual bombing, the decision to keep schools in London closed and children with strangers in the country might have appealed to anyone with a provident and long-term view, but for mothers and children suffering from the separation, it must have appeared as random hardship.

Morrison's press statement falls into two parts: the situation of children already evacuated and the provisions for children still in London. When covering the first point, Morrison uses distancing language and continuously refers to the national government ("those words are not mine; they are the Government's, and they have been written, we may be sure, after the careful thought such an important part of our war effort merits"). He pronounces the government's wish that children already evacuated should stay where they are. He admits earlier problems, but assures the press that children in reception areas receive schooling and are in better health than if they had stayed in London. After politely blaming the press for negative reporting during the early stages of the evacuation ("the press has played its part in calling attention to these difficulties"), he urges them to now draw attention to the effort made by the people in the country. However, Morrison is not really convincing here, maybe because he knows that he is selling a very unpopular policy: "still, there it is—the Government with all their opportunities of summing up the situation, say it's a vital part of the war effort to encourage these children to stay in the country" (Source XIIa, p. 2). For a politician renowned for his oratorical skills, this seems a particularly lackluster performance.

Morrison then introduces the new evacuation scheme for children still in London (internally known as Plan IV). The first major change is that evacuation will only be initiated once there is actual bombing; the second major change is that provisions will only be made for schoolchildren. It has been argued before that integration into a new family and community was easier for urban children than for adults, whose behavior in the country had brought the scheme into disrepute. Morrison emphasized the voluntary nature of the evacuation scheme, but this time it came with a twist.

Leaflets had gone out to all London households on which parents could register their children for the scheme that Morrison describes as a "free insurance policy" for the safety of the children.

> There is, however, an important undertaking which the parent has to sign, and that is to see that he sends his child with the party if evacuation is ordered, and that he leaves the child in the receiving area until the party returns, and I must say that I think the Government is very reasonable in asking that parents should take a firm decision. (Source XIIa, p. 2)

At this point the English evacuation scheme began to look very similar to the German one initiated half a year later (only with just a very limited use of actual camps). Instead of a wholesale preventative evacuation, arrangements would only be made for those participating in the scheme and only when they were needed. Going away would be voluntary, but returning early not an option. There is of course no way to verify if Schirach and his staff in Berlin were at all aware of the initial problems with London's evacuation, but it remains an intriguing proposition that their design took account of events in the enemy's capital.

Attempting to pre-empt the logical conclusion of parents with evacuated children—bring them back to London and let them be evacuated again once there are actual bombs—Morrison tries to educate his audience on the consequences of such short-sighted behavior. Moving the children back and forth is unsettling for the children, interrupts their schooling, complicates rationing, blocks vital transport ways and rolling stock, and makes the next evacuation wave harder to organize. Retrospectively, it seems surprising that with all those valid reasons at hand, neither local nor national government could prevent the drift back to London nor other cities (see Chapter 7 for a further discussion on issues of state–citizen relationships).

There is a supplement from the Education Officer attached to the press conference's transcript: "For the Information of the Press . . . : Government Evacuation Scheme. What about Your Child? Have You Decided?" It urges parents to quickly register for the new scheme that is "another chance." The appeal's urgency stems from a situation that "does embarrass those responsible for making plans," namely that of all the households canvassed in early spring 1940, only 20% gave a clear indication of their preference. Ten percent signed up for evacuation, 10% decided to keep their children in London, and the rest simply refused to make any commitments to register for a controversial scheme at a time when war was more theoretical than felt by Londoners. The LCC had decided to hold off another wave of evacuation (that would have been Plan III) until there was bombing. Without the war, parents could not be convinced to separate from their children, but a year after its declaration, war finally came to London.

London Life During the Blitz

Eventually the Blitz put an end to the Phoney War. By May 1940, the fear of invasion increased. Many London evacuees who had been sent to the Southeast coast had to be relocated to South Wales or other safer areas inland (Gosden, 1976). On August 1, 1940, Hitler ordered preparations for Operation Sea Lion, but based on faulty intelligence he decided that Russia was the weaker target (Kershaw, 2000). In light of a demanding military campaign in the East, attacks on England would have to be limited to air raids destroying infrastructure and demoralizing London's population. Initially Hitler was hesitant to hit London for fear of strengthening British resolve, but after accidental hits by Luftwaffe bombers returning from Thameshaven and Rochester triggered large-scale retaliation bombing, war finally reached the capitals: "World War II now turned into a contest to see which of these two great cities could hold out best under the new horror of repeated aerial bombardments" (Large, 2001, p. 324).

On September 7, 1940, the Blitz began with a massive Luftwaffe attack of 320 bombers and 600 fighter planes raiding London's industrial and commercial centers. The only real opposition came from the barrage balloons. London's demographic layout meant that working-class districts were taking the brunt more than middle-class suburbia. The first districts hit were Stepney, Whitechapel, Poplar, and Shoreditch. There was a chaotic and spontaneous flight from the city. People fled to Epping Forest or the Chislehurst Caves (Donoughue & Jones, 1973). However, the increasingly indiscriminate bombing of targets (or non-targets) all over London led to a feeling of solidarity—after all, it was not only one district or social class that suffered from the attacks.

Finally, the diverse London population had one thing in common: the mythical Blitz Spirit. The famous stoicism and determination was not unique to London, though. The urban populations of Berlin, Hamburg, Tokyo, or Nagasaki behaved in the same way, but the people of London were the first to do so—and they were the first to demonstrate that the new wars would claim civilian lives as much as soldiers' (Inwood, 1998). There might have been an upside to this realization, too. London's population seems to have felt particularly useful and valued during the Blitz.

> The effect of two months of continuous blitz was to spread the habit of adaption from those who were brave and active to those who were not, so

that increasing proportions of the population became brave and active. In the immensity of Greater London, with its peacetime population of nearly nine million, three or four hundred bombers would waste their effort. (A. Calder, 1969, p. 168f)

Despite the resilience of many, London's population dropped by nearly a million to 3,204,000 in the first year of war (Inwood, 1998). In 1941, only 2.3 million Londoners were still in town, a drop of 43% in two years (White, 2001). The heaviest raids to hit London happened between November 1940 and May 1941. Just before the Luftwaffe's full attention was drawn to Russia, it launched the most devastating attack on May 10: 550 planes dropping 700 tons of high explosives started 2,000 fires in London that killed 1,436 people and left 1,800 seriously injured (Inwood, 1998). Nevertheless, even in a week of heavy bombing, about 1,600 children would return home privately from the reception areas (Gosden, 1976). It seems that not even the devastation of the Blitz was sufficient deterrent for homesick children. Later in the war, London parents would argue that the countryside was as unsafe a place as the metropolis since the Luftwaffe had started their *Baedeker Raids* on historic – and hitherto safe—cities like Exeter, Bath, Norwich, York and Canterbury in April 1942 (Gosden, 1976). The next chapter will show how the civil service had to change the government evacuation scheme in order to regain the trust of its recipients.

Berlin

Wartime Berlin—Without the War

Unlike in 1914, when the declaration of war prompted noisy celebrations, this time the people of Berlin were very silent. Shirer describes the mood in Berlin on September 3, 1939 as one of grim determination, while many could not believe that Hitler had actually led them into another war (Shirer, 1984). For many children, war was outside their rational grasp, but if anything it was to be celebrated—after all, the HJ had spent years preparing their charges for such a war by getting them physically fit and as patriotic as it was able to within its role. Claudia Bauer's collection of oral testimonies from Berlin leads her to the conclusion that children did not initially fear war, but rather that adults' feelings of fear and trepidation carried over to them (Bauer, 2010). As in London, the war was visible in Berlin only by shortages and A.R.P. measures. In the winter of 1939/40, lack of coal closed most Berlin schools between 28 January and 28 March. The extra holidays quickly had their own linguistic term: Kohleferien (coal holidays—Stargardt, 2005). Also, already in 1940 there were serious concerns about adolescents' behavior in Berlin: Public opinion was that the youngsters were running wild, the HJ was losing its grip, and there was an increase in nonconformist youth organizations—all in all, the youth were getting scruffier and increasingly criminal. There were a variety of reasons for this development: the erratic schooling and frequent closures of schools, the HJ leadership vacuum (see Chapter 3), the absence of—usually very authoritarian—fathers, and the opportunities afforded by the blackouts (see below; also Kinz, 1991).

Schools were struggling to continue with lessons. School hours became more unreliable since buildings, teachers, and even students were needed for the war effort. School buildings—or parts thereof—were used as army registration centers, first-aid stations, or ration card distribution facilities. Gyms or classrooms became collection points for recyclables or storage space for the voluntary fire brigade. All this led to mergers of schools and teaching in shift systems with students only attending school either in the morning or afternoon. Shortages of air raid shelters and teachers limited student numbers further. Pensioners and older BdM girls officiated as substitutes for the male teachers in military service—by 1942, the pupil–teacher ratio was already at 68:1 (Giles, 1992).

This research focuses on the majority of children who more or less enthusiastically adapted to the NS regime. Existing scholarship indicates that there were still non-conformist adolescents in Berlin and other cities at the outbreak of war, but their number is difficult to quantify and their fate hard to portray. These young people were not organized in the HJ, but in their own—mainly illegal—cliques, *Meuten* (packs), and *Horden* (hordes), like the famous *Edelweisspiraten* or Hamburg's *Swing Kids*. Partly politically motivated, partly just juvenile rebellious, these *Wilde Gruppen*'s relevance is disputed; some claim that they constituted a threat to order in Berlin and the NSDAP rulers (Franck & Asmus, 1983; Kohrs, 1983), while a more differentiated view is that, although "abweichendes Jugendverhalten war keine systemgefährdende Massenerscheinung" (dissenting juvenile behaviour never became a mass movement capable of threatening the system), Goebbels and the HJ deliberately chose to overestimate their importance and deliberately portrayed them as public enemies of NS conformity (Buddrus, 2003, p. 462). For the history of the evacuation they are relevant only as an added incentive for NS leaders to initiate a scheme based on total social control.

Until the autumn of 1940, the war happened elsewhere, and the early successes of the Blitzkrieg in Poland and later the Lowlands and France reassured the people of Berlin of their safety far away from the frontlines. Exploitation of captured areas enabled the regime to send additional food and goods to Berlin so that the quality of life even increased for some.

Keeping schools open and working might have been a priority for teachers and parents, but the children seemed to have enjoyed the new slackness (loosening of social control) afforded by the distant war.

The war might not have reached Berlin yet, but it had changed life in the capital all the same. Protective measures like blackouts and curfews as well as the absence of men drafted for military service led to new opportunities for young people to live out their adolescence. There is a one-page circular from the education ministry that pre-dates the evacuation by half a year (source XIII). While it is not strictly speaking a key source for this study, it still is very valuable as an illustration of the social and political climate that the KLV scheme would have to fit into.

This circular dated February 6, 1940 is addressed to headteachers in schools and civil servants within education ministry branches. Its main concern is the absence of fathers and other male authority figures (e.g., HJ leaders) that puts adolescent boys and girls in danger. To compensate, school staff is ordered (1) to remind their students of the curfew and other regulations, and to impose school-based punishment for infringements; (2) to work with the students in order to prevent them from exposing themselves to danger (although this order is ambiguous, the "erzieherische Beinflussung" requested could be translated as either pedagogical influence or manipulation); (3) to support mothers with husbands in the army in case of parenting problems; and (4) to be vigilant for all signs of moral or physical neglect and to report those students to the local youth authority or NSV office.

This short document is significant for this study's context because it shows that, unlike the English BoE (see London section, above), the NS authorities were not short of assertiveness in their orders. The language used is clear and the requests unambiguous. There does not seem to be any hesitation to expect teachers to drop their professional ethics and do what is, in essence, police work. The NS regime exercised—at least on paper—absolute power over a once-independent profession. Secondly, the document shows that privacy was no longer a fundamental right. Not only were teachers ordered to intrude on their students' free time, they also had to intrude on the parents under the pretext of parenting assistance. As has been mentioned earlier, Germans were used to leading public lives by then, since any attempt at privacy was considered suspicious and secretive. Thirdly, the document confirms points made earlier about the amalgamation of state and NSDAP party institutions. Teachers should report signs of moral decay to either the state authority or the NSV, the party-run welfare organization that had risen to a one-stop contact point for all social problems. At this point there did not seem to be a discernable difference between state and party anymore.

Primarily, this circular shows the authorities were struggling to keep the adolescents under control. Interestingly, the actual threats or perils were not spelled out, but the special inclusion of girls ("und namentlich die weibliche Jugend"—this is one of the very few sources that actually differentiates between boys and girls, mostly the officials in London and Berlin used the gender-blind term *children* in their descriptions of and prescriptions for evacuees) implies that sexual activity became as much an issue as the usual loitering and low-level vandalism. There was a noted increase in burglaries and thefts, and the billeting of soldiers into Berlin caused further upheaval among local female teenagers (Wortmann, 1982). Under these circumstances, evacuation became additionally attractive for its opportunity to keep straying adolescents under constant supervision in camps rather than let them run riot in blacked-out (later bombed-out) Berlin. It seems certain that one of the evacuation planners' aims was to get juveniles out of the city before they became a problem for the authorities.

The Bombing of Berlin

When British bombs finally hit Berlin, they came as a shock to Berlin's population. The people in the capital had arrogantly deluded themselves into a sense of invincibility. In particular, Goering's carelessness (as the one in charge of the Luftwaffe) led to Berlin having no effective air defense at all (Kershaw, 2000). That RAF bombers were not able to inflict more damage on the city might have to do with its inland location; for British fighters, Berlin was as far as they could go to and from in one night. While the real damage might have been limited at first, from September 1940 onwards, public life was severely affected by almost nightly RAF bombings. The government imposed a curfew at 11:00 p.m. for bars, cafes, restaurants, and cinemas in an attempt to have everyone home and close to their designated shelter before the English planes arrived.

There is evidence that most adolescents reacted to the war with the socio-Darwinist attitude and lack of empathy that marked out Nazi ideology (*what doesn't kill you makes you stronger*); they permitted themselves no fear and dismissed the victims of bombs as having had bad luck. Life had to go on. Many youngsters signed up as *Luftwaffenhelfer* (working as messengers and cleaners on the air raid defense flaks) and eagerly awaited the nightly attacks. Oral history accounts suggest that the young people were ashamed of the fears and worries of their elders (Franck & Asmus, 1983). Rather, they would pray that the bombers, if they would come anyway, would arrive after midnight, since this meant that the next day would be off school (Bauer, 2010).

The bombings accelerated problems of schooling that had begun in September 1939. School log books reveal the wartime interferences with schooling in Berlin: the gym was used as grain storage, classrooms had to be vacated for administration staff handling food rationing and similar, teachers were actually drafted for these duties and had to abandon their classes, classrooms were used as makeshift hospitals, students had to use the remaining rooms in shifts, class sizes increased, recycling runs were cutting into school time, students were exhausted from extensive HJ duties, and the playground was used as a parking lot for military and council vehicles. With more and more children disappearing into the KLV, schools were merged into one school building in order to free up valuable space for military purposes. Later in the war, the collection of recyclables actually became a school subject with grades, and children were taken out of normal schooling with their teachers for weeks to help with the harvest (Franck & Asmus, 1983; Goldberg, 1994).

In Berlin, there was an additional twist to the wartime occupation of school buildings. Dr Bremberger, a Berlin-based researcher in the history of Zwangsarbeit (forced labor), was kind enough to provide information on the use of Berlin schools as forced laborers' camps for this study. There are more than hundred cases where the address given on forced laborers' death certificates are those of schools (e.g., *Schule am Hertzbergplatz*). The gym of *Schule in der Halleschen Straße* was a POW camp as early as December 1941; 193 prisoners were listed there (from an email to the author). Again, the regime's motivation cannot be proven retrospectively on the basis of the surviving sources, but the suspicion lingers that the push for evacuation and Schulverlegung might have more to do with the need for buildings rather than concerns of child welfare.

From February 1943 onwards, the children remaining in Berlin only had classes in the mornings. The afternoons were dedicated to military drill, charity work (assisting the elderly, collecting donations, or collecting bones, herbs, and recyclables), or training on anti-aircraft batteries. The last school examinations in Berlin were held in 1943, and during the last months of war most schools ceased to provide schooling altogether (Evans, 2009). For the Luftwaffenhelfer—and all the unofficial children in Berlin— the schools held weekly assemblies, though, to exercise at least a bit of control over the capital's stray children. These assemblies were used for overt propaganda, especially once the war got desperate. The proposed assembly scripts were laden with pathos:

Das muß vor allem die deutsche Jugend wissen; denn der Kampf der Front ist nichts anderes als das gewaltige Ringen ihrer Väter und Brüder um die Erhaltung der Freiheit und um die Sicherung der Zukunft aller deutschen Jungen und Mädel, die heute noch auf den Schulbänken sitzten.... Sie soll verachten lernen alles Schwache, Erbärmliche und Feige in ihrem eigenen Volk, das den Schritt zum Sieg hemmt, und sie muss hassen lernen den Gegner, der sie um Freiheit und Zukunft betrügen will. (The youth of Germany has to know this above everything else: Their fathers and brothers are only fighting to ensure the freedom and a safe future for those boys and girls who are attending school right now. German youth shall learn to despise everything that is weak, pathetic, or cowardly within its own people, as it only delays victory. The youth shall also learn to hate the enemy determined to take freedom and future way from them.) (Order III Nr. 1, 29 June 1944 at: BBF/DIPF GUT SAMML 191)

While schooling became more and more unreliable in Berlin, parents learned that the situation of their children in KLV camps might not have been exactly like the party-endorsed circulars *Elternbriefe* suggested. Reports of overcrowding, lack of privacy, hard work during the harvest, or cruel supervisors would make their way to the capital and widened the gap between propaganda and reality in the minds of parents (Franck & Asmus, 1983; Fürstenberg, 1996). To safeguard the scheme, the regime introduced various bureaucratic obstacles. Mothers wishing to visit their children had to apply for a travel permit stating valid reasons for burdening the wartime transport system. Equally complicated was it for children to visit Berlin. They would have to gain permission from the camp leader, which was usually only granted for weddings, funerals, and fathers' *Fronturlaub* (temporary army leave). Usual reasons given by the officials not to allow parents into the camps were that they upset the daily routine or that they would cause embarrassment to the child (peer accusations of being a mollycoddle). A warmer welcome was extended to NS officers who more and more frequently came to the camps to recruit increasingly younger boys for the army (Fürstenberg, 1996). Sometimes parents took the initiative and, like in England, used the Christmas holidays for picking the children up from the camps or billets under the pretence of a short holiday, but without returning them there in the New Year. Very occasionally, the organization itself had to send children back to Berlin because of problems with the infrastructure, like in camps where the heating did not work (Franck & Asmus, 1983).

On the whole, though, Berlin's evacuation did not create the same upheaval as London's. If anything, the KLV's operation during the first three years of operation was surprisingly uneventful—and there will have to be a discussion as to the reasons for this. It was still a big operation and the officials involved would meet regularly to discuss the state of the KLV.

A Meeting of KLV Executives

From the deposits of the NSLB at the Bundesarchiv comes this interesting and illuminating source. It is a report about a conference in Berlin by a NSLB clerk for the absent Fritz Wächtler (source XIV). The meeting of KLV executives took place on the morning of June 25, 1941 and lasted a bit over two hours. This memo does not constitute its official minutes, nor was it written for publication. It is a recurrent document (a working document for the in-house use of an organisation) and thus promises a level of frankness and openness unattainable from the closely vetted public statements.

Still, the memo starts with a deception. After opening the conference with thanks from the Führer and himself, Schirach announced that at that point in time a total of 619,000 children from Berlin, Hamburg, and the Rhineland were in KLV care, 230,000 of them in camps. These exaggerated numbers have since been subject to revision and correction. The balance sheets of the Reichsschatzmeister (treasury) show the camp population in May 1941 closer to 170,000—making a total of at most 550,000 children in KLV a much more likely estimate (Buddrus, 2003; Kock, 1997). Schirach—unlike later historians—had direct access to the figures from the Dienststelle KLV and probably only wanted to varnish *his* scheme in front of his rivals for authority within the regime.

Schirach then put forward some problems that arose from the operation so far. The most pressing issue for him was many parents' desire to have their children back, not because they were treated badly where they were, but for the good treatment that made the children go native and forget their parents instantaneously. Schirach painted a picture of ungrateful children and parents who put their own emotional needs before the common good. While this might make some sense with regards to the parents, it seems unclear what triggered the remark: "nachdem es nichts Undankbareres gibt, als ein Kind" (since there's nothing more ungrateful than a child). There are two minor points of further interest: One is that Schirach intended to ask Hitler for an extension of the current sixth-month stay to nine months. However, the later discussion will confirm the six-month stay as preferable. The other interesting—and slightly contradictory—contemplation is that assuming an early end of the war, it would still take some time (up to a year) to return all children, since other priority groups (soldiers, coal, and supplies) would have priority access to the transport capacities.

A further problem is raised: it transpired that hotels and B & Bs in spa towns were *plutokratisch* (derogatory term meaning "commercially") used by families without any health problems. This misuse needed to stop at once and future bookings there would have to be accompanied by medical certification—but first of all (and this is an interesting snide remark to fellow party functionaries) the chief of the NS doctors' association Dr. Conti and coal commissioner Walter would have to lead by example and send their own children—that they had withdrawn from the KLV in favor of exclusive hotel accommodation—back to camp. Furthermore, there was evidence of corruption: Rations assigned to a camp accommodated in hotel rooms had been redirected to paying customers by the hotel kitchen. In the future, hotels would only be used when it was feasible to take them over completely.

Both agenda items offer insight into the working of the NS regime at war. A limited perception of reality is evident from the first remark that the children are too happy in camp; it seems that Nazi officials were likely to fall for their own propaganda. Schirach's intention to ask Hitler for a decision shows how much the NS hierarchy was a pyramid with one person at the top who concerned himself with—and reserved ultimate decision on—every aspect of NS policy. From the second point, the power of the state to change people's lives becomes evident. This conference could simply decide on the selection criteria that hoteliers all across the country will have to adhere to. Furthermore, it illustrates the dog-eat-dog mentality of the Nazi ranks. This was not a club with loyal members, but a group of individual careerists who fought each other for access to the Führer.

The document then proceeds to some good news. Schirach announced a breakthrough in curtailing the influence of the churches by taking over their buildings and camps for the KLV. While the conference memo is ecstatic about this blow against the church—a longstanding party ambition—it is also cautious about its publication. While there was a war, the memo states, there would be demonstrable neutrality. This has to be seen in a wider context: For the NSDAP, the KLV became more than just an evacuation, but a tool of leverage to push through party ambitions (e.g., limiting the independence of schools, reducing parental influence, excluding other agents from interference) on the back of the humanitarian effort. The KLV was not subject to politics; it was an integral part of it.

Schirach proclaimed more good news: the opportunities to send children to Hungary and North Italy, the stable level of meat rations to the camps (actually higher than in cities since potential weight gain was used to convince parents), the guaranteed paper and petrol supplies to the organization, the continuous running of KLV trains despite war in Russia, and the improved health of children in camps, although Schirach might be exaggerating here as well: The memo is suspicious of his claim that among 600,000 children there were only 428 accidents and 24 deaths.

The subsequent discussion raised a few more issues like the impending move of doctors to the Eastern front to fight epidemics and replacement in the KLV camps by female medical students, or the outrageous behavior of some urban mothers who let "ihren sexuellen Nöten freien Lauf" (their sexuality run wild). One major concern, though, seems to be very similar to London.

> Die Beauftragten von Köln und Düsseldorf machten dabei die psychologische interessante Mitteilung, daß nach schweren Luftangriffen die Eltern der geschädigten Familien am nächsten Tage erscheinen und ihre Kinder zurückholen wollen. Aus allen Berichten spricht die große Sorge, auf welche Art Eltern abgewiesen werden können, wenn sie einfach aufkreuzen und ihre Kinder abholen wollen. . . . Parteigenosse Schirach erklärte, daß wir außer der Belehrung der Eltern keine Handhabe besitzen. Düsseldorf stellt fest, daß es unmöglich ist, noch einen Transport zusammenzustellen. Die Eltern geben ihre Kinder nicht mehr ab. (Delegates from Cologne and Düsseldorf relayed the psychologically interesting habit of bombed-out parents to demand their children's return the day after the air raid. Concerned officials everywhere demand guidance on how to refuse those parents who just show up set on taking their children home. Comrade Schirach explained that they had no leverage except lecturing those parents. Düsseldorf announced that they would not have enough children to assemble even one train full; parents were simply not letting them go.) (Source XIV, p. 5)

Like in London, compulsion was not yet an option. Even at an intimate meeting of party loyals, Schirach stuck to Hitler's request to the letter. The civil servants' confusion with family behavioral patterns also seemed to have been an issue in both cities, as was an outspoken refusal to send children away, despite obviously dangerous living conditions in the cities. A third familiar point is the organizers' approach to complications. Instead of investigating the root of parental refusal, they were contemplating tools to overrule the unruly parents. In both cities the discussion is about the parents, not the children. There is an edge to that discussion in NS Germany, though. The assumption here was that children were so successfully habituated to life in the paramilitary HJ that their support of the KLV could be taken for granted. The parents refused to let them join the KLV against the children's will—an attitude evident even from this memo, where the high number of returnees has been attributed to parents who could not endure their children's happiness away from home. In the officials' minds, the party was successful in dividing families and creating new loyalties.

All in all, this is a technical memo. It shows that concerns of organizers on both sides of the channel were largely similar—but also that execution was unique to each country's political system. Organizational problems in Germany could be easily solved, since the KLV was a NSDAP priority and everything else would bow to the will of the party. Thus, issues of transport, accommodation, provision, schooling, and so on were under control and only made the agenda if there was discord among the stakeholders. Still, the memo does not act as a showcase for a flawless operation, but demonstrates that concerns and considerations of the organizers were actually quite similar—only the way of tackling differed in line with the political climate.

Reasons for Parental Non-Compliance

In reality, the KLV was a much smaller operation than London's ill-fated Plan II. Even after three years of total war, the majority of children were not in KLV, but staying in private billets (with relatives or friends) or remained in the capital. For the end of the year 1943, Evans (2009) has the following numbers for Berlin: of a total school population of 249,000, only 32,000 children were evacuated with the KLV. Eighty-five thousand remained in the city, and 132,000 were in Verwandtenverschickung. "Thus, up to this point, self-help remained more important than state or Party direction in the removal of children from bombed-out areas of German towns and cities" (Evans, 2009, p. 451). Despite the severity of RAF bombing and substantial propaganda efforts promoting the KLV, parents were hesitant to sign up their (often more easily convinced) children for the party-run official evacuation.

Berlin parents had different reasons not to comply with the regime's requests than their London counterparts. The class differences that led to planning mistakes in London did not apply in Berlin; the NSDAP had always understood itself to be a party rooted in blue- and white-collar working classes and had a lot of experience in targeting these people with its propaganda and apparatus—so much so that the NS regime had accidentally already removed the other stumbling block of the London evacuation: Thanks to a long tradition of fully funded holidays for the underprivileged, both children and parents were used to long periods of separation. Similar programs in England existed, but none of a similar size. Unlike in London, where the evacuation was brought into disrepute during the Phoney War, the KLV was only initiated once Berlin was actually under attack and should have been viewed as a sensible measure by the population. Thus, reasons for parental noncompliance in Berlin had to be rooted in the particular relationship of German people and NS regime. Unfortunately for this study, there was no impartial institution around at that time to survey parents' motivation for what must have amounted to low-level rebellion against the all-powerful NSDAP. One can assume that a general mistrust of the government that led Germany into another world war played a part, as did the parental instinct of keeping a family together in times of crises. Due to an absence of data this has to remain speculative, though. However, there are two aspects of the KLV that have been better researched, and they can help explain the low participation rates in Berlin.

One aspect was the actual living conditions in KLV camps and how they were communicated to parents back in Berlin. The experiences in camps or foster families are not the focus of this research; it must be sufficient to mention that the collected and published testimonies show emotions ranging from excitement about adventurous scout life (e.g., Bandur, 2006) to terrifying suffering at the hands of older bullies (e.g., Hermand, 1993). Particularly, Jost Hermand claimed that a lot of children were subjected to mental and physical abuse in the camps. To a certain extent this was due to the nature of adolescence in a largely uncontrolled environment of dormitories and bike sheds, but it was aggravated by the strict hierarchy and the excessive power wielded in the hands of pubertal HJ leaders. News of ill treatment traveled fast to Berlin—despite attempts of censorship by the camp leaders—and parents became increasingly suspicious of the KLV, an organization that they used to regard with approval. Sometimes there was public humiliation, too. Camp leaders would publicly read out critical letters during assembly. Still, they would forward them to their destination afterwards (Bauer, 2010), where critical reports would cascade within close-knit communities and shape many parents' opinion of the KLV. The Bundesarchiv holds carbon copies of letters written by children to their parents. It remains unclear if the letters and postcards were withheld or forwarded to the parents, but they would surely be magnificent source material for a different study.

Another reason for parental noncompliance lay in the known antireligious stance of the HJ, although this was much more important for the Catholic south than Berlin. The HJ's "hostility to religion was notorious" (Noakes, 1998, p. 429) and while the churches and individual clergymen were eager to provide religious education lessons for the evacuees, the party-loyal camp leaders largely sabotaged their efforts. Religious education was no longer a school subject, but was allowed as an extracurricular activity, which did cut into the children's precious free time.

On the whole HJ, NSLB and NSV successfully excluded the churches from the evacuation and restricted access to the children severely—at the expense of the parents' trust. If they were religious they were likely not to sign their children up for the KLV, especially if the reception area would be dominated by a different denomination (the Protestant north vs. the Catholic south). Even in comparatively secular Berlin, the church sent several clergymen and -women to the reception areas, mainly in Ostpreußen (today's Eastern Poland), in order not to lose a whole generation of church-goers (Braumann, 2004).

Chapter Conclusion

In both cities, evacuation administrators were disappointed with the parents and children of their subject population. While they saw themselves as executioners of a government policy that was in the people's best interest, the people largely refused to cooperate. Both governments had to learn and adapt in order to attain the desired symmetrical relationship between state apparatus and citizens. For the LCC, the Phoney War period proved to be very educational. Members of the Evacuation Branch were initially frustrated about the lower-than-expected participation rate, the complaints from reception areas, and the unauthorized returns from the country—but the sources show that they also learned a great deal about working-class family dynamics at that time. The LCC also learned (from its own mistakes or from the criticism by the press and social study surveys) about diplomacy and about their approach to the target groups. Instead of proudly disregarding concerns about the scheme in London and the reception areas, the Evacuation Branch adapted the scheme in light of previous shortcomings. The modified evacuation scheme Plan IV that was operated during the Blitz should profit from reflective analysis within the LCC (see Chapter 5). Still, the scheme never fully recovered from the wounds inflicted on it by the Phoney War. It seems that even during the Blitz, working-class parents would rather keep their children close by than expose them to the real or imaginary ordeal of the evacuation.

Evidence from this chapter suggests that London parents took compulsory schooling less seriously than parents in Berlin. Whereas outrage in London only started when a large number of children were left without any schooling because they were never evacuated or had already returned from the reception areas, parents and government officials in Berlin did not allow the closure of schools and were already very concerned about the use of school buildings for the war effort and subsequent curtailed timetables (see Chapter 7 for a further discussion on the role of compulsory schooling).

However, maybe this was a consequence of the reverse course of events in both cities. Whereas London had the evacuation first and problems with unsupervised children later, in Berlin it was the other way round. First there was the absence of fathers and male authority figures, the part-closure of schools, and a new libertine lifestyle among some adolescents, and then came the evacuation. When it came, it only came gradually, though. This was positive from an operational point of view, because the evacuation was easier to manage, but it might have given parents too much leisure to listen to the bad news coming in from the reception areas and refuse evacuation for their children. Since many parents were already suspicious of the NS-DAP's attempt to monopolize education, they showed their opposition by not complying with the government/party request to hand their children over to the HJ. The reasons for keeping the children close by (or sending them away privately) were different than in London, but the outcome was similar: When RAF and Luftwaffe started bombing each other's capitals, the cities they targeted were still full of children—although both governments had initiated large-scale operations to get them out, but largely failed to secure the parents' support.

'Luftnotgebiete – kein Platz für Kinder'
Bundesarchiv Berlin Poster Collection 003-011-027

5

Policy Changes

*From the first day of September 1939 evacuation ceased to be a problem
of administrative planning. It became instead a multitude
of problems in human relationships.*
—Titmuss, 1950, p. 109

Changes would have to be made. In neither city was the evacuation successful or popular enough for its planners to carry on regardless. In London, only a minority of the first wave's evacuees stayed in the country, while the others rejoined the children who had remained in the city despite best efforts to reach them with the evacuation scheme. In Berlin, registration numbers remained low and schools, and children carried on with their normal business that was only marginally impaired by the occasional departure of a KLV train. In London, people would fear a German invasion after the fall of France and the Lowlands during the summer of 1940, and in autumn the long awaited Blitz began. In Berlin, air raids increasingly disrupted civilian life, and by summer 1943 it became evident that neither the war would be over soon nor would there be a return to normality in the near future. Still, most of the children remained in the capitals.

Operation Pied Piper, pages 107–131
Copyright © 2012 by Information Age Publishing
All rights of reproduction in any form reserved.

This chapter will look at the changes made to the evacuation schemes as well as the discussions that preceded those changes, their publication, and immediate results. This and the previous chapter are closely linked, so some repetition may be unavoidable. Overall, this chapter is heavier on the narrative than on source analyses, but a few selected documents will be critically reviewed. For London these will be a memo from within the Education Office about interviews regarding the feasibility of compulsory evacuation and a set of documents relating to the *propaganda drive* accompanying the modified schemes. The core sources for Berlin are leaflets for householders that inform about the new evacuation and appeal to parents to comply with the emergency measures. A second set of short sources deals with resistance to the Schulverlegung—they are orders prohibiting the continuation of informal schooling in Berlin.

Before looking at the policy changes it seems prudent to look again at the planners' original expectations of parents and children's behavior—and how and why they were disappointed. The image of self and other gains huge significance in the explanation of the schemes' original shortcomings based on the administrations' inability to incorporate other views of childhood and parenting than their own.

The British civil servants and politicians of the 1930s would have been prep school boys under Queen Victoria, and their expectations would largely be based on their own biographies (please note that male domination only applied to professional state activity; women were politically active in volunteer committees and boards—see Grosvenor & Myers, 2006; Martin, 2003). Prep schools, according to Vyvyan Brendon, ran under the guiding principal of preparing boys for a life in service. Thus, they enforced an informal code instilling a higher sense of sacrifice than could be expected of the *underprivileged* (2009, p. 116). This military-style concept of service would have shaped the civil servants' reasonable expectations of children and parents: When there is a war and the government decides to evacuate the children, children will be evacuated. The possibility of alternative decisions shook the former prep school boys, who after all deemed themselves the holders of majority opinion since they had an exclusive grip on certain spheres of society.

The Third Reich was tailored to Hitler's views, and his image of what children are or should be is crucial for the design of the major organizations catering to young people (HJ, BdM, etc.) and the evacuation. While the British upper classes, as arbiters of opinion, promoted children as little adults and exemplary citizens, the German view is much harder to grasp. There are certainly elements of duty, sacrifice, and honor in Nazi childhood concepts, but also wild references to the *beau savage* within children:

Eine gewalttätige, herrische, unerschrockene, grausame Jugend will ich.... Schmerzen muß sie ertragen. Es darf nichts Schwaches oder Zärtliches an ihr sein.... Ich will keine intellektuelle Erziehung. Mit Wissen verderbe ich mir die Jugend. (I want a violent, imperious, fearless, ferocious youth capable of enduring pain. There must not be anything weak or tender in them. I don't want an intellectual education for them; knowledge only spoils them.) (Hitler in conversation with Hermann Rauschning in 1940, quoted in: Kohrs, 1983, p. 52)

Thus, disappointments followed the realization that children were neither as independent from their parents as British civil servants expected, nor as ready to voluntarily submit to the harsh, military regime of the KLV camps as the men of the Reichsjugendführung anticipated. Two options were open to the planners now: listen to children and parents and take their grievances into account for the forward planning, or just force the children out of the cities regardless of their or their parents' wishes.

Personnel Changes

Not only some of the policies, but also some of the people executing them changed. With Churchill's war cabinet in May 1940, some of the key players in the British evacuation changed. This does not include the short period after the outbreak of war when normal administration was shelved in favour of an Emergency Committee chaired by Herbert Morrison who "in theory . . . was the dictator of London" (Donoughue & Jones, 1973, p. 268). Malcolm MacDonald took over at the helm of the MoH, and Herwald Ramsbotham at the BoE (he would be succeeded by Richard Butler of the Butler Education Act in 1941). After Rich's retirement at the LCC in June 1940, E. Graham Savage took over as Education Officer. This former senior chief inspector at the BoE took over at the height of Plan IV and formed a lasting alliance with his deputy—and successor—Dr. John Brown.

No major alterations happened to the upper levels of the hierarchy in Berlin, but some changes were made within the evacuation's actual executive. Already in February 1941, Möckel handed over the running of the Dienststelle KLV to Heinrich Schulz, who would be succeeded by Eberhard Grüttner in June 1942. By 1944, Richard Heil had taken over at the helm of the Dienststelle KLV—now evacuated to Bad Podiebrad outside Prague— since Grüttner had returned to the front. Bad Podiebrad was not an accidental choice. The spa town close to Prague became the KLV's secret capital. Over 15,000 evacuated children occupied the grand spa resorts there (Kock, 1997). After Heil's car crash on January 8, 1945, Gerhard Dabel became the last office manager of the operation (Buddrus, 2003). At this point the regime was breaking apart. Schirach was estranged from Hitler and thus lost any proximity to real power. In the dissolution of the KLV he had no involvement. The Dienststelle KLV in Bad Podiebrad closed on May 8, 1945, even though some KLV camps continued to exist for up to another two years (Dabel, 1981).

Escalations

Already in January 1940, there was widespread suspicion that London's evacuation scheme was close to collapse. Three thousand children returned to London each week, the operation so far had cost £20 million, and there had been no schooling for more than 500,000 London children since September (Crosby, 1986). The once sympathetic press had turned against the administration. The *Guardian* observed the children running around the cities without schooling and urged the government to reopen schools instead of damning the dame schools (unofficial learning circles by ambitious teachers or parents) that sprang up during that time: "Better the schools than the streets." In light of the small number of children who were actually still in the reception areas the paper advised treating the evacuation as a rehearsal for a time of acute bombing. "For the moment we had better confess that parental feeling (or obstinacy or indifference, as you will) has beaten us" (*Manchester Guardian*, 16.10.1939).

The Fabian Society's damning verdict goes further and claims a complete failure of propaganda and cooperative actions. While the report admits that the reopening of schools was necessary (after all, 84% of children were still or again in London), other actions were damaging and unnecessary: asking parents of evacuees for a levy to contribute to the cost of the evacuation, or publishing photos of the king's daughters in London, which might have been good for morale, but also gave an illusion of safety (R. Calder, 1940). The evacuation's first wave also triggered heated debate in parliament. While Labour MPs were largely defending the evacuees and their parents, Conservative and Liberal Democrats were denouncing them as antisocial, suffering from diseases (especially scabies), having primitive habits, and destroying carpets and mattresses. Overall, the evacuees were an imposition on the owners or tenants of quiet country houses. Labour politicians were hitting back by blaming the situation: the evacuees were under stress, strangers in unwelcoming houses, separated from their parents, and unfamiliar with the country ways (for a full review see Crosby, 1986).

Thus, only weeks after its initiation—and well before the actual air raids that were its sole raison d'être—the scheme was largely discredited and widely unpopular. At the same time German advances on the Western front increased the pressure on the administration to prepare for the onslaught on British soil, and Morrison's press announcements discussed in the previous chapter already hinted at the changes to the evacuation scheme. The administration would review and redesign it several times before the war was over, but it seems that whatever they did, the population would never fully embrace the scheme after the disappointment of the Phoney War. *Once billeted, twice shy* seems to have been the dominant sentiment in the East End. In public, politicians glossed over their defeat with emotional rhetoric, like Minister of Health Malcolm Macdonald's proclamation in the House of Commons: "When we touched the ties binding families together in this country, thank goodness we still touched something which was exceedingly tender and exceedingly sacred" (Manchester Guardian, 14.06.1940). The disappointing unwillingness of parents to comply with government policy thus became a surprise indication of healthy family values.

In Berlin, the evacuation scheme KLV was not so much unpopular as unappealing. Despite regular heavy air raids in 1943, only 32,000 of the eligible 260,000 schoolchildren were evacuated through the government scheme in KLV camps or NSV billets. One hundred-thirty-two thousand children were privately evacuated, and 85,000 remained in Berlin. Sixty-two thousand of these had parents who categorically refused participation with the KLV (Kock, 1997). After Stalingrad, the war turned into a permanent military retreat and no amount of propaganda could camouflage that the war was going badly for Germany in Russia and North Africa. The defection of axis allies like Italy and Bulgaria only added to the despair and disbelief in the capital. At the same time, RAF bombing increased when Churchill decided to redirect Air Force attention away from the Ruhr towards Berlin, a major industrial center in its own right. The first devastating campaign was flown in November 1943, followed by eighteen more attacks, resulting in 9,000 Berliners killed and 812,000 homeless (Evans, 2009).

Unlike in London, where the danger came, went, and returned in the course of the war, the situation in Berlin just got worse. Looting of newly occupied territories might have provided basic necessities for the people of Berlin, but after 1943 no one was fooled that the situation would change for the better soon. What Evans calls "the sharp decline of morale amongst the German population in 1943" (Evans, 2009, p. 467) was evident particularly in the capital, where the socialist and communist legacy had always prevented a total Nazi penetration. The loss of morale was followed by a loss of discipline. The regime was increasingly worried about sexual liberalism, about a lack of social behaviour (evident in events like the trampling to death of 30 people during a rush into the Bunker at Hermannplatz in January 1944—Evans, 2009), and about the looting of bombed-out houses.

Its reaction was to persecute and punish. There is also evidence of dissent by Berlin parents towards the pressure exercised on them to evacuate their children. Party information evenings had to end prematurely due to tumult, parents were disappointed by the vague answers they received to very specific questions, and speakers were laughed at and booed out for their euphemistic presentations of camp life (Buddrus, 2003). By that time parents had heard their (or their neighbors') children's complaints about the downside of living in camp: the permanent drill, the harsh and violent environment, the unfair pecking order in the dormitories, the sexual harassment, the low self-esteem among the physically weak, and the occasional sadistic HJ leader. In particular, the leadership vacuum led to the reign of "infantil-aggressiven Egoismus" (childish aggressive egoism—Hermand, 1993, p. 40). It was not only the rebellious parents who refused the evacuation, though, but also the ones very loyal to the regime. They regarded evacuation as a form of "Fahnenflucht" (desertion). Goebbels had to reassure the wealthier Berliners that the more children joined the KLV the better (Fröhlich, 1998).

London

Changing Policy in London

Only five days after the outbreak of war, a decision was made among ministers in Whitehall that any future evacuation scheme would have to exclude mothers. Their evacuation was immediately viewed as a failure and their conduct and behavior in the reception areas the reason for the evacuation's bad reputation (with the onset of heavy bombing, this policy was relaxed again and mothers with small children readmitted to the priority classes). Future plans for a new scheme of more modest and gradual movements would target schoolchildren only and proceed very quietly, "as it was feared that parents would fetch their children home if they knew that the Government might give them another chance" (Titmuss, 1950, p. 142).

Another near immediate change was made to the financing of the scheme. On October 3, 1939 it was agreed that the prospective revenue of a billeting allowance recovery outweighed the risk of charging parents for the evacuation (i.e., their children's immediate return to London). In retrospect, the attempt proved to be a mistake. The mammoth administrative task executed by already overburdened civil servants produced little more than confirmation that poverty in London was more severe and widespread than previous government figures had suggested. The majority of households were unable to pay the requested contribution. While the evacuation's first year had cost the Exchequer £6,700,000, the recovery from parents amounted to £550,000—and from that the substantial local expenses for the fee's collection, book keeping, and so on had to be paid as well (Titmuss, 1950). Similarly disputed was the means testing of parents who had privately evacuated their children in an attempt to recover some of the billeting charges. The LCC was at the forefront of protests against this unfair and counterproductive practice. The national government had to abandon it eventually (Titmuss, 1950). Instead of cutting costs, the Treasury actually had to accept an increase in the billeting allowance for rural householders. After a near revolt in the reception areas about insufficient funding for the feeding and clothing of the evacuees, new billeting charges were set at: 10s6d for children 10–14 years old, 12s 6d for those aged 14–16, and at an unprecedented 15s for those over 16 (Titmuss, 1950).

In late January the London stakeholders met and designed a modified evacuation scheme: Plan III. There were a few key changes as results of the evacuations progress over the first few months. From this point on, evacuation focused exclusively on schoolchildren, some very young children with mothers, and pregnant women—as they made for the most desirable guests. A new propaganda campaign in the reception areas promoted more tangible benefits to rural householders like the increase in the billeting allowance for older children and the promise to put difficult billets into hostels. Furthermore it was agreed—despite its risk to the scheme, but really without alternative—to reopen of schools in evacuation areas and the return of compulsory attendance (Crosby, 1986). This scheme, to be initiated the moment bombing started in earnest, "was almost completely ignored" (Lowe, 1992, p. 7). By April 25, the registration in London was below 10% of schoolchildren eligible for the scheme. Plan III was never operated. The Phoney War had changed the mood of Londoners: The initial tension was gradually replaced by apathy. "The people preferred to wait and see, for although they had as yet no experience of what the bombers could do, a large proportion did at least know what evacuation meant" (Titmuss, 1950, p. 176).

The LCC, now desperate about the survival of the whole evacuation scheme, indicated that compulsion was desirable (Gosden, 1976), as did a MoH advisory committee (Titmuss, 1950), but the national government rejected the idea. Nevertheless, compulsion remained hotly contested. Even during the second big wave of voluntary evacuation, the papers enthusiastically followed the House of Commons' debates on the topic. On June 14, 1940, the *Guardian* reports Minister of Health Malcolm Macdonald speaking out against compulsion: "Supposing the Government had ordered compulsory evacuation and a large number of parents had not obeyed the order, the Government would have to impose penalties upon them . . . and he would like to hear from members what penalty they would impose on such parents" (*Manchester Guardian*, 14.06.1940).

Only the next day the *Guardian* printed replies to Macdonald's statement stating that "many mothers during the past fortnight had said they wished the question would be settled by the Government and not by them" and that "if you depend on sentiment and rely on mothers to send their children away you will get nowhere" (*Manchester Guardian*, 15.06.1940). Compulsion was on the table, and the LCC had to take position.

Discussing Compulsory Evacuation

In May 1940, a discussion took place at the Education Office about the possibility of compulsion. A confidential note (sources XVa-b) summarizes the views of six divisional officers from different parts of London ("in their variety representing the whole"). The discussion took place at a time before intense German bombing and plays with different scenarios: Should compulsion be introduced before bombing, after bombing, or after the bombing of a city that was not London?

One of the main concerns voiced is Plan IV's focus on schoolchildren (necessitated—as discussed above—by the problematic relationships of urban and rural mothers during Plan II): the exclusion of very young children is seen as evidence for a lack of sincerity on the part of the government. The officers reported the popular sentiment that "we will all keep together, even if bombs fall." Their estimate of noncompliance in a compulsory evacuation scheme reflects this sentiment. The officers calculated that nearly half of London parents would refuse a compulsory scheme for schoolchildren only, whereas noncompliance would drop to about 20% for a scheme for schoolchildren as well as younger children with their mothers. Reactions by parents were characterized as: "If the Government really wish the children to be safe, how is it that the plan is for the evacuation of school children only? Why not for little children too?" (Source XVa Appendix, p. 1)

The officers unanimously agreed that evacuation was very unpopular, so much so that parents who actually left their children in the reception areas faced criticism by their neighbors. The unpopularity might also account for the problems to get London children back into schools. A report from North Kensington claims that parents were worried to send their children to school for fear of them being evacuated without warning.

Furthermore, there was a false sense of security after other A.R.P. measures had been very visibly put in place for the protection of Londoners (barrage balloons, Anderson shelters, etc.). The discussion closed with an unambiguous conclusion: "The officers were unanimous that a policy of compulsory evacuation would be resented, some said bitterly resented, and that it would be actively opposed. The North Kensington man said that 'people would get together' to oppose it" (Source XVa, Appendix, p. 2).

A few months later, Savage claimed in a memorandum to the chairman of the Education Committee that "the blitzkrieg has altered many opinions, and it is now the common view of these experienced officers that only by some measure of compulsion will the 'hard core' of children kept in London by unwilling or indifferent parents be got away to the reception area" (Source XVa, p. 4). At that point in time compulsion could not be enforced, but the issue resurfaced in May 1941, when representatives of vulnerable boroughs like East Ham sought the Education Officer's support for compulsory evacuation in representation to government.

As compulsion could not be enforced (yet), the MoH and LCC agreed on a system of personal visits to parents at home and in shelters. A directive from October 24, 1940 to the dispersal officers in charge of these visits included the following instruction by Savage: "The prime object of the campaign is not so much to give further publicity to the opportunities now open for evacuation as to bring kindly persuasion to bear upon people not yet convinced that they ought to use them" (Source XVb, p. 2).

Savage's attitude here—patronizing as it is—stems from a very realistic assessment of the situation of London parents. Later in the war—after the first winter in blitzed London—the MoH had to give in to the LCC's persistent demands for the evacuation of those children made most vulnerable by the bombs—even against their parents' wishes. Defence Regulation 31(c) allowed the compulsory evacuation of "any children in the Greater London evacuation area certified to be suffering or likely to suffer in mind or body as a result of enemy attacks." It was rarely used for schoolchildren, though, but for a number of under-fives who were sent to nurseries in Suffolk. Compulsory evacuation remained very limited; in 1941 only 470 children were sent out of London against parental will (L.C.C., 1943, XIII; Samways, 1995).

Propaganda Drive

Since compulsion remained unfeasible, the voluntary evacuation scheme had to rely on advertising to increase its popularity. This note from within the Education Office was written at the height of the Blitz (sources XVIa-b). The second large-scale evacuation (Plan IV) had taken over 100,000 children out of London in June and the weekly or daily trains of the "Trickle" evacuation had subsequently doubled that number. The memo opens with some estimates: 200,000 schoolchildren were still in London, 200,000 billeted in reception areas, and a further 100,000 were in the country under private arrangements. Sixty-five thousand mothers and young children had sought their own accommodation in the country, but had been assisted with transport arrangements by the LCC. After the intensification of air raids, facilities officially billeting mothers with children (of school age or under) were again taken up by 50,000. In the same period, the number of unaccompanied schoolchildren sent into billets was *only* 12,000.

Based on the very limited success of past campaigns, the new propaganda drive would have to reach the target groups much more efficiently.

> The essential feature of a new campaign would therefore be an individual appeal to the parents who have not sent their children away. Evacuation is a personal and family problem, which can only be solved by personal discussion. . . . A mother has first to reach a decision either to let her children go or to go with her children; then to go through with the business of registration; and finally to go right through with it by turning up at the station. Many mothers, even though broadly inclined towards going, drop out at one of these difficult stages. . . . They can be helped along considerably towards the desired end by persuasion by someone with authority or someone whom they know and trust. (Source XVIa, p. 3)

These persons of trust and authority were envisaged to be women in the WVS or care committees, but also the LCC staff. The approach here shows that the critical reflection within the LCC (already discussed in previous chapters) continued. There is an appreciation of psychological and emotional considerations, whereas previously only logistical issues made the agenda. The LCC attempted to learn from the low numbers, the complaints, the bad press, and the critical surveys published after Plan II and IV.

This document is a guide for those appointed for the cold calls. Visitors to homes, rest centers, and shelters should be well prepared for the discussions they'd trigger. Key aspects envisaged in this note are safety, health, education, and domestic problems. With regards to safety, the approach should be balanced. "It is necessary to admit frankly that the safety of the reception areas is relative and not absolute," but considering the regular and severe attacks on London it is still preferable to be out of town. Visitors should emphasize that while a child's health and "general development" suffers in London, there are plenty of opportunities for regular sleep and open-air activities in the country. "Whereas education is almost at a standstill in London, full-time education is, generally speaking, being provided in the reception areas." Domestic problems that would stop mothers from leaving London included the care of an aged relative or the fear of separating from the husband in times of crisis. The note recommends pragmatic reasoning here: A wife can increase the likelihood of her husband finding shelter space during an air raid by not taking up one herself. If a wife feels duty bound to cook for her husband, the communal kitchens might be the solution.

The LCC now deemed these personal visitations and discussions more important than costly propaganda. It was crucial that comprehensive listings of the services were made available and that the visitors were equipped with information and answers. Some posters were recommended for the walls of tube stations or other shelters, ideally with a message by the prime minister. While films like *Westward Ho!* might have been effective propaganda, they were watched by fewer and fewer people. "Since the London cinemas have lost most of their audience, it is doubtful whether film publicity can play any part in this new campaign." The suggested methods of reaching parents were press and BBC publicity (mainly detailing the services available), personal canvassing, and posters.

Several items produced from October onwards show the impact of this summary. A printed "Notes for Visitors" gave template answers for a variety of possible questions by mothers, including: "What will happen to my children if I am killed?" and "Who will look after my husband?" An extensive leaflet entitled "Please read this: Important Notice to Mothers" was distributed, and a press advert bearing the headline "Mothers you'd give your life for your children—won't you give them this chance to get away to safety and health" placed in London newspapers. It must have been sobering to collect the results of this extensive and time-consuming campaign of personal visitation. A table shows the outcome for the County of London: the volunteers and LCC staff made over 130,000 visits (plus another 60,000 were noone was at home), but only for 33,000 children did they receive a promise to register. The organizers anticipated various reasons for refusal—and their pessimism was confirmed. For 20,312 children there was a blank refusal with no reason given; another 23,103 were to stay in London since 'husband cannot leave London and family wish to remain together'; and 17,194 children had been evacuated before and mothers were dissatisfied. Other reasons given included unwillingness to entrust children with strangers, the assumption that London is as safe as the country, the mother's commitment to the care of a relative in London, the refusal of children to go away, the expense of the evacuation, or the promise to make private arrangements. Evacuation remained unpopular.

Still, the measures discussed in this chapter show that the LCC was unfazed by the widespread refusal of their provision. Instead of giving up, the clerks at the Education Office were busy canvassing and convincing hostile parents. The actual changes made to the scheme will show that not only did the propaganda change, but also the scheme itself. The LCC took the criticism on board and attempted to rectify the evacuation's gravest problems—at least as much as they could without trespassing into reception areas or BoE and MoH territories.

Policy Changes: Plan IV, the Trickle, and the Doodle Bug Evacuation

Plan IV

It is worth looking at the policy changes collectively, even if it means taking a step back in the narrative's chronology. Plan IV was originally intended for time of intense air raids, but was initiated in June, when there was a growing fear of a German invasion. The Lowlands had fallen, France negotiated for peace, and the NS regime drew up—but later shelved—plans for Operation Sea Lion. For London the fear of invasion was not as immediate as the fact that the Luftwaffe could now turn their full attention to Britain and fly attacks from the much closer air fields in Holland and France. Between June 13 and 18, 61,000 children were moved out of London (103,000 from the greater metropolitan area). Logistically, the operation worked along the lines of Plan II, but with some discernable differences. The LCC was keenly aware that "much of the goodwill of householders and local authorities had already been lost, perhaps irretrievably. The sensibilities of the reception areas were this time more prominent in the minds of the policy-makers" (Titmuss, 1950, p. 357). Thus, one change had to do with the state of the evacuees:

> The lessons of the first evacuation were not ignored; every child was medically inspected the day before departure, by school doctors reinforced by GPs, dirty children were first sent to a hostel to be cleaned up before being billeted in private houses, and no child was allowed to join a party without a minimum outfit of clothing, any shortages being made up from clothes issued from a reserve depot. (Brown, 2005, p. 45)

As mentioned before, other changes were the exclusiveness of the scheme to unaccompanied (mainly school) children and the increased billeting allowance. Lower registration numbers also meant less chaotic distributions of children in reception areas that already had a working infrastructure for evacuees, especially if the children rejoined their own schools. However, another new feature was the inclusion of long-distance travel. Whereas previously the reception areas were close to the evacuation areas, this time London children would make long journeys west to Cornwall and

Wales. The two reasons for this extra strain on the transport network were the comparative safety of areas away from the vulnerable coast as well as previous experiences with lower returnee rates from distant billets (please note that choices for Berlin's reception areas seemed to have followed similar considerations).

Plan V: "Trickle"

Plan IV was for preregistered children only, but when the political situation worsened in summer 1940 and especially after the onset of bombing, many more parents signed up their children for evacuation. The "Trickle" scheme's design actually closest resembled the German KLV scheme. Registrations were taken continuously, and unaccompanied children left London in weekly—during the Blitz daily—trainloads. A total of 64,000 children were thus evacuated, but the plan was suspended in 1942 as a result of the increased reluctance of householders to receive evacuees (Crosby, 1986; Samways, 1995) and the decrease in air raids. After all, "the German raids on London and other cities in 1940 were intended above all to bring Britain to the conference table, and when they did not succeed, they were discontinued" (Evans, 2009, p. 436). It remained true that only bombs were sufficient motivation for parents to part from their children as is evident in the result of a further publicity campaign in 1942. Post-Blitz, only 9.5% of London parents signed their children up for evacuation, while 16.2% positively refused and 74.3% did not reply to the circular letters (Gosden, 1976).

Not even the *Little Blitz*, the intense bombing of London during the first three months of 1944, led to an increased demand in the evacuation scheme. However, the rumors of secret unmanned rocket bombs fueled the Londoners' imagination and subsequently led to the last big wave of evacuees from the metropolis.

The Doodle-Bug Evacuation

The final operation *Rivulet* was initiated in the summer of 1944, when flying bombs V1 (noisy and visible) and V2 (silent and difficult to anticipate) reached the coast and capital. The V weapons were insofar secret, as the LCC did not anticipate—or they underestimated—their impact. The fear of these new weapons was such that some Londoners gave up their homes and slept in the tube shelters (Holman, 1995). The capture of the V1 launch sites in France led to the premature claim that the Battle of London was over, but on September 8, the first V2s landed in Epping and Chiswick "and London became the first city in the world to come under sustained long-distance rocket attack. This was a truth too terrible to tell" (Inwood, 1998, p. 806). The government kept quiet about the new threat;

no mention of the attacks was made on the radio or in the papers, where the damage caused was attributed to gas leaks. The people—"who were angry, demoralized and frightened by the ferocity of these attacks when victory had seemed so near" (Inwood, 1998, p. 808)—were not fooled and started to seriously doubt the government who tried to hush up air raids that claimed half as many casualties as the Blitz.

Already on August 2, Churchill announced that anyone not required for the war effort should leave the capital. In addition to the schoolchildren, provisions were made for hospital patients. Within the month, 275,000 official—and an estimated 1.2 million private—evacuees had left London. Between July 5 and September 2, 118,000 children from the LCC area were evacuated, with the fringe and East coast sending a similar amount simultaneously (Gosden, 1976)—thus giving credit to its codename "Rivulet," more than a trickle but not yet again a river. However, not even at the height of the V2 attacks did the driftback into London stop, despite the rockets killing over 2,000 people there (A. Calder, 1969). The threat only subsided when Allied advances on the continent pushed back the V2 launch sites, and "by January evacuees were returning at the rate of 10,000 a week" (Brown, 2005, p. 60). When the allies captured all V launch sites in Holland in early 1945, it marked the end of the evacuation scheme. From then on, the children's return to London was the challenge.

Berlin

Changing Policy in Berlin

In Berlin, as for the whole of the Third Reich, policy changes would be subject to the power vacuum and self-destructive attitude that were symptomatic for the NS regime. The administration was a pyramidal structure with Hitler at the top, but during the war the Führer was "largely removed from the day-to-day running of the Reich. But no individual, let alone any collective body, had filled the vacuum" (Kershaw, 2000, p. 313). In the same way the war was improvised and chaotic, so was the evacuation's operation. It was ambitious individuals who kept Berlin running, like Gauleiter Goebbels, who after all was in charge of civil defense and had the most experience with air raids among the regime's inner circle (Kershaw, 2000). The power struggle between NSDAP and civil service was also slowly escalating. Evans dates "the eclipse of the traditional State administration in comparison to the Party" for 1943 (Evans, 2009, p. 511).

Even without grand policy decisions, the war and KLV changed schooling in Berlin. From 1941 onwards, schools no longer admitted Poles, Gypsies, and Jews. From 1942 onwards, school libraries no longer issued books by foreign authors. The curriculum was adapted to war propaganda: In handicrafts, students would build model planes, in math they would solve aviation problems, and their essay topics in German would revolve around England's war guilt or the opportunities afforded by military conflict. The HJ even succeeded in establishing "military service counting in lieu of success in the final examination," thus undermining the German Abitur and university entrance qualifications (Giles, 1992, p. 21).

It is worth considering the HJ's changed role from 1940 onwards. The once rebellious, revolutionary group with the strong appeal to adolescents had evolved into the *Staatsjugend*, a compulsory organization for everyone (Kinz, 1991). As a club it lost all its exclusivity, and the young people rebelled against the loss of identity in their own ways. Some deserted and joined the many illegal cliques in Berlin (see Chapter 4), but a more popular low-level form of rebellion was to simply refuse to conform to the expected discipline. The regime's reaction was to enforce obedience by punishment and tighter supervision. This, however, became increasingly difficult, since the war demanded soldiers and thus the HJ was about to have its own leadership vacuum, as most HJ leaders were drafted to the front (Kinz, 1991). With regards to the KLV, the HJ had to make concessions. Regular (and often tumultuous) information evenings for the parents of evacuated children had to be organized in the home schools where representatives of HJ and the education ministry as well as the camp leaders had to be available for questions and answers (Order II Nr. 60/44, 2 October 1944 at: BBF/ DIPF GUT SAMML 191).

The relationship between HJ and state schooling had been an "elementarer Konfliktherd" (substantial source of conflict) from the beginning to the end of the Third Reich (Buddrus, 2003, p. 852), with both institutions bargaining for children's minds and time. With parents' influence widely neutralized through conformity and the churches marginalized within the state system, schools remained as the only competition to the overpowering HJ. It had been Schirach's aim to stir responsibility for education towards the youth organization and dissolve the Reichsministry. Probably the only reason that Rust and his ministry could withstand the pressure was the aforementioned leadership crisis within the HJ.

The KLV camps had offered Schirach the chance to implement his vision of Nazi education; they would become places of largely undisturbed NS indoctrination (Buddrus, 2003). At first it seemed as if Schirach's aspiration would be fulfilled. Young but arrogant HJ leaders would demonstrate their (party-backed) power over the teachers. The daily routine favored activities run by the HJ staff: Only four hours were designated school hours, but seven were marked for indoor and outdoor communal activities and games. In those circumstances, tension and power struggles amongst the competing supervisors were the norm (Fürstenberg, 1996).

However, in the course of the war, teachers would regain some of their authority in the KLV camps, since increasingly desperate drafting of increasingly younger HJ leaders for the army meant that the teachers' competitors for authority in the camps were hardly older than their regular students. Those young, insecure, and inexperienced leaders were no match for the teachers, especially those brought out of retirement. Undisturbed by Nazi indoctrination, they went on to teach Latin and Greek the way they always had (Larass, 1983; Noakes, 1998). Within the isolation of the camps, the elderly teachers had to be everything to the students: parents, educators, disciplinarians, as well as bearer of bad news like the death of a relative (Fürstenberg, 1996). With the shortage of men and older boys, the role of the BdM also increased. At an average age of eighteen, girls would volunteer for duty in KLV camps. They organized funerals and excursions, led the flag salute, oversaw the communication with parents, and so on. Their training for these positions was a three-month BdM course that girls could enroll for straight after school (Lang, 1991).

The one big policy decision concerning the KLV from Berlin had to do with compulsion. There were powerful proponents of compulsion like Schirach and Goebbels (despite describing compulsion as "intolerable" in his diary in September 1940—Fröhlich, 1998, p. 349), but in the end Hitler's personal decision not to put pressure on parents overruled their ambitions (Buddrus, 2003). Apart from Hitler's personal wish for voluntary support, there was a very tangible reason for avoiding compulsion. Propaganda needed the British bomb attacks to hit civilian targets in order to criminalize them. A wholesale evacuation for the Ruhr, for example, would designate that area a war zone and thus subject to different laws (Kock, 1997).

Generally, Hitler resisted compulsory measures since his rule relied on voluntary support. Nevertheless, central government occasionally found it hard to control local practices. Some cities used rations and ration books as a tool to bully parents into participation, despite clear guidance to the contrary from Berlin (Braumann, 2004). Even in the capital, though, some pressure was exercised by stipulating that registration for the KLV was entirely voluntary, but once committed, children could not be withdrawn from the camps for a set duration (a measure also introduced in London; see Chapter 4). The unauthorized return of a child became a punishable offense for the parents from August 12, 1941 onwards (Kressel, 1996).

How compulsory the KLV had become actually was a topic of hot debate among parents, children, and—it seems—NSV clerks. From the transcript of an evacuee's letter, it becomes apparent that already in October 1940 the issue of voluntary participation was important. After describing vividly how some evacuees sneaked out of the camp just to get in touch with the local NSV office, the young author reports on the procedure for early returns:

> Wir müßten an die Eltern schreiben. Sie sollen zur NSV. gehen, und sich dort vom Ortsgruppenleiter (Braun) die Rückfahrkarte geben lassen.... Wenn die Eltern die Rückfahrkarte nicht bekommen, sollen sie fragen ob die Kinderlandverschickung Zwang geworden ist. Wenn dieses der Fall ist, werden wir ja wissen, was wir zu tun haben. (We should write to our parents. They should contact the local NSV officer Braun and demand the return ticket. If parents are refused the return ticket they shall ask if the KLV has become compulsory then. If that is the case we shall know what to do— i.e., escape and return to Berlin independently. NG.) (BA: NS/12/942/a)

Parents and children had relied on the KLV to be voluntary, and this excerpt implies that also NSV officials were assuming just that when advising evacuees to demand the right to leave camps. However, in Berlin the NSV used red tape and rhetoric about the strains of war to refuse parents the return of their children—and in summer of 1943, the city's administration abandoned any pretension about the KLV and ordered the schools to close and leave.

Eltern der Berliner Schuljugend!

With this leaflet addressed to the parents of Berlin's schoolchildren, the government evacuation scheme entered a new phase: The KLV changed from optional to quasi-compulsory since all schools in Berlin would be closed and relocated (sources XVIIa-c). The leaflet is signed by Dr Goebbels, Gauleiter of Reichsverteidigungsbezirk Berlin (new terminology, literally "Reich's defense district Berlin"). It is a remarkably plain document; the complete absence of Nazi insignia and symbols is conspicuous. This one-page leaflet wants to be factual and uncontroversial. It is neither. Simultaneous to this leaflet another one was distributed to the rest of the evacuable population headed "Berliner! Berlinerinnen!"

The leaflet to parents starts with some scaremongering. The first two sentences explain how the Luftterror (aerial terror) has no consideration for civilians, how the bombers fight a war of extermination against defenseless women and children. The leaflet's motives are then laid bare: out of concern, the government is forced to extreme measures. Instantaneously and under the label KLV, all schools are to be relocated in the reception areas of Brandenburg, East Prussia, and Wartheland. Parents will be informed about the details at information evenings organized by either headmasters or local NSV offices. Mothers may accompany the schools, provided they are not needed in Berlin.

The leaflet was published during the summer holidays. It contains a clause for those children on vacation outside Berlin. They may stay wherever they are now and will be informed of their school's new location on their return to Berlin. The document closes with Goebbel's expectation of parental support in order to carry out this scheme for the safety of their children.

It is a short, plain, and direct communication. Its factual design and writing style seems a (deliberate?) contrast to the explosive content. After all, the relocation of schools for an undetermined period of time signals many things: that Berlin is not safe (pretty obvious to anyone living there at that point, but still rarely admitted by the government) and that war is going to last a lot longer still. Actually, at that point anything to do with the KLV was controversial—resentment by parents was at an all time high, so much so that Goebbels delayed the relocation for some months. Only in April 1944 was the move completed, albeit with far fewer children than anticipated or officially admitted.

Linguistically, this leaflet is noteworthy for the implication of compulsion without actually spelling it out. Officially and by the Führer's demand, evacuation remained voluntary and Goebbels could not claim compulsion, despite judging it necessary at this point in the war. Thus, the wording implies compulsion, but it really only implies it. Hoping they do not get lost in translation, here are two examples from the source:

> Mit sofortiger Wirkung werden die Berliner Schulen mit ihren Lehrern klassenweise...verlegt. (Instantaneously all Berlin schools will be relocated with teachers in their form groups).

Schools and teachers are mentioned, but it does not say students. Nevertheless, the term "Klasse" (form group) as in "klassenweise" of course works synonymously.

> Von den Eltern wird Verständnis für die getroffenen Maßnahmen, die im Interesse Ihrer Kinder getroffen werden, erwartet. Ihre Bereitwilligkeit und Einsicht werden dazu beitragen, daß die Verlegung der Schulen reibungslos vonstatten geht. (We expect parents to appreciate the measures put in place for the safety of their children. Your willingness and reason will contribute to the schools' smooth relocation).

In 1943 few dared to fall short of one of the highest-ranking Nazi official's expectations; the wording must have been received as threatening. Additionally, the wording is such that it implies carelessness, neglect, and ignorance in everyone not complying with these reasonable precautions "for your children." There is a major difference, even in German, between "we hope you understand" and "we expect you to understand"—the latter leaves the recipient with far fewer options.

The second leaflet—"Berliner! Berlinerinnen!"—supports this interpretation. Contrary to parents of schoolchildren, the other priority groups—the elderly and women with very young children—receive very clear and precise orders what to do next. While the first paragraph still attempts to convince with politeness ("it is desirable"), the document becomes sharper further down. After explaining three government-approved options for flight from the city, it states: "Es ist verboten, unter Verzicht auf diese Möglichkeiten planlos zu reisen" (Haphazard travel outside these options is not permitted). It seems that the regime did not have a problem to order its people around, only the children—which might have to do with the Führer's particular interest in them and the power struggle surrounding their fates.

The KLV organizers' increasing desperation level is evident from a further leaflet distributed in February 1944 (reprinted in Franck & Asmus, 1983, pp. 208ff). This call to all parents of children still in Berlin uses stronger persuasive language still, but also a new level of frankness about the reality of the war. The wording here has nothing in common with the prior optimistic and upbeat attempts to convince schoolchildren to join the KLV. The leaflet appreciates the parents' dilemma of safety considerations and the desire to keep the family unit together, but comes down clearly in favor of safety.

> Die Eltern müssen sich stets darüber im klaren sein, daß sie die Verantwortung für das Leben ihrer Kinder tragen. Dieser Gewissenszwang ist stärker als alle menschlichen Gesetze und stellt die persönlichen Wünsche der Eltern zurück. ... Es ist immer noch besser, seine Kinder außerhalb in Sicherheit gegen Luftgefahr und Bombenterror zu wissen als für immer auf dem heimischen Friedhof. (Parents have to realize that they are responsible for their children's lives. This moral constraint supersedes all other human laws—and parents' individual wishes will have to yield to it. After all, it is better to have your children abroad but safe from air raids and bombs, than forever close by in the local cemetery.) (Source XVIIc)

At that point, Hitler was very remote from local events in Berlin. Thus, this leaflet freely uses the previously shunned term "Zwang" (compulsion), but still only in a philosophical sense rather than as an actual order. It is the parents' moral compulsion to sign up for the KLV, rather than the government's demand. The document reads much more like a plea than an order; it tries to convince rather than to intimidate. It picks up controversial issues about the conditions in camps and admits shortcomings, but none so big as to make staying in Berlin preferable to going away. Especially the loss of schooling for those staying in Berlin is used as an argument. The document is unusually frank about the prospects of winning the war when it relays that: "Der Schulunterricht in Berlin wird auf keinen Fall wieder aufgenommen" (schooling in Berlin will not resume under any circumstances).

Compared to the factual tone of the previous leaflet, this one is full of emotion. A lot of it might be written in the overly complicated formal German employed by the NS regime, but some passages come from the opposite end of the rhetorical toolbox: they read more like a sermon:

> Alle Opfer, alle Arbeit, alle Sorgen, alles Leid und alle Not, die die ältere Generation in diesem Ringen auf sich nimmt, werden getragen um der glücklichen Zukunft dieser Jugend willen. (The older generations bear all the sacrifices, all the work, all the worries, all the sorrow and all the hardship of this conflict to enable a happier future for the young). (Source XVIIc)

The leaflets discussed here are evidence of many things. For one, they show that propaganda changed during the war and that there was no continuity in the approach to parents of potential evacuees. While they were excluded from the propaganda effort in the first two years (when it was deemed more effective to target the children and rely on their pester power), the attitude changed with the Schulverlegung. Suddenly the publications were much closer to the material used in London: the addressees were now responsible parents who, despite flaws and rumors, will still do the decent thing and send their children to safety, whatever their personal political allegiance or emotional needs. The change in tone also suggests that Berlin's evacuation scheme was struggling badly. The numbers confirm that the KLV was unpopular and Berlin full of stray children. Faced with the obvious, a change in the marketing approach was only sensible. The later leaflets were much more honest about life in Berlin and in the KLV camps than at any time earlier in the war.

Policy Changes: Schulverlegung

The order from September 7, 1943 to evacuate all Berlin schools was greeted with hostility at tumultuous parents' evenings. Compulsion was not spelled out but implied; after all, parents who did not entrust their children with the KLV still had to comply with compulsory schooling. Schulverlegung left children and parents with three choices: either to go with the KLV, to take the stop-train and become a Gastschüler (a guest at a school just outside Berlin), or to stay in Berlin illegally and get some form of home tuition. Thus a fervent search for places in suburban schools around Berlin began where children could join existing classes as guests, while officially still being listed with their own—now evacuated—school. To satisfy Berlin authorities, children had to register under a new address outside Berlin— while it was apparent to anyone that they continued living with their families (Bauer, 2010).

Logistically the Schulverlegung was not a new challenge; the infrastructure was in place anyway and had been positively underused so far. Evidence collected by Franck and Asmus suggests that before the Schulverlegung, only a small minority of children were participating in the government's scheme. One school listed 22 students in KLV, 207 students "detained in Berlin by parents," and 191 students in Verwandtenverschickung. Despite the ambition to move schools immediately and collectively, individual school records show that reality was different. A census taken on September 20, 1943 at girls' school Gertrud-Stauffacher-Schule showed that of 680 students, only 153 took part in the current move; 353 were privately evacuated or Gastschüler in the suburbs; 15 had to stay in Berlin to help the war effort (presumably as BdM nurses or similar); and 159 girls' whereabouts were unknown (school's own archive).

The administration now pushed hesitant parents around with a variety of bureaucratic measures. Those who had not registered their children for KLV nor could prove that they received schooling as Gastschüler would no longer be issued their rationing cards. Children at the verge of secondary schooling could only enroll in grammar schools in the reception areas. After the Schulverlegung, parents were informed that children who were not partaking in the official evacuation scheme, who were not registered Gastschüler, or had otherwise been granted leave would be expelled from their school. Once *the war was won* and schooling back to normal, those children would be last on the list for readmission (Order III, 2 Gen. 721/44, 24 June 1944 at: BBF/DIPF GUT SAMML 191).

In April 1944, the *Berliner Hauptschulamt* (local education authority) announced that all schools were now evacuated and their buildings used for the war effort (Franck & Asmus, 1983). In reality, most parents had made different arrangements for their children. According to Kressel, only 13.4% of eligible children had gone with the KLV by April 1944. He calculates that 37,709 children went with the Schulverlegung, 140,155 children were privately evacuated, and 87,373 remained in or around Berlin (Kressel, 1996, p. 114). Kock estimates that in June 1944, 100,000 schoolchildren were still in a Berlin without schools (Kock, 1997, p. 223). Much later, in early 1945, some schools attempted partial re-opening with teachers that had remained in town for adult evening classes. Compulsory evacuation— or rather closing the schools and insisting on compulsory schooling—was a desperate step for a regime unwilling to publicly admit the true state of the war. Still, parents would rather rely on self-help than public provision. For perspective, though, it is important to keep in mind that the controversial step taken here really just meant that Berlin's evacuation now looked like London's Plan II did three years before (the crucial difference was the variant value of compulsory schooling). Berlin's government changed the KLV for good by dropping any pretense that this was not an evacuation. Even the change of the label, from KLV to Schulverlegung, had a domino effect on the power dualism in favor of the teachers. The compulsory evacuation was no longer an HJ adventure, but a simple location change of an established school. Thus the teachers, rather than the increasingly younger HJ and BdM leaders, were now in charge of the camps (Dabel, 1981).

Evidence of Opposition

In Berlin it seems that ordering the dispatch of all schoolchildren was very different from actually achieving their departure. Here are two short documents that illustrate the limits of the regime's power over schools and teachers (sources XVIIIa-b). While the order was simple—move all schools, teachers, and schoolchildren (with the exception of Flakhelfern) out of Berlin—the execution was everything but smooth. Only after half a year did the authorities announce completion of the Schulverlegung, but even then it was an illusion. Like in post-Plan II London, Berlin was full of unsupervised children who either half-legitimately were registered as Gastschüler in surrounding boroughs or dodged registration and Schulpflicht altogether. The sources presented here show that the teachers did not abandon those children, despite their explicit orders.

The first document is dated August 18, 1943 and constitutes an order from the Stadtpräsident (contemporary term for Mayor) to teachers, headteachers, and governors. Its first two topics are redesignations of reception areas and the desirability of teachers' spouses to accompany the KLV. Then it deals with children and parents:

> Es wird behauptet, dass Lehrer Unterrichtszirkel für in Berlin zurückgebliebene Schulkinder gebildet haben. Dadurch werden Kinder, die durch

den Abtransport in Sicherheit gebracht werden sollen, in Berlin zurück-
gehalten. Ich mache darauf aufmerksam, dass ein solches Verhalten den
Absichten des Führers widerspricht. Ein derartiger ohne Genehmigung
der Aufsichtsbehörde eingerichteter Privatunterricht ist unzulässig. Eine
Genehmigung wird nicht erteilt. (There are claims that some teachers have
formed unofficial tutoring groups for children left in Berlin. This detains
children in Berlin who should have already been sent to safety. I want to
point out that this behavior contradicts the Führer's intentions. Private lessons are prohibited if they are not authorized by this office. No authoriza-
tions will be granted.) (Source XVIIIa, p. 2)

So, teachers were providing some lessons and it seems that there were
more than just a few isolated cases of unofficial tutoring, otherwise the authorities would not have drawn attention to the possibility by issuing a pro-
scription. It further seems that even after private lessons were made illegal,
provision continued. Two weeks later, another order—or rather appendix to
the previous ones—came from the Stadtpräsident's office. It shows the officials' increasing desperation and annoyance with headmasters and teachers.

Es ist mir mitgeteilt, daß die Schulappelle in einzelnen Bezirken dazu be-
nutzt werden, den Kindern häusliche Schularbeiten aufzugeben. Bei den
Eltern wird dadurch der Eindruck erweckt, daß trotz der Schließung der
Schulen eine ersatzweise Beschulung durchgeführt wird. (I have been informed that in some districts school assemblies have been used to provide
schoolwork for children to do at home. The implication for parents is that,
despite the closure of schools, there is some sort of replacement educational
service for their children.) (Source XVIIIb)

The document goes on to state that this act would deter hesitant parents to sign up for the move since some provision was still to be had in
Berlin. Needless to say, the order to headmasters is to refrain from doing
anything during assemblies that might give parents the impression that
some form of schooling ("ersatzweise unterrichtliche Betreuung") was still
available in Berlin. Interestingly, these were the same assemblies that in the
minds of the NSDAP officials should have been used for patriotic indoctrination (see Chapter 4).

It seems that the delay in clearing Berlin and the regime's inability to
clear it completely was partly down to the refusal of schools to partake in
the Schulverlegung—or to teachers who judged rebellious children's need
for education as high as that of the compliant ones.

Chapter Conclusion

In both countries, participation numbers of the governments' schemes dropped swiftly after initially high levels. The organizers' response to that was an increase of pressure up to near-compulsion. However, the planners in London eventually reacted to public opposition and changed tactics, while in Berlin the intimidation continued. Thus, the changes to the evacuation schemes mirrored political reality. In England, government and civil service were under public scrutiny and could not persist with unpopular policies indefinitely; eventually the scheme had to adapt to the needs of the parents. In Germany, however, no such system of checks and balances existed under Nazi dictatorship; thus, the officials in charge did not feel the need to rethink or revise their policies, but only to increase the pressure on parents and children.

In London, compulsion was discussed but dismissed. Instead, the planners changed the scheme and its propaganda. The evacuation got progressively smaller, both by absolute numbers and target groups. Schoolchildren remained the main focus since the LCC had better access to them than to the adult population—and because they stirred up comparatively little controversy in the reception areas. Their dispatch was scaled down and more flexible as well: Plan IV was a logistical challenge, but since in absolute numbers only 20% of the earlier Plan II participated, it was easily manageable by the experienced LCC staff. From then on, small but regular departures would bring the children to increasingly distant locations. Propaganda changed, too. Instead of advertising, the LCC now relied on an extensive system of personal visitation and individual persuasion. The changes seem sensible, but the scheme could not recover from the initial loss of trust. In the end, the evacuation planners were torn between pride for their achievements and disappointment about the lack of public support for their efforts.

In Berlin, no one was there to make the necessary policy changes. Hitler had removed himself from day-to-day business, Schirach was no longer in the regime's inner circle, and the officials in charge of the KLV had themselves evacuated to a fa-away reception area close to Prague. The improvisation continued—with every local officer inventing his own set of policies about compulsion and pressure. For two years, the KLV ran alongside normal life and schooling in Berlin, partly unnoticed or resented, partly appreciated and celebrated. Berlin's governor Goebbels initiated a single desperate policy change in 1943: the closure and move of all schools. However, not even the sobering admission of a dire political situation changed all that much. While the regime was still trying to bully parents and teachers into submission, for them self-help (e.g., private evacuation, Gastschüler-ing or unofficial tutoring) remained the favored option. Thus the two schemes went in opposite directions. While the English one remained voluntary and became smaller, the German one got bigger and more compulsory. Neither one, though, was ever as successful as the planners anticipated.

6

The End of the War

By September 1944, Londoners had hoped that the theater of war had moved to the continent for good and were shocked and surprised by the sudden V1 and V2 rocket attacks. However, once the rocket launch sites were captured and the Wehrmacht driven out of France and the Lowlands in early 1945, the war was indeed over for the capital. London could now start the long road to reconstruction from the physical and psychological damages of war. Bringing the children home should have been an integral part of that recovery, except it was not. The city was in no condition to receive additional population yet—it could hardly feed and shelter the ones already there. This chapter will look at how the LCC organized the return of the evacuees and how the children tried to adjust to life after the war.

By the end of 1944, very few Germans believed that the war could be won. The enemy had long entered German territory and the army's retreat was obvious, not only to the ones living on the frontiers of the Reich. Many KLV camps had been deliberately placed in the newly occupied Eastern territories to bolster the German occupying presence there. The Berlin children who had been sent there for their safety when their city was exposed to

Operation Pied Piper, pages 133–156
Copyright © 2012 by Information Age Publishing
133

ever-increasing Allied air raids suddenly found themselves very close to the battle lines. The KLV organization needed to react, but they were running out of options: There were simply no safe places left to send the children to and they would not get permission to do that anyway, for Hitler's fear of appearing defeatist (paired with the slow collapse of the administration) blocked any sensible policy. The camps' fates were down to the teachers who ran them. The regime was about to disintegrate; pragmatic self-help was left as the only option to keep the evacuees safe.

This chapter completes the narrative of the evacuations. The schemes' conclusions will illustrate the transformations that happened to the agents, citizens, and their relationships. For London, the sources concern the organized return of evacuees: a bureaucratic act of little controversy but enacted on the background of the collective and individual tragedy of war. The sources from Berlin show the brief absence of bureaucracy in the last months of the war and its recovery under Allied control. Looking at both nations' very dissimilar ends of the war and the emergence of new municipal authority should be useful to consolidate claims about jurisdiction and authority made about the respective cities in the conclusion. This chapter further offers a brief review of the evacuations' legacies that are as varied and numerous as the analytical or popular studies they initiated. Interest in the evacuations' social, psychological, and political impact is not diminishing as it gets beyond living memory. In this chapter, three central aspects of legacy will be reviewed: the evacuation's impact on education, its impact on social reform in London, and the controversial issue of a German generation brought up by the HJ.

London

The End of the War

For London, the war ended on 27 March 1945, after the last major V2 attack on Stepney. During the four and a half years of war, London lost large parts of its population to flight, evacuation, diseases, and enemy action in London and abroad. This was especially true for the most damaged boroughs in the capital's East End: Stepney lost over half of its population; the City, Shoreditch, and Poplar about 45%; and Southwark, Bermondsey, and Finsbury about 38% (Inwood, 1998). For those children still in town and those returning from evacuation, the derelict city became one massive playground. Greater London lost 116,000 houses, with another 288,000 in need of major repair (Inwood, 1998). There was general relief about the end of the war and cheerfulness that it was won, but simultaneously it became apparent that despite victory there would be several years of austerity still to come.

There seemed to be little doubt on the part of the policymakers that social intervention and government planning during the war would also help London's recovery afterwards. Already in October 1940, Churchill promised that London would rise from the ruins more healthy and beautiful, and the destruction of the Blitz actually accelerated the city's rebuilding after the war. London would profit from Labour's surprise election victory in 1945 and subsequent ambitious welfare state legislation. London's most dire problem was the housing shortage—especially since the LCC area's population grew by 800,000 in the five years after the war. Private building was at a standstill, and the LCC had to react with an emergency repair plan that made 103,000 damaged dwellings habitable by 1947 (Inwood, 1998). The following years would see rapid new buildings and repair works with the LCC desperately trying to compensate the increasing shortage in urban dwellings that it fueled itself with the ambitious slum clearance program.

To have a house to return to was, after all, a key requirement for those displaced by war. The source analysis here will show that there were many reasons not to immediately return to the capital, but the lack of a home was the biggest. Londoners were scattered all over the place: Many men were still on military duty abroad, and a lot of bombed-out women and children were staying with friends and relatives or in public shelters. Families and communities that once were closely knit now had to re-establish each other's whereabouts and arrange for the immediate future. What Londoners really craved was a return to normality, to an uninterrupted daily life of work, shopping, evening entertainment, and family life. Thus the evacuees' return was both challenging and crucial.

While it had been obvious from March 1945 onwards that the threat to London was over and that the remainder of the war would be fought on German territory, the evacuation scheme could not close down immediately. The small chance of a continuation of the rocket attacks and the big housing crisis made the Ministry of Health delay the organized return of London children. Only in May 1945, all the emergency schools closed for a few weeks to allow teachers and inspectors to survey the state of London parents, checking the location of families, the condition of houses, and so on. It was a tedious enterprise. Not only private homes had been destroyed, but also many schools. Of 1,200 school buildings in London, only 50 were undamaged. Two hundred and ninety schools were either completely destroyed or severely damaged, and a further 310 had extensive bomb damage (Maclure, 1990). A further complication was that the release of school buildings requisitioned for the war effort took time. By October 1945, 516 schools were still otherwise occupied (Gosden, 1976).

The Organized Return of the Children

For the MoH and LCC the organized return of evacuees was a top priority—its execution was not easy, though, as is evident from these documents (sources XIXa-c). The first step of the return arrangements would be a survey of the evacuees' parents, during which LEAs should obtain possible reasons why children should not (yet) return. The MoH directive from October 1944 states:

> Mere unwillingness on the part of the parents or guardians to receive their children should not be allowed to act as a bar to the children's return, but there will be individual cases in which, for one reason or another, the child cannot or should not return home for the time being. (Source XIXa, p. 1)

Apart from reasons that had their origin in the evacuation areas, the MoH listed two connected to the evacuees' progress in the reception areas: the near completion of secondary schooling or actual employment, provided it was "of a really progressive nature." For those returning home, free transport arrangements would be in place, but the directive remains a bit vague there ("the arrangement for travel both by rail and road will be settled... by the Senior Regional Officer of the Ministry of Health"). The document makes up for that by being very specific when discussing the pre-journey medical checks, the children's luggage, and especially their ration books. Food for the journey was to be organized via the "local food executive officer."

In the end, the return of evacuees to London would be executed with as much bureaucratic fervor as their departure. The MoH's nine-page circular 68/45 from 10 April 1945 set out the return arrangements in great detail—even though no date for the return had been set at that point. The plan was to be executed immediately upon the local authorities' receipt of a telegram with the content "Operate London Return Plan." That telegram—and further detailed instructions—was eventually sent on May 2.

The plan is straightforward, deals with a lot of paperwork (ration books, medical cards, etc.), seems to have been issued without controversy in the policy making process, and does not bear detailed analysis here. The bulk of it is about responsibilities and timings for certain aspects of the journeys, but there are some items that are interesting with regards to the developments of the war. Again, the LCC takes charge and the plan demonstrates that the concerns of London trumped the needs of the reception areas. This was deemed sensible since London was heavily destroyed and suffering from the strain of returning people—but the rural hosts could have equally demanded to be finally relieved of their burden since it was no longer a wartime necessity. Nevertheless:

> In view of the difficulties of the housing situation in London, it is of the utmost importance that evacuees who have not adequate accommodation immediately available for their occupation in the evacuation area should be given no assistance or encouragement to return there. (Source XIXb, p. 1)

On June 7, 1945, E. A. Hartill at the LCC Education Officer's Department compiled a list of returnees up to that date. The document states that official arrangements completed the return of 20,000 children in the LCC area and another 17,000 in the rest of the Metropolitan Evacuation Area. This meant that 19,000 children were at that point not part of the arrangement—either because they were "already at home, having returned before the evacuation scheme closed down," or because of "long-term difficulties" that kept children in the country. An earlier list compiled by the Education Officer's office on June 5, 1945 registers those difficulties in more detail. For some of the 563 children listed, the problems seemed to be temporary; they were expected to return home within four weeks. For others, the reasons for not returning were more permanent: the homes of 203 children were blitzed and awaiting repairs, 22 children's parents could not be traced, 43 children's fathers were still in the forces and their mothers dead or missing, 16 children's parents were removed from London, four were orphans, and in 17 cases the care committee recommended that due to the unsuitability of the homes (no narrower definition given—but the low number indicates practical problems rather than class cultural judgments) the children should remain away. Other reasons for a delayed return (or not returning at all) were not really difficulties, but rather issues that developed during the course of the war. Forty-five children stayed in the reception areas to finish their secondary education, seven children remained because they were working there, 43 children stayed permanently in Barnado's Homes, and for 95 children the parents made private arrangements for them to stay with their foster-parents longer in order to sort things out better at home.

A subsequent, undated list provided more explicit explanations of "domestic difficulties" that stopped children from returning home. Some cases could be reasonably explained by the war: when parents were divorced or separated and had not decided custody then, or mothers had become war widows and worked full time. Other listings refer to human tragedies that made children *residuals* of the evacuation scheme. They could not be returned home because:

"Mother deceased, father remarried"
"No mother, ignored by father and stepmother"
"Mother deserted family, father in H.M. forces"
"Mother deceased, girl of 15 keeps house"
"Father in prison, mother ill" (selected from Source XIXc)

A handwritten, undated table stored with these typed documents shows the difficulties the children, parents, and officials faced at the end of the war. Table 6.1 is a transcript, just to illustrate the range and dimension of problems.

What these sources show is that the end of the war did not lead to an immediate return to normality at all. Too many lives had been severely af-

TABLE 6.1

Reason	County of London	Original Metropolitan Evacuation Authorities
Already returned	1,491	596
Parents arranging return	778	521
Returning later for educational reasons	343	211
Parents arranging for child to remain	1,840	298
Mother working—does not want child to return	41	18
Mother ill or being confined—illness in the home	251	89
Child ill	41	17
Child in Barnado's Home, etc.	155	—
No trace of parents at address given	951	176
Parents cannot be traced	615	158
Both parents in H.M.F.	—	7
Mother dead or missing + father in HMF or cannot accept child	325	127
Parents separated or divorced	79	84
Both parents dead	56	12
Insufficient accommodation or home unsuitable	948	166
No home	1,752	462
P.A.C. children[a]	—	6
Misc.	102	77
Total	9,763	3,025

[a] Children of Public Assistant Cases under Poor Law Authority (unverified).
Source: Source XIXc

fected by the war and the LCC could but register all the tragedies and problems that would constitute the aftermath of the evacuation. Bringing the children home was logistically easy, but pointless if there was no home to return to. The bureaucracy had to patiently wait for the people of London to find each other and make their city habitable again.

The Aftermath

The war turned a settled society into a society of refugees (Mellegard, 2005). It was a long war, and evacuees who had sometimes been separated from their own families for years—formative years at that—often found it difficult to rejoin their London household. At the same time, the adults in London had changed as well. Fathers returning from battle might have been psychologically affected by the horrors of war and subsequently seemed distant and strange to their children—especially when they tried to impose a regimental style of parenting after being away from civilian life for so long. Mothers emerged from the war more independent and confident, since they had been working and earning money in the war effort. Post-war London witnessed divorces on an unprecedented scale. For many evacuees their parents were strangers with occasionally very different parenting styles than the country hosts. There is evidence that many children resented having to go home and found it hard to readjust. In particular, overseas evacuees found the city grey and dreary.

The civil servants accused of psychological ignorance in the early stages of the war now seemed keen to prove their newly developed sensitivities. The MoH produced a leaflet that would help teachers, social workers, nurses, and so on in charge of visiting families with former evacuees to check on the progress of the reintegration (source XX). It is a comprehensive document offering guidance for likely emotional problems encountered by parents trying to re-attach to their children. Its guiding principle seems to be: care workers should emphasize to parents how dramatic a change their children underwent by leaving their rural playground for the city and to reassure parents that everything will be fine in the end.

The authors empathized with the difficulties parents might have to even recognize their offspring: "they may have been attractive little things, dependent, babyish: they may have become self-reliant, boisterous, determined." Many children had not been home for several years—and especially in families where the father had joined up some family members had not seen each other for years. Estrangement and possible puberty needed to be considered by parents. After all, "children cannot be expected to stand on their own feet for some years and then automatically become docile, obedient, considerate and helpful to their parents."

Difficulties might also arise from a marked difference in the living standard of the foster family and the child's own family, from the freedom afforded by country life and the constraints of the city, from the evacuees' status in their rural communities as something special (either to be envied or pitied), or from plain homesickness for the host family. Evacuees were particularly vulnerable to the feeling of being an outcast or intruder into a set community—parents were therefore well advised to get children back into their former peer groups, boy scouts, and schools fast. Some children might have been treated badly in their billets. Usually they would have returned or fetched back earlier, but even now they might relay to their parents stories of the hosts' misconduct.

> Children who return may tell highly coloured stories of unsatisfactory treatment and the conditions in their billets. This may be all part of the same picture; the child finding readjustment difficult and hoping to attract sympathy and attention. Parents must use their common sense and realise that such stories are likely to be exaggerated and may be based on nothing but imagination.

A recent BBC broadcast claimed that approximately 15% of evacuees were abused or treated badly during their stay in the country and the historians on tape lamented the lack of professional help extended to families in the psychologically difficult post-war years (Mellegard, 2005). Source XX rather suggests that contemporaries were aware of the problems, since the passage quoted above could also be read as an attempt to shift responsibility away from the MoH. After all, parents who suspected their children to have been abused in their billets might turn to the organization in charge of the evacuation for explanations and compensation.

Furthermore, those who had stayed in London were often dismissive of those *who got out.* The war had made the London children hard and had forced them to grow up faster than would have been necessary in the safety of the country. London children had developed—out of necessity—a self-reliance and independence that made it difficult for them to reintegrate into formal schooling after the war (Inwood, 1998). "Deference and discipline seemed to have deserted the generation born in the late 1920s and 1930s, whose formative years, in inner London at least, were so comprehensively disarranged" (White, 2001, p. 268)

There is no suggestion, though, that being an evacuee was necessarily safer or more pleasant. Being an unwanted stranger, a burden to the host family and rural community could not have been easy. It is safe to say, though, that uprooting a whole generation of children and making them live through a war—regardless if in safety among strangers or with loved ones in danger—had a long-lasting emotional impact. Mike Brown (2005), Bob Holman (1995), Martin Parsons (1998), and Ben Wicks (1998) all collected oral history evidence of former evacuees and war children that testifies to their struggles to settle down and form durable emotional attachments as adults.

It is difficult to ascertain the total number of evacuees during the war for the constant flow of children in and out of London. The LCC numbers are only of limited value here, since the records only show official departures, but not the private returns. Titmuss (1950) made an educated guess based on the MoH and BoE records for the nationwide government scheme (Table 6.2).

These figures mirror the course of the war: The biggest wave of evacuees left the cities during the panic at the outbreak of war in September 1939, but a lot of them returned home during the Phoney War. Participation increased again during the Battle of Britain (winter 1940–1941) and then steadily declined until the end of the war—with the exception of the V1 and V2 attacks on London in the autumn of 1944. Please note that even five months after the ceasefire, there were still 13,250 unresolved cases of evacuees with nowhere to return to on the files.

TABLE 6.2

	Unaccompanied Children	Teachers and Helpers
September 1939	765,000	89,000
January 1940	420,000	43,400
August 1940	421,000	27,000
February 1941	480,500	25,000
September 1941	435,700	21,000
March 1942	332,000	18,000
September 1942	236,000	13,000
March 1943	181,000	9,000
September 1943	137,000	6,400
March 1944	124,000	5,400
September 1944	284,000	6,800
March 1945	132,000	4,000
September 1945	13,250	—

Source: Titmuss, 1950, p. 562

Some regional effects and numbers defy explanations. Titmuss can only speculate why some cities were more successful than others in evacuating their population. For no apparent reason, Leeds sent twice as many evacuees as similarly sized Sheffield. Isaacs has no solution for the fact that half of the Cambridge evacuees from the London Borough of Islington returned home independently, but only a quarter of the demographically similar Borough of Tottenham did the same (Isaacs et al., 1941; Titmuss, 1950). Surely those are promising anomalies for future research.

The question of the evacuation's success is often linked to its primary aim of saving lives, even though there are no verifiable claims to be made about that without the help of alternate realities. It must suffice here to say that according to official records there were 29,890 civilian casualties and 50,507 seriously injured in London during the war. The capital suffered more than other cities, as is evident from the overall proportion: even though only 20% of the English population lived in the capital, it had half of the country's casualties (White, 2001). Titmuss calculates the total of civilian deaths due to enemy action in Great Britain at about 60,000, of which fewer than 8,000 were children under sixteen years. He decisively attributes this comparatively low figure to the success of the evacuation (Titmuss, 1950).

After the War: The Evacuation's Legacies

The evacuation's narrative would not be complete without a fitting epilogue. The one here will take the form of a brief summary of the government scheme's impact on post-war education and social reform. Already in the summer of 1940, many were concerned that the education system—which had been far from satisfactory before the war—would collapse. Simultaneously, there were those who maintained that far from losing out, the children actually profited from the war experience: "evacuation, it was often argued at the time, was basically good education, even if it led to bad formal schooling'" (A. Calder, 1969, p. 49). The evacuees might have benefited from the opportunities afforded by being in the country, but the majority of London children were not there. For those children who stayed in or returned early to London, there was a real loss of education. Already in 1943, a BoE survey showed increased levels of illiteracy and absenteeism (Lowe, 1992). Even the evacuation's organisers had to admit that while the operation fulfilled its primary goal to save lives, it failed in ensuring continuous schooling (Lowndes, 1969). Gosden speaks of a polarization: "the war of 1939–45 apparently had the effect of increasing both the proportion of children who got very little and the proportion who got a great deal from the schools" (Gosden, 1976, p. 72).

Probably inadvertently, the children's contributions to the war effort triggered a revival of the child labor discussion. In cities and countryside, "children were understood to constitute a population group on whom it was legitimate to draw in times of crisis" (Mayall & Morrow, 2011, p. 247), whether as messengers, nurses, or cheap farm hands. The evacuees' help with the harvest revived rural opposition to compulsory schooling—and the war was used to undermine and sabotage school attendance, with some councils allowing longer holidays for harvest help (*Potato Holidays*) or turning a blind eye on abuses of the Children and Young Persons Act. Thus educational loss was the biggest where seasonal demands were highest (Gosden, 1976). This development mirrored parallel ones in the Third Reich: From the very beginning, the HJ had included its members first in civil social services and later the war economy. Unlike English adults' surprise at the children's ability to contribute, German parents were long used to the rivalry between school (education) and HJ (work)—and largely supportive of the useful (if unacademic) work done by the youngsters.

Private boarding schools felt the impact of war less than others. There is the extreme example of Dragon School Oxford: The school stayed put on its premise, there was no food shortage, students did not engage with the war effort, met no evacuees, and there was no shortage of teachers (Brendon, 2009). However, most boarders did notice the war, either because they had to engage in new activities like knitting for soldiers, digging trenches, growing vegetables and so on, or because there were cloth shortages that led to more eclectic football kits and the embrace of "make do and mend." Nevertheless, Vyvyan Brendon argues that, if anything, the war only widened the gap between the boarding elite and the rest, that while some had uninterrupted access to education, a lot of evacuees (and especially returnees) lost years of schooling unrecoverable after the war. Optimistically, she claims, though, that "the war made such inequality of opportunity more obvious and more unacceptable" (Brendon, 2009, p. 135). However, the pre-war networks and *old school tie* mentality, which proved such vital assets during the war, endured.

Teachers were vital for the evacuation, both as educators and as supervisors: they were the first point of call for the displaced children and looked after them in and outside lessons. Gardner and Cunningham identified wartime evacuation as a "turning point in the development of teacher–pupil relationships" (1997, p. 331), arguing that urban teachers had to rethink their previous role based on formality, distance, and symbolic separation (Hendrick, 1997) in the face of a suddenly much more intense level of care required by the collective move to the country. Gardner and Cunningham claim that "evacuation might be...the dominant collective experience which shaped, directly or indirectly, the priorities of the nation's classroom teachers in the post-war years" (1997, p. 335).

The evacuation's legacy (as an accumulation of factors mentioned above) was that in post-war England, both the people and the administration revitalized their interest in state schooling and child welfare. The 1944 Education Act was evidence of a new belief in the "power of education to transform society and the economy" that held for another twenty years (Lowe, 1992, p. 4), although the biggest actual change was probably a new willingness to spend money on education despite budgetary restraints in the austere post-war period.

The evacuation changed more than just education. Already in 1939, the impressively perceptive LCC officer Monica Cosens—after touring London's reception areas during the Phoney War period—concluded that:

> In the new world that we have presently to build, is this evacuation experience to be one of the things that will force us to accept a levelling up of the income of the insecure section of community, even though we shall inevitably experience a levelling down of our comparative middle class ease? (Cosens, 1940, p. 3)

Popular perception is that the evacuation revealed to rural England the poverty and misery hitherto contained to some urban districts—and for some commentators the evacuation was *the* catalyst for the Welfare State (e.g., Gardiner, 2005; Holman, 1995; Süß, 2011). Middle-class gratefulness was also seen as influential for the post-war social reforms. The working classes had—by their endurance and steadfastness, in short: the Blitz Spirit—proved themselves worthy of a better education and health system (Crosby, 1986). A whole class' social standing suddenly changed: "this time it wasn't the paupers who asked for help but citizens who were victims of war" (Holman, 1995, p. 137).

The source analyses and conclusions here suggest that this picture needs differentiating, though. It seems incredible that it needed an evacuation to show rural England the squalor of the poorer parts of large industrial towns. Social commentary on urban poverty had been available for a good hundred years already, a tradition started by Tocqueville, Engels, and indeed Dickens. The middle-class politicians and civil servants knew the need for reform well enough: Education and health reform plans had been an integral part of the political discourse in the 1920s and 1930s. Plans for social reforms had been in LCC drawers since the mid-1930s and the national government—at least on paper—subscribed to the 1942 Beveridge Report that attempted to tackle *want, ignorance, disease, squalor* and *idleness* (Inwood, 1998).

A more promising approach might be to view the evacuation as what most contemporary commentators saw it: a failure. It revealed that the middle class politicians and civil servants did not understand life outside their class and could neither persuade nor force the working class into compliance with their policy. Crosby dryly concludes: "it would seem, then, that the greatest significance of evacuation to post-war Britain lay, ironically, in its failure as a policy" (Crosby, 1986, p. 156). It became apparent that the government, if it wanted to cater to and represent all people, needed to be more sensitive to its diverse population than it had previously exhibited.

There can be no doubt that the evacuation forced social comparisons between urban poverty and rural wealth, but this was not a one-way street. The middle-class hosts might have been shocked, but so were the newly aspiring working classes who were well aware of the rejection their wives and children faced in rural England and critically reviewed their loyalty with the Conservative-led coalition government. "Working class men in their pubs and on the job kept pace with the latest tale of middle-class irresponsibility and heartlessness. They had trusted and believed in the conservative government to lead their wives and children to safety: it was a trust betrayed" (Crosby, 1986, p. 148).

The social reforms probably followed a political survival instinct that the exclusion of a growing and increasingly powerful class could no longer be maintained. There might have been aspects of new solidarity and gratefulness in the overall policy decisions, but it is surely not cynical to propose—as Crosby and Lowe (see above) have done—that the reforms were also tools to maintain political control over a newly confident part of the population (Wicks, 1988). Thus, the evacuation influenced the social reforms, but it did so in more ways than its popular perception implies.

Berlin

The End of the War

While the war became more and more distant to the people of London at the beginning of 1945, the Third Reich was increasingly desperately fighting a *total war* they knew they could no longer win. Legislation introduced in 1944 allowed the drafting of men aged 16 and women aged 17 for the defense of the Reich—and many were recruited straight out of KLV camps. The violence on both sides peaked months before the capitulation. "At the beginning of 1945 Germany witnessed the greatest killing frenzy that the world has ever seen" (Bessel, 2009, p. 5). At no time in the war were there more casualties. The Allies flew their most intense bombing campaigns—the destructions of Hamburg, Cologne, and especially Dresden became vivid reminders of the war's futility. Six hundred thousand Germans lost their lives during the air raids. The advance of the Red Army in the East turned millions of Germans into refugees; they fled westwards to escape the revenge of a people that had suffered more than any other under the NS regime and WWII. While the regime started to systematically destroy evidence of the Holocaust and other atrocities committed during their reign, the German people were profoundly shocked about the level of violence unleashed by their government.

Alongside the violence came the quick deterioration of state authority and infrastructure:

> The Nazi political system collapsed, and what remained of it in the spring of 1945 was abolished by the Allied occupying powers. Millions of German soldiers had been killed or wounded, and millions more were in Allied prisoner-of-war camps. The country's transport system was largely at a standstill; electricity and gas supplies were cut; telecommunication systems no longer functioned; water and sewerage systems were severely damaged, food supply was precarious and many people faced the prospect of severe malnutrition; disease was rampant and medical services were severely disrupted. (Bessel, 2009, p. 4)

And then there was the Battle of Berlin. While the capital was never subjected to air raids of the same magnitude as Hamburg and Dresden, it took severe blows. The most damaging RAF raid happened on February 3, 1945, with 3,000 dead and 2,000 injured (Kershaw, 2000). However, the real threat came from the East. In anticipation of the final ground battle, the civil service worked with hectic energy "despite their rapidly shrinking sphere of influence, like cartoon characters running off the edge of a cliff and keeping going despite the yawning abyss beneath" (Evans, 2009, p. 721). There was no leadership anymore, no discernable government structure, just a Führer who—removed from reality—hid in the bunker underneath Berlin. Above ground, the people were getting desperate and 5,000 chose suicide over the dreaded Russian revenge, with parents sometimes murdering their children before killing themselves (Stargardt, 2005).

In April the citizens—by then mainly women, children, the elderly, and invalids—prepared for the ground onslaught by the Red Army. It took a fortnight of street fighting with 200,000 Russian and 50,000 German casualties until Berlin fell (including two more prominent suicides by Hitler and

Goebbels). Ninety percent of the Hitlerjugend boys in charge of the last desperate attempt of defending Berlin died there and then (in Germany's total war, six million children under the age of 16 fought as combatants—Gardiner, 2005a). On April 30, a destroyed and broken Berlin surrendered (with some street fighting continuing until May 2), and on May 8 the whole of the Third Reich followed.

During the last months of war—and despite official announcements to the contrary following the Schulverlegung—there were still children in Berlin. They went to school, although not to get taught, but to help with the school building's new function as a hospital or refugee camp. They would bring the powdered milk, serve tea, or scrub the floor. Since all the teachers were either evacuated or in the Volkssturm (the army of civilians, young and old, to defend the capital), the schoolchildren would be supervised by older girls or women of the BdM or NS Frauenschaft (Franck & Asmus, 1983). A census taken in September 1944 at Steglitzer Gymnasium (275 students) showed that only 80 students were in a KLV camp in Bohemia, 134 were Gastschüler at schools around Berlin, 56 remained in Berlin without schooling as Luftwaffenhelfer (anti aircraft gun assistants), two worked as HJ leaders, and a further three could not be accounted for (Fürstenberg, 1996). The KLV had not succeeded in getting the children out of harm's way, and they would become the principal defenders of Berlin against the Red Army.

The Closing Down of the KLV

There is no paper trail of the KLV's conclusion, mainly because it was never properly concluded. From January 1944 onwards, evacuation became more and more pointless, since there were fewer and fewer safe areas in the Reich to send the children to (Buddrus, 2003). Berlin might have been the prime target of allied advances, but no evacuation could work without reception areas. At the same time there was a collapse in communication and coordination between Berlin, the Dienststelle KLV and the distant reception areas. It did not help that the KLV administration had been evacuated to Bad Podiebrad in Bohemia, with only a skeleton staff of five remaining in Berlin (Buddrus, 2003). Within the NS state and its chaotic power system based on proximity to the Führer, the KLV had an ambiguous place. It was not important enough for Hitler's permanent attention, but big enough to secure its stakeholders (HJ, NSV, to an extent the NSLB) a bigger share of the power available within the regime (Kock, 1997). Thus it was officially continued against a background certainty that the war was lost, but would be fought without surrender to the end.

Buddrus claims that by January 1945, the Berlin administration admitted defeat since all reception areas had been lost to the enemy. They closed the scheme (Buddrus, 2003), but even in March 1945, just weeks before surrendering, the HJ—probably in an uncoordinated solo effort—planned further KLV transports, despite the obvious lack of safe areas to send the children to (letter to headteachers, March 29, 1945 at: BBF / DIPF GUT SAMML 191). In reality, the KLV was never officially closed, but simply ceased to exist in the chaos of the last weeks of the war. The tight bureaucracy and efficient state apparatus that had ensured the KLV's logistical success over the years now failed those who needed it: the children left in Berlin exposed to immanent attack and the children evacuated to camps in the Eastern provinces of the Third Reich that were gradually recaptured by the Red Army.

> Um die Eltern während der Lagerzeit von ihren Kindern fernzuhalten, hatte die NSDAP zahlreiche bürokratische Vorschriften aufgestellt. Für die sichere Rückführung der Kinder aus den KLV-Lagern gab es jedoch keinerlei Richtlinien. Die Partei, die die Eltern entmündigt und die Kinder für sich und ihren Führer beansprucht hatte, ließ diese nun im Stich. Die Kinder blieben auf der Flucht sich selbst und dem persönlichen Mut oder dem Versagen ihrer Lehrer und Betreuer überlassen. (The NSDAP had invented myriads of bureaucratic obstacles to keep parents away from their children, but for the safe return there was no paperwork. The same party that incapacitated parents and claimed their children for the party and Fuhrer now abandoned them. Children were left to fend for themselves and depended on the individual teachers and supervisors' bravery or lack thereof.) (Fürstenberg, 1996, p. 27)

There are gripping accounts of the tumultuous and spontaneous flights from the reception areas. Former evacuee Renate Bandur remembers her camp of older girls having being abandoned by the adults one morning. The teachers had fled and left the teenagers to either hide from the Americans or attempt to return home. She and her friends had a turbulent journey back to Berlin on military buses, refugee trains, and so on (Bandur, 2006). There are also many reports of children who did not make it back and starved or froze to death, got bombed or shot, or permanently got stuck between the ever-changing front lines on their long way back from the Eastern reception areas (the flight and family reunion of children displaced by war has recently been the subject of scholarly studies—e.g., G. D. Cohen, 2011; Zahra, 2011). Those children who found themselves in the comparative safety of Bavaria, for example, were likely to stay there. They continued to be supervised by their teachers, worked on farms, helped with the rebuilding, did not have formal schooling, and were later returned to

Berlin under the auspice of the Allies. In some cases this dragged out until May or June 1946 (in rare cases even up to 1948, depending on the organizational zeal of the occupying force in the former reception areas).

A Difficult Journey Home

The lack of official documentation regarding the end of the KLV and return of children to Berlin could have been an obstacle for the continuation of this policy study, but thankfully some school archives retained their own documentation of the turbulent transition from war to peace in the form of directives, correspondence, and annuals. Karl Döbling at Eckener Schule (an urban grammar school in Berlin Tempelhof that emerged from two former single-sex schools) was kind enough to provide valuable material about the difficult return of the evacuated children for this study. Additionally, the Bibliothek für Bildungsgeschichtliche Forschung holds the deposits of a similar school: the former Luisenstädtisches Gymnasium in Berlin Prenzlauer Berg. For this study the collection of correspondence between the school (and headmaster) in Berlin and the teachers on the move with their KLV camp in the Southeast is particularly relevant (sources XXIa-d).

The teachers of the Luisenstädtisches Gymnasium were less patient than others. In July 1945 they demanded the return of their school—or rather the KLV group that really only reflected a minority of the school's population—to Berlin. The reply from the leader of Berlin's education authority (Amt für Volksbildung) is a rare example of defiance by a German clerk against his own bureaucracy. In the turmoil of uncertainty that affected every decision at the time of the Allied government takeover, he formulated a pragmatic return plan that was both unorthodox and successful.

He had to refuse the request for a truck, since they were all needed in to bring building materials to Berlin, but advised the teachers stranded in Oberhof (Thuringia—a Russian occupied zone) to ask the local mayor for one. If he refused, the teachers and children could always go down to the train station and buy tickets to Berlin. Any excess luggage or sick children should remain in the care of Oberhof's mayor for the time being. Two thousand Reichsmark were enclosed with the letter to bridge certain financial difficulties (a possible reference to a culture of bribery developing in the occupied zones). A handwritten letter from August 27 by Alfred Homeyer, the teacher in charge of the KLV group, to the education authorities shows the success of this simple plan. On request, the train authority in Oberhof had granted the Luisenstädtisches Gymnasium the use of one passenger and one freight carriage to be hooked on to other trains going north. It took the party only two days to return in comfort to the capital.

However, there was a difference between the occupied zones. The above might have worked in the Russian zone, but for Berlin children stranded in Bavaria, for example, the situation was different. After all, Berlin's status and affiliation within post-war Germany was still unresolved. In the winter of 1945, the Allied government categorically denied requests for the return of KLV children to Berlin before the spring of 1946 and threatened parents contemplating individual returns with the withholding of rationing cards.

In April 1946, Allied occupying powers had not completed the regime change, but already German bureaucracy had recovered enough red tape to instigate really complex return arrangements for the remaining children still outside Berlin. The first half page of the instructions given to the Eckener Schule from the *Beauftragte der Stadt Berlin für die verlegten Berliner Schulen in Bayern* (the clerk responsible for schools stranded in Bavaria) on April 17, 1946 is really a complaint about the wrong format of lists previously submitted to him.

The actual return arrangements were largely similar to the ones in London. The return journeys were centrally organized, schools would be informed of their date of travel, the Red Cross would look after the children at meeting points and stations, luggage needed to be labeled correctly, and teachers needed to have their paperwork in order (including de-nazification certificates: documents that proved the bearer's limited involvement with the Nazi regime). Unlike in London, where children without (traceable) parents would stay in the country, the German camp structure necessitated their return with the groups. It was down to Berlin to sort them out with relatives, in billets or orphanages.

More detailed travel information was provided in an attached generic leaflet on KLV returns dated April 4, 1946. This document is very specific about the eligibility to travel and details at great length that only those with explicit travel permissions could be considered and that all others would be categorically denied access to train or truck. The language is very explicit here—and a probable hint to the aforementioned culture of self-help and defiance of state authority:

> Alle anderen Kinder und Erwachsene sind von dieser Rückführung ausgeschlossen. Meldungen und Anträge hierfür sind völlig zwecklos. Niemand ist befugt eine Sondergenehmigung zu erteilen. Ich warne vor Versuchen unrechtmäßiger Rückführung, sie ziehen harte Maßnahmen nach sich. (All other children and adults are excluded from this return journey. There is absolutely no point in further requests or communications. No one is allowed to grant any kind of special permission. Any attempts of unofficial return journeys will be severely punished.) (Source XXIc, p. 1)

The political and economical situation was such that only unaccompanied children who had been separated from their families for some years were allowed to return in order to prevent estrangement from their families. The unresolved political situation of Berlin and problems providing for the most basic needs of its inhabitants led to the official policy of not allowing more people in, especially children who seemed to have a comparatively comfortable life on Bavarian farms.

Much of this document reads like a LCC directive and hints at fundamental similarities among bureaucracies. It contains the same level of (and attention to) detail and slight obsession with micromanagement. The document covers a wide range of issues including notification of travel dates, notice to police and rationing office, pre-travel medical inspection of children (*Infektionskrankheiten, Ungeziefer*—infectious diseases and vermin), disinfection of train carriages, catering on the trains, and the provision of blankets. Only occasionally it becomes apparent that this is not England, but the country that has brought on its own destruction and now had to start from nothing: "Falls Güterwagen für Personenbeförderung verwendet werden, sind diese mit frischem Stroh auszulegen, mit Abortkübel und Torfmull, mit Nachtbeleuchtung zu versehen" (If freight trains are used for passenger transport they have to be equipped with fresh hay, a toilet bucket with peat dust, and a nightlight.) (Source XXIc, p. 2).

Rebuilding from Ruins

Those children who had actually survived the Battle of Berlin and the others who returned from evacuation to the city had to intellectually grasp that everything they had believed in was wrong and that their parents had supported or tolerated a criminal regime that brought death and devastation over Europe. At the end of the war, 50 million people had died and a further 35 million were permanently injured. 20 million children became orphans by and during the war. Six million Germans or 9% of the pre-war population died in the war (Franck & Asmus, 1983).

Luckily for the children, the mental struggles over guilt and disbelief could momentarily take second place to the very physical tasks at hand. The city had to be rebuilt: When children and teachers finally made it back to Berlin, they first had to repair or rebuild their bombed-out school from roof to basement. Intact buildings did not necessarily lead to a return of schooling, though. Some schools first had to be renamed, the Allied authorities had to agree on a curriculum, and all teachers had to subject themselves to de-nazification procedures and be approved by the new military authorities. De-nazification became a complex procedure lasting up to four years.

Teachers' eligibility for teaching in schools was assessed by their previous military ranks, the date they joined the NSDAP, and the wartime teaching content that could be traced. Many teachers had to leave and reapply for their positions. It also became apparent that the city's new administration had no idea about the whereabouts of its children. A letter from the Magistrate to the districts' mayors quite bluntly invited any information on numbers and fates of schools and students (from the school archive Eckener Oberschule, June 28, 1945).

Schooling was not the top priority anyway. It would take weeks and months for children to actually reunite with their families, if there was one left to reunite with. Making the ruins habitable took a lot of effort, as did the work that had to be done to contribute to the household. With the fathers dead or imprisoned, the older children had to take over much more responsibility. Daily survival in a destroyed city took up the children's energy and time; a return to formal education—although a political priority—must have seemed a distant luxury. Most Berlin schools aimed to reopen for the school year beginning in September 1945. However, there were many obstacles to overcome yet, as is evident from the documents at Eckener Schule: Children were malnourished and lacking shoes and proper clothing, some children had not returned from the KLV, the heating did not work, there were shortages of all the school equipment, textbooks had to be approved by the military government, the curriculum —especially with regards to religious education and history—was not yet finalized, there were not enough teachers and some were still awaiting the result from the de-nazification process. The return to normality was further hindered by frequent recycling runs and excursions to the forest to collect firewood for the community (Döbling, 2007). As in London, the children in Berlin were hardened by the war and could not easily adjust to formal schooling (Stargardt, 2005). Only slowly did school become routine again.

It is difficult to get reliable numbers for KLV participation among Berlin children. While numbers for the capital must remain speculative, reliable estimates for the nationwide scheme are available. Buddrus' reading of an unpublished 1944 draft of an HJ history confirms Kock's earlier estimate of approximately 850,000 children in over 6,000 KLV camps and a further 2.3 million evacuated with the NVS into billets with or without their mothers (Buddrus, 2003; Kock, 1997; Maylahn, 2004). Buddrus refutes Kock's claim, though, that KLV participation peaked in 1941. Rather, the numbers from the Chancellor of the Exchequer do not reflect the real participation levels since money reached the evacuees in many different ways due to the regime's confusing sharing of power and responsibilities among stakeholders (Buddrus, 2003). There seems to be no doubt, though, that the KLV's legend is bigger than its actual size. Of all German children, only about 2% lived in KLV camps—the vast majority of urban evacuees relied on private arrangements by their parents or were sent into family billets (Kock, 1997).

As a charitable holiday program, the KLV preceded the Nazi regime and the war, and it survived both as well. Even today 1.5 million German children spend their summer holidays each year in one of the 50,000 KLV-like camps across Germany. They are organized by sporting clubs, churches, and charitable organizations. On the whole they are well established and run quietly, except when sexual or violent misconduct among the teenagers meets insufficiently trained supervisors (Becker, 2010).

After the War: The KLV legacies and the Kriegskinder Generation

Those who were children in Germany during WWII grew up under the spell of Nazi propaganda and indoctrination. They saw the criminal system at work all around them but did not empathize with the obvious victims. Children left in Berlin would see the malnourished forced laborers who were publicly punished in substitution for the victorious enemy far away. The children in Berlin had consciously witnessed the disappearance of Jews as well. When the KLV collapsed, the evacuee children saw the corpses and the skeletal KZ prisoners on their flight, but only rarely connected this to their own fate. "In this complete nationalisation of empathy lay the fatal work of Nazism, which had legitimated any act of barbarity towards *Untermenschen* as long as it helped the German cause. Despite all the evidence before them, many Germans did not reflect on what they were seeing" (Stargardt, 2005, p. 376).

It seems that not many even questioned the dichotomy in the regime's own attitude to children. After all, childhood remains an elusive concept for this generation. At one point you were a child worth protecting by extensive government provision, the next you were a soldier in battle. The war destroyed conceptual childhood very effectively.

Surviving the war was one thing, but making sense of the post-war world an equally daunting one: "They [the children] had little experience of a pre-Nazi state and therefore, by necessity, were unable to adapt to the changes in their own lives and to those around them caused by the social, ideological, political and geo-political circumstances surrounding them" (Parsons, 2008, p. 146).

Many children turned to their families again as the primary social unit, but families had been mentally and geographically torn apart by the war. Families—provided they existed at all—were fragile bedrocks. Sons and daughters had maybe witnessed their mothers being raped during the first weeks of occupation, or knew what favors they had to trade in order to provide for the family. These topics became instant taboos (Stargardt, 2005). The children did not always welcome the return of defeated fathers and resented the return to an authoritarian, patriarchal family structure. Fathers also found it hard to reintegrate into civilian life with a family they barely knew. The atrocities they participated in or witnessed would haunt and emotionally stunt them. Guilt did not help the recovery of families. While some mainly mourned for the loss of their prior social status, some were only now permitting themselves to open their eyes to the catastrophe that had happened all around them in their names. It was a steep fall from *Übermensch* to monster.

Post-war, there would be elements of collective amnesia in the former children's recollections about their past. Many Germans who spent their childhood under the supervision of the HJ later had no recollection of indoctrination or mental abuse from their time at school or in KLV camps. In the face of that evidence, Geoffrey Giles concludes that simple condemnation of the Nazis cannot be enough and that historians today need to investigate "the nature and the extent of the damage, and the means by which the Nazis, for all the chaos of wartime schooling, in some ways nearly succeeded" (Giles, 1992, p. 26). There is a need for further investigation, but this is not the place for it.

It is the place, though, to note a surprisingly common feature of witness accounts from the KLV: the claim that indoctrination in camps was a lot less obvious than in Berlin. The target group seems not to have noticed that the emphasis on community spirit, the competitive outdoor activities, and a daily routine built around physical fitness and obedience was intended to prepare the next generation for war (Fürstenberg, 1996; Gehrken, 1997). For some camps it might be true that the geographical detachment from the capital softened HJ leaders and teachers, but most camps imposed a strict military regime. In the memories of the evacuees, the actual school lessons are much less well remembered that the camaraderie, the adventures, activities, and games (Fürstenberg, 1996). It seems that indoctrination has been associated with words too much.

The KLV saved lives—and undoubtedly it did—but it has to be seen as an integral part of the Nazi regime's attempt to separate children from other influences and mould them in the image of ideology-ridden Aryan heroes who willingly self-sacrifice themselves for the greater cause. The way children were ignorant of this (not particularly ulterior) motive at the time and as adults in their later recollections is evidence of more than successful self-preservation. The Nazi regime knew *their* children and succeeded in mirroring their own ambitions in the needs of adolescents to an extent that would have secured them devoted followers (or cannon fodder) in the future. As it was, the end of the war was a moment of rupture that the children did not comprehend and spent the rest of their lives recovering from.

Chapter Conclusion

The people of London celebrated a victory they had earned by suffering through several waves of air raids and years of uncertainty and shortages. As the danger subsided, the children were supposed to come back home, but in many cases could not. The war had changed London and London families. Many homes were rubble; there was a severe shortage of habitable space. Many parents were dead, divorced, or missing. Even if children could return immediately, they might not have had the happy reunion they had anticipated. The evacuees had grown and changed; they came home as strangers. There was not much the LCC could do to prepare families for this, especially not since they had shown a marked ignorance of all things emotional in the past and were only just learning multi-perspective approaches (e.g., there was no conception of pos-traumatic stress then). What they did was register the problems meticulously and offer advice on potential psychological issues in a leaflet for the social workers in charge of making the readjustment work. The war had been won, and the evacuation was brought to an orderly conclusion, but the experience would have a long-lasting impact. Immediately, it affected education: Teachers and the Board of Education emerged from the war with new confidence based on an increased national interest in schooling. Formal education was to become much more widely available. Evacuation as a policy might have failed on many accounts, but even as a failure it at lease prompted a closer acquaintance of the different social classes and stimulated discussions about their relationship and power.

The end of the war in Germany would see suffering on an unprecedented scale, and nothing could shield the children from that. In Germany the KLV did not so much conclude as collapse. In the turmoil of war, a lot of children had to depend on their teachers or—if they had abandoned them—their own wits. It was a political decision not to return the children to Berlin, but with defeat immanent everywhere it is difficult to say which location would have offered the better comparative safety anyway. The camps were in the way of the Russian advance and its inmates took flight to the West. Their journeys back home were hampered by hunger, death, rape, imprisonment, and a collapsing infrastructure. The flight from the Red Army brought them to Bavaria, Thuringia, and other Southern areas—and for many it would take another year after the end of the war before they saw their families again, if indeed the total war had left them with a family. The children who had stayed in Berlin probably suffered worse; they had sacrificed themselves in the continuation of a lost war. Those who did survive found it hard to readjust to family life and impossible to understand the drastic changes in their political and social environment. The violence, destruction, and physical and psychological hardship endured by children, either on their perilous flight or during the Battle of Berlin has scarred a whole generation of Germans who had to rebuild the country from ruins. They went on to become the country's Golden Generation, but they could never recover the childhood they lost to the Hitlerjugend and the KLV.

Thus, both evacuation schemes ended in ways that reflected their country's emergence from the war. London might have been bruised, but its people emerged victorious. The evacuation scheme could be brought to a happy conclusion—at least logistically. The emotional problems facing estranged families in austere post-war England would stay with the former evacuees and their parents for much longer. Berlin was defeated and destroyed. Its survivors had to rebuild their lives (and belief system) from scratch. The KLV, once a symbol for the providence of National Socialism, collapsed and vanished—as did the rest of the criminal regime and administration. The former evacuees had to fend for themselves while their country lay in ruins.

7

Comparisons

There are good reasons why historians often recoil from comparisons. Events in history seem unique to their social, political, and geographical environment—and the evacuation of schoolchildren from London and Berlin might be no exception. Both government schemes were heavily influenced by their contexts. However, the side-by-side narrative of the previous chapters also revealed a lot of common ground for comparison. A lot of considerations, discussions, and problems were common to both capitals, despite their very different political and social environments. The particular appeal of a comparative study then becomes the insight of the workings of either regime gained from looking at the different solutions to similar problems. Collating the unique experiences of civilians in one city to the ones in the other has an inherent promise of more reflective analysis due to real—rather than theoretical—alternatives. Again, it is important to stress that the aim here is not to measure a democratic system's success over a totalitarian one or vice versa, but rather to show behavioural patterns that are either common to even diverging societies or unique to their social and political environment.

Operation Pied Piper, pages 157–175
Copyright © 2012 by Information Age Publishing
All rights of reproduction in any form reserved.

This section is about interpretative work, about the dialogue between past and present that historians invariably engage in (Evans, 2000). It is about trying to make sense of both evacuations' histories by piecing the evidence together and checking it against each other—always with sensitivity to chronology and context. It is also about cutting through layers of interpretation: Parents interpreted the scheme and refused it their support, the civil servants then interpreted the shortfall in participation numbers, while the historian later views the civil services' reactions through his own interpretative lens. Ultimately the aim is to offer limited historical generalizations that are "objectively possible and cognisant of enabling conditions" (Ragin, 1987, p. 3). This comparison will focus on three selected themes—or uniform assessment criteria—that have emerged as most promising within the framework of this policy study. The first is *operational aspects*, with a strong emphasis on the discussion of compulsion within the evacuation, the second theme is *the state, its agents and citizens*, with a priority look at questions of power and agency, and the third theme is *children and childhood* from the perspective of the agents in charge of the evacuation.

Operational Aspects

The Level of Compulsion

Some level of compulsion would have made both evacuations' planners' lives easier—and the sources show that they at least contemplated it. In London, discussions of compulsion only appeared when—to the LCC's documented surprise (Source VII)—a large part of the working class population refused to split families up despite the threat of war. Subsequently, compulsion was discussed, but dismissed (Source XV). The historiography then carried the claim that London's evacuation was voluntary forward to this day. It is only by comparison to events in Berlin that questions about the validity of that claim transpire.

To recap: The developments in the capitals were happening in reverse. In London, all the schools were closed and moved out with the whole of the teaching profession, but not with a whole lot of children. Due to the obvious demand for schooling by those children who never left or independently returned to the city, the LCC had to reopen schools gradually. In Berlin, parents initially had a real choice. They could send their children away with the KLV or keep them in Berlin—there would be educational provision at either end (to a level that would at least satisfy the legislature). Only in 1943, Goebbel's Schulverlegung put real pressure on parents—suddenly those parents who did not trust the regime, could not find a host school in suburbia, or did not have relatives in the country had to contemplate the illegality of having their children close by (Sources XVIII). Of course, only one year later those considerations took second place to sheer survival in the increasing chaos of a forlorn war.

Both cities' populations were very concerned about coercive measures with regards to their children and opposed them at the outset (see Sources II and Chapter 5). Both evacuations' executives struggled with parents who did not share their priorities, or even realities (on the assumption that realities are socially construed). In London, the LCC eventually dismissed compulsory measures on the practical ground of the impossibility to enforce them. In Berlin, Hitler refused them because he craved voluntary support. However, there was a difference of opinion between the people of both cities about the definition of *compulsion*.

German contemporary commentators and historians have viewed the policy change in Berlin from KLV to Schulverlegung in 1943 as a change from voluntary evacuation to compulsion, since parents were suddenly left with very few options. After schools and teachers had departed, parents still had to comply with the *Schulpflicht* (compulsory schooling). If they did not want to break the law, they had to find guest places in suburban schools outside Berlin or arrange for Verwandtenverschickung. Since many parents did not have opportunity to do so, they had to hand over their children to the KLV or to break the law—hence the historians' perception of a de facto compulsion from September 1943 onwards.

It is noteworthy, though, that the controversial Schulverlegung was actually identical in design to London's evacuation scheme. There too, schools and teachers collectively left the city in 1939, forcing parents into the same dilemma. Nevertheless, politicians and historians have repeatedly testified to the evacuation's voluntary nature, despite oral sources to the contrary (e.g., "I do not think there was any decision made by parents to keep or send away a child, all went without a fuss," in Chapter 3). It seems that the historiography's claim of voluntarism is mainly based on the persistent claims by the London organizers to that effect. Held to the same standard as Berlin's KLV, the English evacuation was *de facto* compulsive.

For the comparison it is important to look at why—despite their similarity—the evacuation schemes have been viewed differently. The key reason might be the different status of compulsory schooling in both countries. Parts of Germany (e.g., the duchies of Württemberg, Brunswick and Saxony-Gotha) had introduced school attendance laws in the mid-seventeenth century and mighty Prussia followed a century later. Initially, the rural population put up opposition, but by the German unification in 1871, both concept and practice of compulsory schooling were well established and widely accepted. Within the NS regime with its high level of social control, school attendance was not a subject of discussion—and wherever it became one it could be easily enforced. Persistent truants could be taken out of their family homes and placed with foster parents.

By contrast, England was one of the last European countries to introduce compulsory schooling. It was only in 1870 that the school boards attempted to enforce attendance against fierce opposition by the rural population and urban lower classes. Maybe the civil service (unwittingly) exploited the soft status of compulsory schooling in their paradoxical proclamation that evacuation was voluntary, but all children had to go to school, although the LCC had closed all schools in the evacuation area. It seems that compulsory education had to give—probably because it did not have the same legacy and status in England as in Germany. Parents might even have welcomed the opportunity to shake off their children's habit of going to school instead of doing something productive around the house.

Thus, the evidence in this study shows not so much an asymmetry in the scheme as such, but an asymmetry in its contemporary and subsequent assessment. The countries' contexts were highly different, but looking at them simultaneously reveals alternative interpretations: London's evacuation was compulsory, if only compulsory education would have been taken seriously.

The Role of Teachers

A crucial difference between the government schemes seems to be that in London the evacuation was run by and for the schools, whereas in Berlin it ran alongside normal school business. While the teachers were crucial for London's evacuation, their German colleagues were deliberately excluded from the HJ-run KLV program. Looking at school logbooks and chronicles from the time confirms the schools' view that the KLV was something that ran parallel to the normal routine—at least up until the Schulverlegung in late 1943. The KLV is rarely mentioned and children sent away were simply noted as "landverschickt." In the camps, the NSLB-approved teachers' duties were limited to lessons in the morning, whereas the larger part of the day (and the night) was the responsibility of the HJ leaders. It was only when the war seriously curtailed the availability of young party faithfuls that retired teachers—relics from the Kaiserreich and Weimar—took over roles comparable to the teachers' involvement with the English evacuation.

The different roles of teachers across the channel (i.e., the NS regime's mistrust in the profession) might again have their root in the uneven development of state schooling in England and Germany. The Prussian tradition of training teachers well, paying them well, and giving them all the social security that came with being a civil servant led to autonomous and proud professionals in the classrooms. The Nazi regime was well aware that their support was not a given, not even after years of Gleichschaltung. Schirach recommended keeping teachers out of the KLV plans and operation from day one (see Source V), and later developments showed that from even their ousted position they competed quite successfully with the Hitlerjugend when it came to authority over the children. The reality of the camps led to a natural dominance of the older, experienced adult over the teenager with the uniform. Especially at the very end, it was down to the teachers to safeguard their pupils in perilous times of flight, fighting, and hiding—provided they rose to the challenge and did not simply disappear. The Sources XXI show the extraordinary efforts of teachers, both in Berlin and abroad, to reunite the students with their schools during post-war chaos.

In wartime England, teachers in state schools were neither well trained for their role nor well paid. Their social status could not compete with that of the German *Studienrat* (for further comparative analysis see Green, 1990)—which on the whole must have made them easier to handle from the government's point of view. Indeed, the evacuation was executed in complete accordance with the teaching profession (and teacher's unions), and their support made it a logistical and social success. Not even at times when up to half a million children were running around London without schooling or social care did the profession rebel. That the LCC, BoE, and MoH took their time contemplating strategies for what to do with the stray children and their leisure is indicative of the low social status education— and in particular compulsory education—used to have in England. More disconcerting, though, is that the press was a more outspoken critic of the loss of education ("Better the schools than the streets"—see Chapter 5) than the teachers and professionals at the BoE.

The evidence here suggests that English teachers had not yet the professional identity and integrity they would need to defend their agenda (the education and welfare of children) against competing political demands. Alternatively, one could read the teachers' silence as evidence of their fierce loyalty to the administration, although this would be a surprising attitude by those traditionally in charge of children's welfare in a situation where their charges were elsewhere and neglected. After all, teachers were committed to the children—the spontaneous teaching groups and home tuition schemes that sprang up everywhere in London during 1940 are sufficient evidence of that—but it seems that their confidence had not been nurtured for as long as that of their German counterparts. However, this is only a snapshot of the complex roles of wartime teachers. Some research has already been done on these *invisible evacuees* (e.g., Cunningham & Gardner, 1999; Davies, 1992; Limond, 2000), but there is certainly scope for more. A promising starting point might be to look at the gendered construction of the teaching professions in England and Third Reich, but the sources here are not sufficiently explicit to confirm speculative assumptions about gender-based confidence levels. Furthermore, it is important to emphasize that the conclusion above is a simplified analogy: One could easily argue that German teachers, despite their integrity, consented to minority-bashing curriculum changes (like *Rassenkunde*) and thus did more harm than good despite their sense of duty—but that discussion would be well outside this study's scope.

The Distance from the Cities

This a comparatively minor point, but still worth mentioning en passant. Both governments decided to send their children away to safety but had very different ideas of how far away to send the children. In London, planning revolved around logistics; the train companies decided distances on assessments of their rolling stock's capability to operate in between the normal peak commute that was not to be interrupted (Source III). Thus, the majority of children in Plan II ended up in a 60-mile radius around the metropolis—and began returning independently once there was no war, occasionally on bicycles. Titmuss realized the importance of distance for the numbers of returnees: only 19% of London children evacuated to Somerset returned independently, while 35% of those sent out to Hertfordshire found their own way back home (Titmuss, 1950). The short distances enabled children and parents to jeopardize the government scheme so much that for the second wave of London's evacuation (Plan IV), the planners at the MoH chose destinations distinctively further away than during the first wave, such as Cornwall and Wales (Brown, 2005).

In Berlin, the planners seem to have gone to great lengths to create huge (and unnecessary) distances between home and reception area. Children from Cologne and Dusseldorf were sent to the Baltic coast, while Berlin children were sent to Austria and the newly occupied Eastern territories. No paperwork confirms a political decision to send children far away in order to prevent independent returns and manifest the detachment from families and social environment, but since it defies any rational logistical planning it was very likely just that. Especially at a time of wartime shortages of trains, staff, and fuel, it seems a purely political choice to put a strain on the Reichsbahn in order to achieve the HJ's exclusive access to the children by simply detaching them geographically from parents and church. Official explanations about the shortage of supplies in urban areas and superior infrastructure in some reception areas (Kock, 1997) do not justify the seemingly random geographical assignments.

Intentionally or not, the evacuees became ambassadors (or colonizers) for their country in occupied territories and the public face of the NS regime. The propaganda confirms that especially in the Generalgouvernement (today's Poland) the children were used to strengthen the German occupation. In some cases, distant destinations were a sound economic choice, too, since supplies and buildings that would have to be paid for in the German heartland could simply be requisitioned in occupied territories. Especially where food was already in short supply, like in Slovakia, the evacuees would not have been very welcome guests. There are accounts from Denmark where open hostility by Danish locals led to the involvement of the Wehrmacht as a protective force for the KLV camps (Kock, 1997).

It is appealing to speculate if Schirach and Moeckel made their geographical choices after intensive study of London's problems with unofficial returnees. After all, Berlin's evacuation was only initiated at a time when London's scheme already went into its second phase. Of course this is speculative, but the choice of faraway reception areas in the KLV planning could be an indicator of how closely German intelligence was watching developments in England. There is ample evidence that Goebbel's staff kept a close eye on Britain's evacuation programs—after all, the German press exploited the overseas evacuation as example of the English upper class' selfishness. Maybe the schemes' similarities, especially with regards to the provision for smaller children (see Chapter 3), were not accidental or result of logical deliberations with similar outcomes, but simply a case of copying the enemy's plans.

The State, Its Agents, and Citizens

Difficult Relationships

A government evacuation scheme would always be controversial, and to some extent the planners had anticipated that. The sources, however, show how much they underestimated the controversy. On the contrary, the initial plans in both cities (Source I for London, and Source V for Berlin) must now be seen as overly optimistic about the government's ability to reach and convince its population. The evacuation substantially changed the relationship between state (as an umbrella term for elected politicians, civil service bureaucrats and—in Third Reich contexts—party functionaries) and people. It also changed the notion of citizenship. Social theory viewed British citizenship as changing from active involvement in Victorian times to a more passive consumption in the interwar years—although this is a cautious claim since citizenship in 1930s Britain defies sweeping generalizations. Even after the extension of the franchise in 1918, "working-class engagement with the democracy appeared to be in decline at both a local and national level" (Beaven & Griffiths, 2008, p. 216). Where it was once the urban elite philanthropists who defined and pursued social agendas, by the late 1930s—and as a direct result of the working class self-sacrifice during WWI—it was the acknowledged role of the state apparatus to provide civic guidance to an increasingly dispersed society. Class issues that had been well suppressed in Imperial Britain started to compete with the primacies of nation and family: "The Victorian schemes of social citizenship that had attempted to sidestep the thorny issues of class inequalities through emphasising the importance of individual self-improvement seemed out of step with the harsh realities of this new postwar world" (Beaven & Griffiths, 2008, p. 212).

The evacuation scheme fit the new expectations of increased government provision. Unlike the earlier introduction of compulsory schooling, for example, the evacuation failed not because of what it was, but how it was executed. The people expected the state apparatus to strike the right balance between expert government and popular sovereignty (Held, 2006)—that is, to consult the potential beneficiaries of a government scheme about their expectations and requirements before expertly executing consensual measures.

In Berlin, on the other hand, the population did not expect an evacuation scheme and initially reacted to it with surprise and hostility (see Chapter 2). After all, the regime had reassured them that the war would be fought and won elsewhere. In 1940, German citizenship among those who would actually qualify for NSV provision was divided into two groups: the vocal supporters and profiteers of the regime and the others in inward emigration. Suspicious of the course of the nation, the latter had declared the family as center of their lives—which would make sending the children away with the party a so much harder decision. The regime was not ignorant of these sentiments—hence their attempt to cloak the evacuation scheme as an adventure-packed free holiday and directing it at the children rather than their parents.

Kressel proposes that symmetrical occurrence of noncompliance by the people is an act of emancipation. In neither country did the collective closing of ranks to the outward enemy trigger more than just superficial solidarity among the population within. Quite the contrary, Kressel shows a universal *Entsolidarisierung* (erosion of solidarity) among members of different classes and within the same class or community. In the course of the war, the family unit became much more important as a reference point than the belief in government provision. Kressel sees the emancipatory tendency in turning away from one's government in favor of one's family, which might have been comparatively easy in liberal England, but in Nazi Germany this amounted to treason and required great individual courage. The increasingly desperate measures initiated by the German government reflect the worries by those in power about the disobedience of their people (Kressel, 1996). He summarizes: "Unabhängig von Staats—und Regierungsform setzte der Krieg also Prozesse in Gang, die eine größere Unabhängigkeit und ein größeres Selbstvertrauen gegenüber den Regierenden bewirkten" (Regardless of the nature of state and government, the war triggered developments that resulted in greater independence from and increased self-confidence towards those in power.) (Kressel, 1996, p. 226).

It was obvious to the planners that despite their efforts to the contrary, the cities were full of children during the most devastating air raids. The government provisions did not reach its intended recipients; citizens refused to participate in schemes devised for their benefit for different reasons (see Chapter 4). Just because both evacuations were a disappointment in numbers does not mean that the people of London and Berlin had similar concerns about them. The sources show that beyond the common emotional hardship brought on by separation, parents made their decisions based on trust in the schemes within the unique social and political context of their societies.

For one, the political landscape was different. London entered the war during an area of social continuity and ambitious city government by Morrison-led Labour. The class structure and social roles remained largely unchanged; the middle class that became the dominant political and cultural force in the 19th century continued to exercise power, albeit with increasingly social agendas that would benefit the lower classes. At the same time, Berlin underwent a complete social reshuffle. The bourgeois cultural and political elite had been driven out under Nazi rule and had been replaced by the lower middle classes and working class as the arbiters of political power. The NSDAP had a social agenda and looked after its own—however, many parents were unsure how far they wanted to take their affiliation with the party. Demonstrative loyalty with the regime was a reason for some to participate in the KLV, but others minimized their compliance with the regime to the bare minimum required to lead an undisturbed life in Nazi Germany. This might be an important factor the schemes had in common: In the mind of the recipients they were designs and institutions *by others*—

be it another social class (the London middle class) or ideological view (the committed Nazis of Berlin's HJ).

These perceptions had little to do with the designs of the actual schemes, but obstructed them from the outset. The civil servants at the LCC worked hard on the scheme's very successful logistics but neglected to ascertain their clienteles' willingness to actually participate in an operation that was planned by one class for another, and indeed by one gender for another. Emotional aspects were considered secondary until they severely disrupted the government scheme. From that point on, the clerks at the LCC became quick learners of the public and academic criticism to their scheme—and rectified their obvious ignorance of working-class family dynamics. Still, while the behavior of parents and children during the Phoney War period must at least have been comprehendible to LCC officials, the number of returnees as well as parents refusing evacuation during the Blitz left them confused. Within states or cities, democratic theory has assumed a congruent and symmetrical relationship between policymakers or executioners and policy recipients, as well as between output of government and the needs of the people (Held, 2006). The evacuation, at least the one under Plan II, seems to have been a failure on this account. The officials largely misjudged the concerns of their citizens, and subsequently had to work much harder to regain popular trust (never fully successfully) when dealing with the unscheduled high numbers of children remaining in or returning to London during the Phoney War period and Blitz.

Psychology had always been at the forefront of contemplations in Berlin—as can be seen from early decisions like the evacuation's label and advertising audience. However, when faced with disappointing participation rates, the KLV planners' adaptability to parental concerns and reservations did not increase but decrease. The KLV executives initiated only small changes to their scheme beyond increasing the pressure to participate. Nevertheless, Kressel's claim that the schemes' designs reflected their political contexts needs refining. This study aimed to show that the schemes actually were largely similar, but that the manner in which their executives handled them (especially in the face of public criticism) is the superior indicator for the different political landscapes. The documents examined here clearly show how much successful government provision relies on participatory citizenship. In both cities, the executives—be it civil servants in London or party functionaries in Berlin—were too detached from the recipients. In London, separation was a matter of social class. In Berlin, the separation was deliberate: the party institutions set themselves up as rivals to parents and aimed to bypass parental influence. The conclusion here must be that both schemes' perceived failures resulted from the inability of their organizers to engage with the communities they were supposedly serving.

In some ways, the evacuation schemes mirrored the course of the war: the Third Reich was very successful during the Blitzkrieg, but then slid into more and more desperate stages of a military conflict it could not win—but kept going on regardless until collapsing. The war had been the regime's lifeblood; it had utilized it to stabilize its power, change the political system, and exercise extreme levels of social control under the guise of a permanent state of emergency. Not so in England: The state authority structure established in the interwar years was largely preserved during the war; there was a distinct sense of local and national administrative continuity throughout the turbulent period (Süß, 2011). It took the British some time to gear up for war, but after Dunkirk the whole of society accepted the war as one of all people, which brought the classes—and their understanding of each other—inevitably closer. The London evacuation scheme, while never as successful as anticipated, lost a lot of its controversy after the onset of the Battle of Britain.

Questions of Power and Agency

The evacuations were enormous operations involving and affecting millions of people in both cities and rural areas. They naturally needed the involvement of several governmental and nongovernmental agencies. However, the narrative here revealed that there was controversy about which agency would take the lead and direct the others. In London, the evacuation changed long-established political power structures. This affected the relationship of local and national government, and that of ministries towards each other. During the preparation stages, the LCC had to fight the national government to take evacuation seriously and allow for serious planning and succeeded the Home Office as the key agent after the Munich crisis. The documents clearly show the transition, especially with regards to how important that in-house memo, the 1938 Appreciation (Source I), became in the development of the government scheme. The BoE emerged from the war stronger and with more authority, and at least partly this was due to the evacuation: It triggered increased public interest in education, led to a new confidence among public-sector teachers who successfully managed a mammoth task, and provoked the influential surveys under the auspice of Susan Isaacs, Margaret Cole, and others.

In Berlin, Hitler assigned responsibilities alone and ad hoc—no other agency but the HJ stood a chance to run the evacuation, especially not the suspiciously autonomous schools. In contrast to London, there was no drawn-out planning process that would have allowed consultation or obstruction by other agencies; the planners had a fortnight to organize the logistics for the dispatch and receipt of evacuee children (see Chapter 2). In London, the municipal civil service was crucial, but in Berlin it had to accept a supporting role (see Chapter 1). The evacuation thus fitted in with the NS regime's autocratic and anarchic rule of the country. Furthermore, the KLV might have been regarded as a tool to increase power for some agencies from the outset. It was only when the HJ mutilated itself by sending more and more of its officers and members to the front of a lost war that other agents took over some of the responsibility—the schools and the teachers—who then had to clean up the mess left to them after the surrender.

The sources show the disappointment of the evacuations' planners with the lack of public support for what they deemed utterly sensible measures, be it in the LCC's defensive bulletins and press releases (Sources VIII and XI) or in the increasingly desperate tone of German leaflets (Sources XVII). The evacuations' executives did not at first understand working-class families' realities and priorities (see also Chapter 5). It is interesting to note that the LCC actively tried to make the range of their responsibilities explicit and to shift blame to its rightful owners—reception area officials, central government, obstructive families. This petty attitude probably stems from the power struggle the LCC was subjected to during the planning stages and their clear mandate of a local agency. In Berlin, the Hitlerjugend and Reichsjugenführung would not allow public discussion of individual agencies' blame. Whatever the internal squabbles (and sources XIV and XVIII clearly show internal disagreement), publicly the regime's executives would show unity.

The sources also reveal that the LCC was flexible enough not to bury its head after the initial disappointment, but fought hard to regain its clienteles' trust. The documents show reflective analysis on part of the evacuation's planners (especially source XV); they modified both scheme and propaganda to eventually appeal to the vulnerable population in their charge. The KLV executive also adapted the scheme in the face of popular opposition. However, there is little evidence of reflective analysis: Source XIV and the subsequent Schulverlegung show that instead of questioning the scheme, the agents rather questioned their people's loyalty and common sense and chose to bully parents and children into compliance

Policy is a process rather than a product—and the evacuation schemes' transformations during the war testify to different courses these processes can take. In England, the politicians, administrators, and civil service were subject to public scrutiny and could only ignore public opinion for a limited time. For their political wishes to become practice, they had to eventually match those of the people. In Berlin, no such public scrutiny existed anymore, and the KLV executive's simple solution was just to continuously increase the pressure on children and parents. This strategy's lack of success did not trigger a change of policy (Kressel, 1996). Still, the regime pretended to exercise total control—up to the point when its unique self-destruction led to a power vacuum that was filled with pragmatic agents who dropped the political agenda for the safekeeping of the children.

In the last stage of the war, there is no longer a common ground for comparison. While the LCC began to prepare for the orderly return of the evacuees, the KLV collapsed into anarchy. The brutality and suffering at the end of the war—both in Berlin and the eastern reception areas—almost defies logical analysis. The Third Reich destroyed itself—and with it any suitable agency to oversee the return of the children. Again, the evacuation scheme reflected the greater political reality. Victorious London had suffered losses and destruction, but its civil service was ready to return the evacuees (or arrange their continuous absence) and to rebuild the city. Emotional traumas had to be overcome, estranged families to be reunited, but in comparison with Berlin the death toll among children was exceedingly low. The German capital lay in ruins, and most of its children died pointlessly defending it or were scattered around the country on perilous flights or in makeshift camps. The civil service (that had so feverishly worked up until the surrender) came to a complete standstill and awaited de-nazification and instructions from the new Allied military government. In the wider context of the continent's post-war reorganization, the fate of Berlin's evacuee children must have been a minor issue. Pragmatic solutions were called for, and the sources from local schools (Sources XXI) show how enterprising individuals took over agency at a time when the bureaucracy failed them.

Motives and Purposes

This study has deliberately paid little attention to the political motives behind the evacuation schemes. Official records are by their nature rather unsuitable for political or philosophical discussions, thus this study's emphasis on execution rather than motivation. There is the additional danger that the extension of philosophical discourse could gradually erode the foundations for comparison: While the schemes are comparable in their local and logistical elements, a wider comparison of the overambitious, inhumane, and self-destructive NS regime with the ailing post-Empire British kingdom would inevitably lack suitable parameters. Still, it is useful to pay some attention to overt and ulterior motives among those responsible for massive operations that so profoundly affected millions of children's lives. The existence of similar schemes hints to a "von der politischen Verfasstheit unabhängige Vorstellung darüber, wie im Krieg die Zivilbevölkerung zu schützen sei" (common notion about the protection of civilians independent of the state's political system) (Süß, 2011, p. 19)—and the historiography so far has come some way in analyzing the motives and sincerity of the two governments. Their findings will be offered here and checked against the evidence from the present source analysis.

Kressel concludes, in his comparative study of Liverpool and Hamburg, that the protection of civilians was the first and foremost ambition of either municipal government. He explains differences in secondary motivation on the basis of the respective political systems. In England, a comparatively liberal and democratic country, the government attempted to openly communicate the necessity of evacuation as a measure to safe lives, put parents' mind at rest, reduce demands on shelter capacities, and enable women to work in the war effort (by March 1941 there were 190 residential nurseries for small children with some 6,000 places in the reception areas, L.C.C., 1943, XII, 6.)—but also did not hide the additional strategic need for organized flights from the cities rather than transport chaos (Kressel, 1996). Despite getting the children out of harm's way—and quite literally out of the way—there have not been suggestions of secret agendas or ulterior motives behind the operation, regardless of its accidental impact on social policy in Britain. The controversy in England has not been about the civil servants and politicians' motives, but their ability and competence.

Dictatorial Germany attempted to camouflage the evacuation as a holiday program—and only after that transparent cover was blown did admit and communicate to parents the dire need of the government's scheme. The children's safety might have been a sincere motive, but it was not the only one. Similar to London, another aim was to relieve mothers of parental duties so they could work in the war economy (Franck & Asmus, 1983)—obviously in pragmatic contradiction to the *Kinder, Küche, Kirche* female role in Nazi ideology. Additionally, the KLV allowed the regime to showcase their caring side and ensure grateful parents' voluntary support in the *total war* (see Chapter 2). Goldberg proposed further motives: the organized evacuation made mothers geographically independent, which meant they could be deployed wherever the war effort needed them most. Also, the evacuated children acted as additional occupying forces in recently annexed territories, where their presence and patronizing behavior vividly reinforced the new regime's power (Goldberg, 1994). Furthermore, and despite successful attempts of Schirach in Nuremberg or Dabel in his

1981 publication to label the KLV as a purely humanitarian operation, historians now propose an additional and more sinister motivation:

> Insofern diente die Erweiterte Kinderlandverschickung nicht einem "Schutz der Jugend" an sich, sondern stellte in erster Linie den Versuch dar, künftiges *Kanonenfutter* kurzfristig zu sichern, vor zufälliger Vernichtung zu bewahren, um es später effektiv und gezielt einsetzen zu können. (Thus, the primary aim was not the safety of the children, but the attempt to secure future *cannon fodder* from random destruction for the short term in order to deploy them later more effectively and precisely.) (Buddrus, 2003, p. 898; see also: Fürstenberg, 1996)

Looking at the death count among children in the last weeks of war (see Chapter 6), one has to admit the possibility that the whole KLV scheme was a ploy to first separate children from competing influences, indoctrinate them in the seclusion of the camps, utilize them as colonizers in the east, and finally use them as part of the nation's effort to pointlessly defend German territory in a forlorn war. The official sources do not confirm this—but they do not contradict it either.

Children and Childhood

With regards to the cultural construction of childhood, the sources clearly point to a major difference in the two countries: the expectations of the children's involvement with the war. While the London planners and propaganda were upfront about shelter from war as the evacuation's raison d'être, Schirach decided early on to keep the two things apart. The KLV propaganda rarely mentions the war and does not use the danger levels in the capital as its justification. Sleep interruption by sirens was the maximum concession made in admitting the presence of the war. The KLV should have no or only little connection with the war in the evacuees or parents' minds (see Chapter 3).

The English government wanted to protect children from the war. Young people may have contributed to the war effort with a variety of tasks—as has been demonstrated by Berry Mayall and Virginia Morrow, who have questioned the prominent portrayal of passive evacuees and posit wartime children as a "reserve army of labour" (Mayall & Morrow, 2011, p. 256), but their participation in the war was nowhere close to the level of involvement envisaged by the NS regime for German teenagers. They would form an integral part of the war strategy and economy. All English children of school age were treated the same (see below) and could participate in the evacuation up until the age of 18, but German children formed three distinct groups in the KLV concept. After all, older children had already been organized in the HJ before the evacuation, and they had learned to be useful and independent. Within the NS state, adolescents were expected to contribute at home, in the community (recycle runs, donation collection), and in their youth organization; they had left the carefree stage of childhood earlier than their cousins across the channel. Thus the distinction of three age groups in the KLV: children who needed government protection (up to the age of ten), youth who trained for adult (and military) life in the KLV camps, and the rest who were declared adults at the age of 14 (the end of compulsory schooling—see Source V). With that the KLV nodded towards its preferred target group: the lower middle and working classes where children's threshold to adulthood would be earlier anyway.

It is important, though, to point out that no claim here is universal nor divisions clear-cut: after all, substantial amounts of English children were boy scouts and girl guides and thus subject to identical concepts of duty and usefulness as HJ or BdM girls. At the same time, German grammar school students could participate in the KLV until the end of their formal schooling at around 18. Even the claim that in England *all children were treated the same* is somewhat misleading, since the official records do not dwell on the social segregation in English society. All children who needed government provision were indeed treated the same; the social selection happened earlier when affluent parents bought their children's safety privately through their superior contacts and family connections in the country—or indeed other countries. It needs to be cautiously noted that public records come with limitations—as do all historical records.

It was a unique feature of Third Reich concept of childhood that being a child in Germany was not the same as being a German child. A substantial amount of children were deliberately excluded from the KLV. Jewish children could not participate, and neither could (in contemporary terminology) delinquents, underachievers, bedwetters, epileptics, and children with acute illnesses. Deaf and mute children could only travel in designated groups, but were on the whole discouraged to participate. The charitable KLV pursued quite openly a selective policy of worthy recipients (Kock, 1997). Even in the 1943 Schulverlegung, when all children were supposed to leave Berlin, the delinquents and bedwetters would get their own camps. The irrational and discriminatory "racial" Nazi policies in pursuit of the *gesunder Volkskörper* would not stop at the KLV.

Historians have linked the accommodation of German adolescents in camps rather than in families to be evidence of a uniquely Third Reich ambition for children. It has been viewed as part of Schirach's plans of monopolizing children's education and molding children as future soldiers. What happened in the camps might support those claims, but not the establishment of camps as such. After all, during the British planning stages, evacuee camps were favored by many (see Chapter 2). In 1939 the National Camp Corporation was established in England with the aim of providing camps for teenagers in peacetime and wartime. Each camp offered accommodation for up to 350 children, and they were used for difficult billets within the evacuations scheme. As holiday retreats they did not offer the infrastructure for permanent habitation (especially not for teaching) and were run with a strict military attitude. In 1942, there were over 600 camps for children who with their activities (harvest, forestry) contributed to the war economy—although those activities were sold as educational (Gosden, 1976).

However, the NS regime knew no moral boundaries to the exploitation of children in the later stages of the war. Once regular schooling collapsed, boys between ten and 14 could volunteer as Luftwaffenhelfer and remain in the vulnerable cities in order to assist with anti-aircraft defence (Sources XXI). It was the girls, though, who really stabilized the home front. At first, they were used as helpers at the reception of refugee transports, sorted ration cards, delivered merchandise to shops by hand-drawn carts, did chores for the aged, sang morale-boosting songs in factories, and compensated the mothers' absences in the family homes. When war became more desperate they would also work in factories, as messengers for the post office, as Red Cross nurses, as kindergarten teachers, and various A.R.P. measures—or indeed as supervisors in KLV camps. All of these activities happened at the expense of regular schooling (Goldberg, 1994). Fürstenberg poignantly concludes:

> Die Kinderlandverschickung muß auch unter dem Aspekt der Machtausdehnung der NSDAP auf den Erziehungssektor gesehen werden. Hier bemühte sich der nationalsozialistische Staat im großen Rahmen, Kinder dem Einfluß ihrer Familie zu entziehen, für die eigenen Ziele zu schulen und als eine mobile Generation überall dort einzusetzen, wo es die Partei für richtig hielt (Ernteeinsatz, Luftwaffenhelfer, Volkssturm u.a.). (The NSDAP used the KLV to tighten its grip on state education. The NS state went to great lengths to separate children from their parents' sphere of influence, to educate them for their own goals, and as a mobile generation use them wherever it deemed necessary, for example, for the harvest, for air raid defence, and as a fighting force in the Volkssturm.) (Fürstenberg, 1996, p. 32)

The evacuation schemes clearly reflected the regimes' expectations of children and the societies' concepts of childhood, but it is also important to point out the uniqueness of the evacuee experience. It was not civil servants who actually looked after the children, but individual householders did—and they applied their own individual views of children. Thus, even within comparatively similar evacuation schemes, the individual experience can hardly be generalized. Former evacuee Jost Hermand's bleak summary applies to the KLV more than to the English evacuation, but as a testimony of the uniqueness of experiences it is valid for both:

> Aufgrund dieser unbestimmten Machtbefugnisse, bei denen je nach Situation fürsorgliche oder tyrannische Tendenzen die Oberhand bekommen konnten, ist es nicht leicht, im Hinblick auf die Lager... irgendwelche generalisierenden Urteile zu fällen. Es gab in ihnen fast alles: väterliche und mütterliche Besorgtheit, gläubiges Vertrauen auf das ursprünglich Gute im Menschen, naiven Idealismus, aber auch faschisierende Indoktrinierung, öde Routine, bewußte Verrohung und Brutalisierung, wenn nicht gar übelsten Sadismus. (It is impossible to come to a general conclusion about the camps where, as a result of unresolved authority issues, paternal or tyrannical tendencies could prevail. Any camp could have paternal or maternal compassion, religious belief in the good of humanity, naïve idealism—but also fascist indoctrination, bleak routine, intentional brutalisation, and even outright sadism.) (Hermand, 1993, p. 23)

Chapter Conclusion

There is justification for both academic comparisons in general and a comparative study of policies developed before and during the war in London and Berlin. The societies under scrutiny shared enough common ground to successfully apply parameters for comparison such as operational aspects, role of government, decisions of agency, and concepts of childhood. The comparative approach enables both the presentation of common attitudes and explanation of differences in the planning and execution of the evacuation schemes. While some questions have to remain unanswered due to the asymmetrical survival of sources, other answers come easier by comparatively collating developments across the channel.

The discussion of the evacuations' levels of compulsion should benefit from this study. The comparison shows that the long-held view of a voluntary scheme in England and coercive measures in the Third Reich needs to be questioned. Compulsory schooling—and each country's own attitude to it—is the key factor for this discussion. Berlin's government did not make the KLV compulsory, but insisted on compulsory schooling while simultaneously closing all metropolitan schools. By that, it really just copied what the LCC had done four years prior. Other key results from the comparison of operational aspects are that English teachers were probably less confident to voice criticism because they did not have the same professional legacy as their Prussian counterparts, and that the distance between evacuation and reception areas was important, deliberate, and maybe even evidence of an intimate knowledge of the enemy.

The evacuations influenced and were influenced by the relationship between state and people. While the bureaucracy in democratic London might have been ignorant of its own working-class families' attitudes at first and patronized them with a scheme that did not consider their needs, it could not persist in doing that, but had to learn and reconsider; the evolution of the evacuation scheme over time shows this well. The developments in Berlin showed that the autocratic Nazi government neither learned nor reconsidered, but used their absolute power for increasingly draconian measures of persuasion.

At least in NSDAP-run Germany, the question of agency was easily resolved: the NSDAP (or rather its youth organizations) would be in charge of the KLV at the expense of other suitable agents such as the teachers—who only regained authority when the NS state collapsed. During the evacuation's planning stages, a lot of effort in London went into a struggle for agency among different ministries and government branches. The importance of this power struggle is evident from the later roles of the winners: the LCC, BoE, and MoH played key roles in England's post-war recovery.

The governments' motivations to initiate evacuation schemes were linked to their respective views of childhood. London's evacuation had some military merits but was mainly designed to save the lives of children, who had nothing to do with the war. In Nazi Germany, older children were an integral part of the war. HJ ideology forced children into work for the war economy, and the KLV was not just a measure to save lives, but also to exclusively prepare them for fighting the war.

Thus the evacuation schemes had as much in common as the states operating them. The schemes reflected the political and social realities of London and Berlin. The benefit of the comparison is not only to showcase that, but also to provide additional evidence for explanations about successes and shortcomings in each city. It is the hope that peeking across borders will further our understanding of events in one place.

8

Conclusions

A s policies, the government evacuation schemes in London and Berlin were bold, contested, controversial, and (at least measured by real participation) ultimately failures. Although the schemes were set in their cities distinctive political and social contexts, they shared numerous common features and were subject to similar discussions. At the same time, some elements of the governments' schemes for their schoolchildren were unique to their city's situation and defy generalization across borders. It was this study's aim to assess the extent of the similarities, explain the differences, and compare policy developments in each city by collating them with each other.

The schemes had very uneven preparation stages. In London, questions of agencies overshadowed what otherwise could have been sufficient planning time. The source analysis here shows how policy powerhouse LCC emerged to spearhead London's evacuation. The ideas and impulses from the capital shaped the national scheme as a whole and contributed substantially to its overall logistical success. The massive organized exodus of children at the outbreak of war in September 1939 and their dispatch into

Operation Pied Piper, pages 177–181
Copyright © 2012 by Information Age Publishing
All rights of reproduction in any form reserved.

billets was hailed as a humanitarian and operational achievement, but the surprising absence of air raids during the Phoney War and subsequent independent returns of the majority of children damaged the scheme's reputation. In Berlin, there was little preparation. Hitler demanded an instant evacuation scheme in the wake of the first arrival of British bombers over Berlin in late August 1940. Questions of agency were quickly resolved by the appointment of Schirach's HJ as the executive of an evacuation scheme that was not allowed to be perceived as one. The Germans compensated for the lack of preparation time by utilizing the established KLV charity travel operation and NSDAP bureaucracy. In the initial planning, schools and teachers were not involved—and for the first years the KLV did not seem to affect them much: the records here show that despite some children disappearing into the camps, schooling in Berlin was not majorly affected.

Schooling in London came to a standstill, since all schools and teachers had been evacuated. Once the returnees joined the children who had stayed in London all along, there was no or only little educational and welfare provision for them in the metropolis. They were running wild, jeopardized the reputation of the evacuation scheme, and became symbolic of the LCC's failure to properly persuade parents of the government provision. Close-knit working-class families largely refused to participate in a scheme that was devised by boarding-school-educated middle class civil servants ignorant of the lower class children's role within families. Even before the onset of the Blitz, the LCC had made substantial changes to its scheme in order to regain its citizens' trust, and the eventual arrival of German bombs became the crucial incentive to evacuate. Nevertheless, both London and Berlin were full of children when bombs finally fell, despite the governments' efforts to the contrary.

The evidence shows the LCC to be adaptable and eager in their perseverance to keep the scheme running. This required the bureaucrats to overcome their own ignorance about communities dominated by different social classes and family dynamics. Eventually, the civil servants reached some parents, but the scheme never fully recovered from the initial loss of trust. Mistrust and noncompliance was equally high among parents in Berlin. However, for the NS regime this was no cause for reflective analysis. Instead, the party functionaries insisted on the mythical—but increasingly hollow—*Volksgemeinschaft* type of citizenship as legitimate reason to increase pressure on intractable parents. From autumn 1943 onwards, all Berlin schools were closed and children coerced to join their age-appropriate form of evacuation. Still, revised numbers show that private evacuation or the (often fake) registration as Gastschüler just outside Berlin accounted for the majority of children, whereas only a comparatively small minority spent the war in the KLV camps.

Throughout the war, London's evacuation had peaks and lows in line with the course of the war. Participation numbers were particularly high during the Blitz and the V rocket attacks, but never as high as during the first wave in September 1939 that dispatched over 500,000 London children. When the war had left London for good, the LCC officials busily organized the return of evacuees to a substantially damaged city. Homes and families had been destroyed during the Blitz, and for many children return was impossible, problematic, or at least emotionally challenging. In England, the war shifted many people's priorities, and the evacuation became symbolic of some of the post-war changes, including renewed interest in education, social welfare reforms, and new working class confidence. Berlin's evacuation was never concluded, but simply collapsed during the last months of war. From autumn of 1944, the lack of safe reception areas made the KLV increasingly pointless, but it was the power vacuum that followed the dissolution of the Nazi regime that had catastrophic consequences for both evacuees and children left in Berlin. Evacuated children fled from the camps and attempted to return to Berlin in the chaos of war, while the ones left in Berlin fought a desperate and deadly battle against the Red Army. After the war, Berlin and its people lay in ruins. Those children who had survived and made it back to the capital now had to rebuild their schools, city, family relationships, and ideological outlook. The KLV became symbolic of a youth policy by a murderous regime that attempted to exercise total power over its children.

This study's dual ambition was to separately situate the evacuations schemes in their local historical context and then compare them against evidence from the other city. Not surprisingly, the evacuation schemes had as much in common as the states operating them. The schemes reflected London and Berlin's respective unique political and social realities—but also shared a lot of common features. The schemes' concepts were either similar (e.g., the NSV's provision for younger children was largely identical with London's scheme)—and where they were not, the alternative had at least been discussed in the other city (e.g., the erection of camps outside London). Both evacuations also had in common that the civilian population did not accept the government provision uncritically, that private provision catered to a lot more children than the official schemes, and that the municipalities failed in their ultimate ambition to evacuate the majority of children from the cities under attack.

The benefit of the comparative approach is the opportunity to view local decisions against real alternatives. The comparison revealed the need to review the evacuations' level of compulsions against the respective statuses of compulsory schooling, since seemingly similar schemes have been assessed differently afterwards. For German historians, the closure of schools in connection with the regime's insistence on the Schulpflicht was sufficient evidence to mark the KLV compulsive from 1943 onwards, while the closure of London schools did not carry similar connotations. The comparison also showed that the teachers' role in the evacuation schemes was determined by their profession's differing status in each society. Within the long tradition of German state schooling, the teachers had retained a proud independence that made them unsuitable executives of the KLV scheme, but eventually they would be in charge of a generation utterly disrupted by war. In England, teachers were willing and largely uncritical operators of the evacuation scheme, which would have been uncontroversial if the majority of children were indeed evacuated—but they were not. The loss of education was biggest among those children for whom evacuation was refused and those who independently returned to London.

The comparison also illustrates how the evacuations changed the relationship of citizens and their governments. While in London the mythical revelation of urban poverty to the unsuspecting rural middle class population is widely regarded as a trigger for social reform, it is equally true that the newly confident working classes voiced their disappointment with state provision—the evacuation—and forced sensible concessions out of anxious governments. In Berlin, the class struggle worked differently: The lower middle and working classes had been the ones most fervently supporting the NS regime. Only after the war did the middle class return to its previous vanguard position. The Nazi apparatus (and thus the agents of the KLV) disappeared after the lost war, but in London the evacuation's agents—the MoH, BoE, and LCC—all emerged stronger from the war and assumed authoritative roles within post-war reconstruction.

This study also found major differences in the political construction of childhood in London and Berlin. English children were seen as passive objects of parental and governmental care; the evacuation's primary motive was to shelter children from the war. Children in the Third Reich had to assume a more active role in both war and war economy. The KLV is rightfully considered a NSDAP attempt to monopolize education and to prepare adolescents for fighting the war and stabilizing the home front far away from competing influences by parents and church.

Both, the similarities and the differences, find their representation in this study's title. The Education Committee in London gave the evacuation its codename Operation Pied Piper, probably in a light-hearted attempt to lend some child-appropriate imagery to a scheme that would see all children leave the city in an organized fashion. However, the German KLV scheme seemed to have much more in common with the fairytale's sinister content. After all, the disappointed rat catcher of Hamelin duped the children into participation with his instrument and led them out of town against their will for reasons that were ultimately more selfish than altruistic. The London evacuation might have been Operation Pied Piper by name, but in Berlin it was by nature.

Register of Key Documentary Sources in This Study

The listing follows this format:

> *Title*
> > Date, Author (if available), Status, Pages
> > Archive or Holding, Deposit no.

Chapter Two

London

(Source I)
Evacuation of the Child Population—an Appreciation
> (May 1938, submitted 2 June 1938), George A. Lowndes (attributed),
> unpublished, 4 pages
> London Metropolitan Archives (LMA): EO/WAR/1/3

(Sources II)
> (IIa) *Air Raid Precautions, Education Officer's Dept., Minutes of Conference with Heads of Secondary Schools and Junior Technical Institutes*
> 15 May 1938, anon., unpublished, 13 pages
> LMA: EO/WAR/1/4

> (IIb) *Air Raid Precautions, Education Officer's Dept., Minutes of Conference with Heads of Elementary Schools*
> 15 May 1938, anon., unpublished, 11 pages
> LMA: EO/WAR/1/4

Operation Pied Piper, pages 183–188
Copyright © 2012 by Information Age Publishing
All rights of reproduction in any form reserved.

(Source III)

> *Short Range Emergency Scheme for Evacuation of the Child Population of School*
> *Age whose Parents Consent to their Evacuation Separately in School Units*
> 23 September 1938, Edmund M. Rich, unpublished, 5 pages
> LMA: EO/WAR/1/4

(Sources IV)

> (IVa) *Borough of Chelsea – An Experiment in Civil Defence*
> 19 June 1939, S. Boyle, Booklet for Guests
> LMA: EO/WAR/1/23

> (IVb) *Proposed Test of Evacuation Scheme*
> 12 June 1939, W.J.O. Newton, unpublished, 3 pages
> LMA: EO/WAR/1/23

> (IVc) *Report to A.R.P. Committee – Government's Evacuation Scheme – Chelsea*
> *Test (Draft)*
> (June 1939), Edmund M. Rich, unpublished, 2 pages
> LMA: EO/WAR/1/23

—————

Berlin

(Source V)

> *Betr.: Entsendung der schulpflichtigen Jugendlichen aus Berlin und Hamburg*
> (September 1940, submitted 27 September 1940), Baldur von Schirach,
> Österreichisches Staatsarchiv Wien, Bürckel/Mat 4651, Bd. 1
> Reprinted in Kock, 1997, pp. 348ff

(Source VI)

> *Betrifft: Landverschickung der Jugend luftgefährdeter Gebiete*
> 2 October 1940, Bernhard Rust, transcript, unpublished, 2 pages
> Bibliothek für Bildungsgeschichtliche Forschung des Deutschen Insti-
> tuts für Internationale Pädagogische Forschung/Archiv Berlin (BBF/
> DIPF/Archiv): GUT PRIVAT 008–229

Chapter Three

London

(Source VII)

> *Evacuation Scheme – Bulletin No. 25*
> (September 1939), W.J.O. Newton, unpublished, 7 pages
> LMA: EO/WAR/1/34

(Source VIII)
Evacuation Scheme – Bulletin No. 27
(September 1939), W.J.O. Newton, unpublished, 7 pages
LMA: EO/WAR/1/34

▬▬──────
Berlin

(Source IX)
NSV.-Bekanntmachungen B78/Folge 42: Arbeitsanweisung für die erweiterte Kinderlandverschickung
15 October 1940, anon., 7 pages
BBF/DIPF/Archiv: GUT SAMML 191

(Source X)
37. Ew.-Transport (DJ.u.JM.) am 14. Mai 1941
9 May 1941, Karl Behrens, 1 page, typed letter
Archives of KLV e.V.
Published in Dabel, 1981, p. 18

──────────
Chapter Four

London

(Source XI)
Criticism of the Evacuation Operation
with an appendix: *Verminous Conditions – Note by Medical Officer*
(October 1939), anon. – LCC staff, unpublished, 8 pages
LMA: EO/WAR/1/210

(Sources XII)
(XIIa) *Government Evacuation Scheme – Press Conference*
6 March 1940, Herbert Morrison, Press Conference Transcript, 4 pages
LMA: EO/WAR/1/75

(XIIb) *Government Evacuation Scheme – What about Your Child? Have You Decided?*
28 March 1940, Edmund M. Rich, Press Submission, 1 page
LMA: EO/WAR/1/75

▬▬──────
Berlin

(Source XIII)
Gen Nr.2 II
6 February 1940, Der Oberpräsident der Rheinprovinz, Abteilung für höheres Schulwesen: Jungbluth, unpublished, 1 page
BBF/DIPF/Archiv: GUT PRIVAT 008–192

(Source XIV)
> *Bericht über die Arbeitstagung für KLV. in Berlin*
> 26 June 1941 (misdated 26 May 1941), anon., unpublished, 6 pages
> Bundesarchiv Berlin (BA): NS/12/942/a

Chapter Five

London

(Sources XV)
> (XVa) *Memorandum from the Education Officer to the Chairman of the Education Committee*
> (October 1940), Graham Savage, unpublished, 4 pages
> with an appendix:
> Compulsory Evacuation
> (May 1940), anon., unpublished, 2 pages
> LMA: EO/WAR/1/48

> (XVb) *Government Evacuation Scheme*
> 24 October 1940, Graham Savage, unpublished, 2 pages
> LMA: EO/WAR/1/48

(Sources XVI)
> (XVIa) *Evacuation – Propaganda Drive*
> 16 October 1940, anon., unpublished, 6 pages
> LMA: EO/WAR/1/48

> (XVIb) *Mothers – You'd give your life for your children . . .*
> (October 1940), Ministry of Health, preview copy of press advert, 1 page
> LMA: EO/WAR/1/48

Berlin

(Sources XVII)
> (XVIIa) *Eltern der Berliner Schuljugend!*
> (August 1943), Joseph Goebbels, leaflet, 1 page
> BA: ZSG/140–74

> (XVIIb) *Berliner! Berlinerinnen!*
> 1 August 1943, Joseph Goebbels, leaflet, 1 page
> BA: ZSG/140–74

> (XVIIc) *Luftnotgebiete sind kein Platz für Kinder!*
> (February 1944), anon., leaflet
> Reprinted in Franck and Asmus, 1983, pp. 208f

(Sources XVIII)
> (XVIIIa) *Betr. Verlegung von Schulen*
> 18 August 1943, Der Stadtpräsident der Reichshauptstadt Berlin: Dr.

Schamvogel, unpublished, 2 pages
BBF/DIPF/Archiv: GUT SAMML 191

(XVIIIb) *Im Nachgang zu meinem Erlaß vom 27. August 1943 – III Gen. zu 1237/43*
3 September 1943, Der Stadtpräsident der Reichshauptstadt Berlin: Hübner, unpublished, 1 page
BBF/DIPF/Archiv: GUT SAMML 191

Chapter Six

London

(Sources XIX)

(XIXa) *Government Evacuation Scheme – Organised Return of Unaccompanied Children to certain Evacuation Areas*
18 October 1944, Ministry of Health, unpublished, 5 pages
LMA: EO/WAR/1/131

(XIXb) *Ministry of Health Circular 68/45*
10 April 1945, S. J. Wilkinson / Ministry of Health, unpublished, 9 pages
LMA: EO/WAR/1/131
National Archives Kew (NA): ED 138/53 – 429

(XIXc) *London County Council, Education Officer's Department, Government Evacuation Scheme – Return Arrangements*
With an appendix: handwritten table
7 June 1945, E. A. Hartill – LCC, unpublished, 2 pages
LMA: EO/WAR/1/131

(Source XX)

Ministry of Health Circular 95/45: Return from Evacuation of Unaccompanied Children Resettlement and Adjustment to Family Life
28 May 1945, S. J. Wilkinson, unpublished, 5 pages
NA: ED 138/53–438

Berlin

(Sources XXI)

(XXIa) *Letter from Bezirksamt Berlin-Mitte, Amt für Volksbildung to Luisenstädtische Schule*
18 July 1945, (signature illegible), unpublished, 2 pages
BBF/DIPF/Archiv: GUT SAMML 207 – 5, 7

(XXIb) *Betr. Rückführung der Luisenstädt. Schule*
27 August 1945, Alfred Homeyer, handwritten and unpublished, 1 page
BBF/DIPF/Archiv: GUT SAMML 207–45

(XXIc) *Betr. Rückführung Berliner Kinder (Verlegte Schulen (KLV) und Einzel-kinder)*
4 April 1946, Der Landesbeauftrgate für die Heime der verlegten Schulen in Bayern (KLV): Hartmann Franz Xaver, unpublished, 2 pages
Archive of Gertrud-Stauffacher-Schule, Oberschule für Mädchen at Eckener Oberschule, unlisted

(XXId) *An die Leitung des Schulheims*
17 April 1946, Der Beauftragte der Stadt Berlin für die verlegten Berliner Schulen in Bayern: Zettl, unpublished, 1 page
Archive of Gertrud-Stauffacher-Schule, Oberschule für Mädchen at Eckener Oberschule, unlisted

Bibliography

Other Primary Sources, Archival Material and Contemporary Surveys

Adams, W. G. S., & Emden, A. B. (1947). *London children in war-time Oxford: A survey of social and educational results of evacuation by a Barnett House study group*. London, UK: Geoffrey Cumberledge–Oxford University Press.

Calder, R. (1940). The school child. In M. Cole & R. Padley (Eds.), *Evacuation survey: A report to the Fabian Society* (pp. 145–156). London, UK: Routledge and Sons.

Clark, F. L. G., & Toms, R. W. (1940). *Evacuation: Failure or reform*. London, UK: Fabian Society.

Clarke, J. S. (1940). London. In M. Cole & R. Padley (Eds.), *Evacuation survey: A report to the Fabian Society* (pp. 200–209). London, UK: Routledge and Sons.

Cole, M., & Padley, R. (Eds.). (1940). *Evacuation survey: A report to the Fabian Society*. London, UK: Routledge and Sons.

Cosens, M. (1940). *Evacuation: A social revolution*. London, UK: Charity Organisation Society (reprinted from Social Work)

Freud, A., & Burlingham, D. T. (1943). *War and children*. New York, NY: Ernst Willard.

Isaacs, S., Brown, S., & Thouless, R. (Eds). (1941). *The Cambridge evacuation survey: A wartime study in social welfare and education*. London, UK: Methuen & Co. Ltd.

L.C.C. (1939). Report of A.R.P. Committee w/r Chelsea Evacuation (LMA EO/WAR/1/23). London, UK: London County Council—Education Officer.

Operation Pied Piper, pages 189–200
Copyright © 2012 by Information Age Publishing
189

L.C.C. (1943). The Story of Evacuation (LMA EO/WAR/1/1). London, UK: London County Council—Education Officer.

Mann, E. (1938). *School for barbarians: On the educational policy of the German National Socialist Party.* New York, NY: Modern Age Books.

MIRS London Branch. (1944). *Basic handbook: The Hitler Jugend (the Hitler Youth Organisation).* London, UK: Supreme Headquarters Allied Expeditionary Force–Evaluation and Dissemination Section–via scribd.com.

Padley, R. (1940). The national scheme. In M. Cole & R. Padley (Eds), *Evacuation survey: A report to the Fabian Society* (pp. 10–67). London, UK: Routledge and Sons.

Rich, E. M. (1938). Letter to the National Union of Teachers / 10.06.1938 / EO/WAR/1/3. London, UK: London Metropolitan Archives.

Wagner, G. (1940). *Our wartime guests: Opportunity or menace? A psychological approach to evacuation.* London, UK: Hodder & Stoughton.

Contemporary Newspaper Coverage, Broadcasts, and Films

BAZ. (24.09.1940). Flüchtlingsdampfer angeblich auf der Fahrt nach Kanada torpediert. *Berliner Allgemeine Zeitung.*

Berliner Lokal Anzeiger. (01.10.1940). 'Erweiterte Landverschickung für Kinder'. *Berliner Lokal Anzeiger.*

BNN. (14.10.1940). 'Plutokratenkinder bevorzugt!'. *Berliner Neueste Nachrichten.*

Das 12 Uhr Blatt. (09.10.1940). 'Berliner Kinder fahren ins Paradies'. *Das 12 Uhr Blatt.*

Dickinson, T. (1940). *Westward Ho!* United Kingdom: Ministry of Information.

Eldrige, J. (1940). *Village School.* United Kingdom: Ministry of Information.

Jennings, H., & Watt, H. (1940). London can take it! United Kingdom: Ministry of Information / Warner Bros.

Manchester Guardian. (14.06.1940). 'Why Child Evacuation is not Compulsory'. *Manchester Guardian.*

Manchester Guardian. (15.06.1940). 'Compulsory Evacuation of Children Urged'. *Manchester Guardian,* pp. 8.

Manchester Guardian. (16.10.1939). 'Is Evacuation a Failure?'. *Manchester Guardian,* pp. 6.

Manchester Guardian. (17.07.1935). 'Air Raid Circular–Commons Protest–Its 'Terrible Implications''. *The Manchester Guardian,* pp. 3.

Manchester Guardian. (28.11.1940). 'The Chaos of the Schools'. *Manchester Guardian.*

Manchester Guardian. (29.08.1939). 'Evacuating School Children–Excellent Cooperation in Successful Rehearsal'. *The Manchester Guardian,* pp. 4.

Sainsbury, F. (1941). Living with Strangers (pp. approx. 11 minutes). United Kingdom: Ministry of Information.

Times. (01.09.1939). Evacuation To-day. *The Times,* pp. 11.

Times. (02.02.1939). 'Evacuation of Children–Camps for Schools'. *The Times,* pp. 8.

Times. (06.02.1939). 'Evacuation of Children–Camp or Bedroom Accommodation'. *The Times,* pp. 8.

Times. (06.02.1939). 'New Scheme for Evacuation–Immediate Survey of Private Houses'. *The Times,* pp. 12.

Times. (09.08.1944). 'Evacuation in Full Swing–Scheme Operating Smoothly'. *the Times,* pp. 2.

Times. (10.02.1939). 'Civil Defence Pay–M.P.s and Evacuation Camps'. *The Times,* pp. 9.

Times. (12.07.1939). 'Popular Dislike of Evacuation–Mr. H. Morrison's Statement'. *The Times,* pp. 9.

Times. (21.03.1939). 'Evacuation in 1803'. *The Times,* pp. 19.

Weidenmann, A. (1941). Ausser Gefahr (pp. 25 Min.). Germany: D. F. G. Reichsjugendführung–www.archive.org/details/1941-Ausser-Gefahr.

Literature

Ackroyd, P. (2000). *London: The biography.* London, UK: Chatto & Windus.

Amenta, E. (2003). What we know about the development of social policy: Comparative and historical research in comparative and historical perspective. In J. Mahoney & D. Rueschemeyer (Eds.), *Comparative historical analysis in the social sciences* (pp. 91–130). Cambridge, UK: Cambridge University Press.

Arthur, M. (2004). *Forgotten voices of the Second World War: A new history of the Second World War and the men and women who were there.* London, UK: Ebury Press.

Bandur, R. (2006). *Von Berlin in das Sudetenland, Meine KLV-Lagerzeit von 1944–1945.* Bochum, Germany: Projektverlag.

Bauer, C. J. (2010). *Ferien vom Krieg; Berliner Kindheitserinnerungen 1939–1947 (Hrsg. Heimatmuseum Reinickendorf).* Berlin, Germany: Jaron Verlag.

Beaven, B., & Griffiths, J. (2008). Creating the exemplary citizen: The changing notion of citizenship in Britain 1870–1939. *Contemporary British History,* 22(2), 203–225.

Becker, S. (2010). Panische Angst. *Der Spiegel, 30/2010,* pp. 34–35.

Beevor, A. (2002). *Berlin: The downfall 1945.* London, UK: Penguin.

Benz, W. (2000). *Geschichte des Dritten Reiches.* Munich, Germany: C. H. Beck.

Bessel, R. (2009). *Germany 1945: From war to peace.* London, UK: Simon & Schuster.

Boberach, H. (1982). *Jugend unter Hitler.* Dusseldorf, Germany: Droste Verlag.

Boberach, H. (Ed.). (1984), *Meldungen aus dem Reich 1938–1945, die geheimen Lageberichte des Sicherheitsdienstes der SS.* Herrsching, Germany: Pawlak Verlag.

Bracher, K. D. (1969). *Die Deutsche Diktatur: Entstehung, Struktur, Folgen des Nationalsozialismus.* Köln Germany: Kiepenheuer & Witsch.

Braumann, G. (2004). *Evangelische Kirche und Erweiterte Kinderlandverschickung.* Bochum, Germany: Projektverlag.

Brendon, V. (2009). *Prep school children: A class apart over two centuries.* London, UK: Continuum.

Brown, M. (2005). *Evacuees: Evacuation in wartime Britain 1939–1945.* Stroud, UK: Sutton Publishing.

Brown, M. (2009). *Evacuees of the Second World War.* Oxford: Shire Publications.

Bryan, T. (1995). *The great western at war 1939–1945.* Sparkford (Somerset), UK: Patrick Stephens Ltd.

Buckton, H. (2009). *The children's front: The impact of the Second World War on British children.* Chichester, UK: Phillimore.

Buddrus, M. (2003). *Totale Erziehung für den totalen Krieg: Hitlerjugend und nationalsozialistische Jugendpolitik* Munich, Germany: Institut für Zeitgeschichte–K G Saur.

Burke, P. (2005). *History and social theory* (2nd ed.). Cambridge, UK: Polity Press.

Burleigh, M. (2000). *The Third Reich: A new history.* London, UK: Macmillan.

Calder, A. (1969). *The people's war: Britain 1939–45.* London, UK: Jonathan Cape.

Churchill, W. S. (1948). *The Second World War, Vol. 1: The gathering storm.* London, UK: Cassell.

Cohen, G. D. (2011). *In war's wake: Europe's displaced persons in the postwar order.* Oxford, UK: Oxford University Press.

Cowen, R. (2002). Moments of time: A comparative note. *History of Education, 31*(5), 413–424.

Crawford, K., & Foster, S. (2007). *War, nation, memory: International perspectives on World War II in school history textbooks.* Charlotte, NC: Information Age Publishing.

Crook, D., & McCulloch, G. (2002). Comparative approaches to the history of education. *History of Education, 31*(5), 397–400.

Crosby, T. L. (1986). *The impact of civilian evacuation in the Second World War.* London, UK: Routledge.

Crump, N. (1947). *by rail to victory: The story of the L.N.E.R. in wartime.* London, UK: London and North Eastern Railway.

Cunningham, P. (2000). Moving images: Propaganda film and British education 1940–1945. *Paedagogica Historica, 36*(1), 389–406.

Cunningham, P. (2004). Sources as interpretation: Sources in the study of education history. *History of Education, 33*(1), 105–123.

Cunningham, P., & Gardner, P. (1999). Saving the nation's children: Teachers, wartime evacuation in England and Wales and the construction of national identity. *History of Education, 28*(3), 327–337.

Dabel, G. (Ed.) (1981). *KLV: die erweiterte Kinder-Land-Verschickung, KLV Lager 1940–45.* Freiburg, Germany: Verlag Karl Schillinger.

Davies, O. L. (1992). The invisible evacuees: England's urban teachers during the first autumn of war, 1939. *History of Education Society Bulletin*, XLIX, 53–60.

DHM. (2010a). *Die Hitler-Jugend (HJ): Deutsches Historisches Museum.* Retrieved from www.dhm.de/lemo

DHM. (2010b). *Die NS-Volkswohlfahrt: Deutsches Historisches Museum.* Retrieved from www.dhm.de/lemo

DHM. (2010c). *Schule im NS-Regime: Deutsches Historisches Museum.* Retrieved from www.dhm.de/lemo

DHM. (2011). *Antisemitismus: Deutsches Historisches Museum.* Retrieved from www.dhm.de/lemo

Döbling, K. (2007). *100 Jahre Eckener-Schule in Mariendorf–Chronik der Eckener- und der Gertrud-Stauffacher-Schule (1907–2007).* Berlin, Germany: Eckener Gymnasium.

Donoughue, B., & Jones, G. W. (1973). *Herbert Morrison: Portrait of a politician.* London, UK: Weidenfeld and Nicolson.

Earnshaw, A. (1995). *Britain's railways at war.* Penryn, UK: Atlantic Transport Publishers.

Erne, E., & Schneider, C. (2009). *Herrenkinder.* Germany: Salzgeber.

Evans, R. J. (2000). *In defense of history (2nd ed.).* London, UK: W.W. Norton & Company.

Evans, R. J. (2006). *The Third Reich in power, 1933–1939.* London, UK: Penguin.

Evans, R. J. (2009). *The Third Reich at war: How the Nazis led Germany from conquest to disaster.* London, UK: Penguin.

Franck, N., & Asmus, G. (Eds). (1983). *Heil Hitler, Herr Lehrer. Volksschule 1933– 1945. Das Beispiel Berlin.* Reinbek b. Hamburg, Germany: Rowohlt Verlag.

Fröhlich, E. (Ed.). (1998). *Die Tagebücher von Joseph Goebbels.* (Vol. 8: 1940). Munich, Germany: K. G. Sauer/Institut f. Zeitgeschichte.

Fürstenberg, D. (1996). *Kinderlandverschickung 1940–1945: Wen der Führer verschickt, den bringt er auch wieder gut zurüc.* Berlin, Germany: Kunstamt Steglitz.

Gardiner, J. (2005a). *The children's war: The Second World War through the eyes of the children of Britain.* London, UK: Imperial War Museum / Portrait.

Gardiner, J. (2005b). *Wartime Britain 1939-1945.* London, UK: Headline Review.

Gardiner, J. (2010). *The Blitz: The British under attack.* London, UK: HarperCollins.

Gardner, P., & Cunningham, P. (1997). Oral history and teachers' professional practice: A wartime turning point. *Cambridge Journal of Education, 27*(3), 331–342.

Gärtner, N. (2010). Administering 'Operation Pied Piper': How the London County Council prepared for the evacuation of its schoolchildren 1938– 39. *Journal of Educational Administration and History, 42*(1), 17–32.

Gehrken, E. (1997). *Nationalsozialistische Erziehung in den Lagern der Erweiterten Kinderlandverschickung 1940 bis 1945* Braunschweig: Forschungsstelle für Schulgeschichte und Schulentwicklung–TU Braunschweig.

Giles, G. J. (1992). Schooling for little soldiers: German education in the Second World War. In R. Lowe (Ed.), *Education and the Second World War: Studies in schooling and social change* (pp. 17–29). London, UK: Falmer Press.

Goldberg, B. (1994). *Schulgeschichte als Gesellschaftsgeschichte: die höheren Schulen im Berliner Vorort Hermsdorf 1893–1945.* Berlin, Germany: Edition Hentrich.

Gosden, P. H. J. H. (1976). *Education in the Second World War: A study in policy and administration.* London, UK: Methuen & Co. Ltd.

Graf, R. (2003). Interpretation, truth and reality. *Rethinking History, 7*(3), 387–402.

Green, A. (1990). *Education and state formation: The rise of education systems in England, France and the USA.* London, UK: Macmillan.

Grosvenor, I., & Myers, K. (2006). Progressivism, control and correction: Local education authorities and educational policy in twentieth-century England'. *Paedagogica Historica, 42*(1), 225–247.

Harris, J. (1992). Political thought and the welfare state 1870–1940: An intellectual framework for British social policy. *Past & Present, 135*, 116–141.

Hartl, P., & Knopp, G. (1999). Der Brandstifter. In G. Knopp (Ed.), *Hitlers Helfer* (Vol. 1). Muenchen, Germany: Bertelsmann.

Held, D. (1989). *Political theory and the modern state: Essays on state, power, and democracy.* Stanford, CA: Stanford University Press.

Held, D. (2006). *Models of democracy.* Cambridge, UK: Polity Press.

Hendrick, H. (1997). *Children, childhood and English society, 1880–1990.* Cambridge, UK: Cambridge University Press.

Hendrick, H. (2007). Optimism and hope versus anxiety and narcissism: Some thoughts on children's welfare yesterday and today. *History of Education, 36*(6), 747–767.

Hermand, J. (1993). *Als Pimpf in Polen: Erweiterte Kinderlandverschickung 1940–1945.* Frankfurt a. M., Germany: Fischer Taschenbuch Verlag.

Hess, S. J. (2006). *Civilian evacuation to Devon in the Second World War.* Exeter, UK: University of Exeter.

Hobsbawm, E. (1995). *Age of extremes: The short twentieth century 1914–1991.* London, UK: Abacus.

Holman, R. (1995). *The evacuation: A very British revolution.* Oxford, UK: Lion Publishing.

Horchem, H. J. (2000). *Kinder im Krieg: Kindheit und Jugend im Dritten Reich.* Hamburg, Germany: E. S. Mittler & Sohn.

Howard, M. (1981). *War and the liberal conscience.* Oxford, UK: Oxford University Press.

Huber, H. and Müller, A. (Eds). (1964). *Das Dritte Reich: Seine Geschichte in Bildern und Texten.* München, Germany: Verlag Kurt Desch.

Imlay, T. (2007). Democracy and war: Political regime, industrial relations, and economic preparations for war in France and Britain up to 1940. *The Journal of Modern History, 79*(1), 1–47.

Inwood, S. (1998). *A history of London*. London, UK: Macmillan.

Irving, D. (1996). *Goebbels: Mastermind of the Third Reich*. London, UK: Focal Point.

Jackson, C. (2008). *Who will take our children? The British evacuation program of World War II*. Jefferson, NC: McFarland.

Kater, M. H. (2004). *Hitler Youth*. London, UK: Harvard University Press.

Kellerhoff, S. F. (2006). *Berlin unterm Hakenkreuz* Berlin, Germany: Berlin Edition.

Kershaw, I. (1999). *Der NS-Staat–Geschichtsinterpretationen und Kontroversen im Ueberblick*. Reinbek b. Hamburg: Rowohlt.

Kershaw, I. (2000). *Hitler: 1936–1945 nemesis*. London, UK: Allen Lane.

Kinz, G. (1991). *Der Bund Deutscher Mädel: ein Beitrag über die außerschulische Mädchenerziehung im Nationalsozialismus*. Frankfurt a.M., Germany: Peter Lang.

Klaus, M. (1985). *Mädchen im Dritten Reich, der Bund Deutscher Mädel (BdM)*. Cologne, Germany: Pahl-Rugenstein.

Klee, E. (2008). *Das Personenlexikon zum Dritten Reich: Wer war was vor und nach 1945*. Koblenz, Germany: Edition Kramer.

Koch, H. J. W. (1975). *The Hitler Youth: Origins and development 1922–1945*. London, UK: Macdonald and Jane's.

Kock, G. (1997). *Der Führer sorgt für unsere Kinder: die Kinderlandverschickung im Zweiten Weltkrieg*. Paderborn, Germany: F. Schoeningh.

Kohrs, P. (1983). *Kindheit und Jugend unter dem Hakenkreuz: Nationalsozialistische Erziehung in Familie, Schule und Hitlerjugend*. Stuttgart, Germany: J. B. Metzler.

Kressel, C. (1996). *Evakuierung und erweiterte Kinderlandverschickung im Vergleich: das Beispiel der Staedte Liverpool und Hamburg*. Frankfurt a.M., Germany: Peter Lang.

Lang, J. v. (1991). *Der Hitler Junge. Baldur von Schirach: der Mann, der Deutschlands Jugend erzog*. Munich, Germany: Knaur.

Larass, C. (1983). *Der Zug der Kinder–Die Evakuierung von 5 Millionen deutscher Kinder im 2. Weltkrieg*. Munich: Meyster.

Large, D. C. (2001). *Berlin: A modern history*. London, UK: Allen Lane, Penguin.

Larsen, M. (2009). Comparative education, postmodernity and historical research: Honouring ancestors. In R. Cowen & A. Kazamias (Eds.), *International handbook of comparative education* (pp. 1045–1060). Dordrecht, NL: Springer Science + Business Media.

Le Tissier, T. (2007). *The Battle of Berlin*. Stroud, Gloucestershire, UK: Tempus.

Lichbach, M., & Zuckerman, A. (Eds.). (2009). *Comparative politics, rationality, culture and structure* (2nd ed.). New York, NY: Cambridge University Press.

Limond, D. (2000). [R]emain[ing] true to...vocation and...conscience: Teachers in Britain and Norway under national socialism as conscientious objectors, war resisters, and anti-Nazis resisters, 1939–1945. *Paedagogica Historica, 36*(2), 631–652.

Lowe, R. (Ed.). (1992). *Education and the Second World War: Studies in schooling and social change*. London, UK: Falmer Press.

Lowndes, G. A. N. (1969). *The silent social revolution: An account of the expansion of public education in England and Wales 1895–1965*. Oxford, UK: Oxford University Press.

Maclure, S. (1990). *A history of education in London 1870–1990*. London, UK: Allen Lane–the Penguin Press.

Macnicol, J. (1986). The effect of the evacuation of schoolchildren on official attitudes to state intervention. In H. L. Smith (Ed.), *War and social change* (pp. 3–31). Manchester, UK: Manchester University Press.

Mahoney, J. (2003). Knowledge accumulation in comparative historical research. In J. Mahoney & D. Rueschemeyer (Eds.), *Comparative historical analysis in the social sciences* (pp. 131–176). Cambridge, UK: Cambridge University Press.

Mahoney, J., & Rueschemeyer, D. (Eds). (2003). *Comparative historical analysis in the social sciences*. Cambridge, UK: Cambridge University Press.

Mahoney, J. & Villegas, C. (2007). Historical enquiry and comparative politics. In C. Boir & S. Stokes (Eds.), *The Oxford handbook of comparative politics* (pp. 73–89). Oxford, UK: Oxford University Press.

Mann, J. (2005). *Out of harm's way: The wartime evacuation of children from Britain*. London, UK: Headline.

Manvell, R., & Fraenkel, H. (2006). *Doctor Goebbels: His life and death*. London, UK: Greenhill Books.

Marr, A. (2008). *A History of modern Britain*. London, UK: Pan Macmillan.

Marr, A. (2009). *The making of modern Britain: From Queen Victoria to V.E. Day*. London, UK: Pan Macmillan.

Martin, J. (2003). The hope of biography: The historical recovery of women educator activists. *History of Education, 32*(2), 219–232.

Mayall, B., & Morrow, V. (2011). *You can help your country: English children's work during the Second World War*. London, UK: Institute of Education.

Maylahn, E. (2004). *Auflistung der KLV-Lager*. Bochum, Germany: Projektverlag.

McCulloch, G. (2004). *Documentary Research in Education, History and the Social Sciences*. London, UK: RoutledgeFalmer.

Mellegard, V. (2005). *Evacuees* (running time: 60 minutes). Great Britain: BBC 4.

Mierzejewski, A. C. (2000). *The most valuable asset of the Reich, Vol 2, 1933–1945: A history of the German National Railway*. Chapel Hill, NC: University of North Carolina Press.

Miller-Kipp, G. (Ed.). (2001). *"Auch Du gehörst dem Führer": die Geschichte des Bundes Deutscher Mädel (BDM) in Quellen und Dokumenten*. Weinheim: Juventa Verlag.

Morris, M. (2009). *Goodnight children, everywhere: Voices of evacuees*. Stroud, UK: The History Press.

Morrison, H. (1960). *Herbert Morrison: An autobiography*. London, UK: Odhams Press.

Myers, K. (1999). National identity, citizenship and education for displacement: Spanish refugee children in Cambridge, 1937. *History of Education, 28*(3), 313–325.

Naasner, W., & Schmidt, A. (1995). *Vorbermerkung zur Sammlung des KLV e.V.* Koblenz, Germany: Bundesarchiv Deutschland.

Noakes, J. (Ed.). (1998). *The German home front in World War II.* (Vol. 4). Exeter, UK: University of Exeter Press.

Ozga, J. (2000). *Policy research in educational settings: Contested terrain.* Buckingham, UK: Open University Press.

Parsons, M. L. (1998). *I'll take that one: Dispelling the myths of civilian evacuation 1939–45.* Peterborough, UK: Becket Karlson.

Parsons, M. L. (2008). *War child: Children caught in conflict.* London, UK: Tempus.

Parsons, M. L., & Starns, P. (2002). Against their will: The use and abuse of British children during the Second World War. In J. Marten (Ed.), *Children and war: A historical anthology* (pp. 266–278). New York, NY: New York University Press.

Platt, J. (1981a). Evidence and proof in documentary research: 1–Some specific problems of documentary research. *Sociological Review, 29*(1), 5–52.

Platt, J. (1981b). Evidence and proof in documentary research: 2–Some shared problems of documentary research. *Sociological Review, 29*(1), 53–66.

Porter, R. (1994). *London, UK: A social history.* London, UK: Hamish Hamilton.

Ragin, C. (1987). *The comparative method.* Berkeley, CA: University of Californian Press.

Rempel, G. (1989). *Hitler's children: The Hitler Youth and the SS.* Chapel Hill, NC: University of North Carolina Press.

Reuth, R. G. (1990). *Goebbels.* Muenchen, Germany: R. Piper.

Roth, W., & Mehta, J. (2002). The Rashomon effect: Combining positivist and interpretivist approaches in the analysis of contested events. *Sociological Methods & Research, 31*(2), 131–173.

Rowe, S. F. (2001). *The external/internal conflicts during war and social change: The emotional impact on evacuated children during the Second World War and the long term effects.* Colchester, UK: University of Essex.

Rusby, J. S. M. (2006). *Childhood temporary separation: Long-term effects of wartime evacuation in World War 2.* London, UK: Birkbeck.

Saint, A. (Ed.). (1989). *Politics and the people of London: The London County Council, 1889–1965.* London, UK: Hambledon Press.

Samuel, R., & Thompson, P. (Eds). (1990). *The myths we live by.* London, UK: Routledge History Workshop.

Samways, R. (Ed.). (1995). *We think you ought to go: An account of the evacuation of children from London during the Second World War based on the original records of the London County Council.* London, UK: Greater London Record Office.

Schäffer, F. (2010). *Nationalsozialistischer Lehrerbund (NSLB) 1929–1943*. Retrieved from www.historisches-lexikon-bayern.de

Schirach, B. v. (1967). *Ich glaubte an Hitler*. Hamburg, Germany: Mosaik Verlag.

Schoeps, J. H. (Ed.). (2007). *Berlin: Geschichte einer Stadt*. Berlin, Germany: be.bra Verlag.

Scholtz, H. (1985). *Erziehung und Unterricht unterm Hakenkreuz*. Goettingen, Germany: Vandenhoeck & Ruprecht.

Schueler, K. A. F. (1987). *Logistik im Russlandfeldzug*. Frankfurt a. M., Germany: Verlag Peter Lang GmbH.

Scott, J. (1990). *A matter of record: Documentary sources in social research*. Cambridge, UK: Polity Press.

Shirer, W. (1984). *The Nightmare Years 1930-1940*. Edinburgh: Birlinn Ltd.

Siegrist, H. (2006). Comparative history of cultures and societies: From cross-societal analysis to the study of intercultural interdependencies. *Comparative Education, 42*(3), 377–404.

Simon, B. (1991). *Education and the social order 1940–1990*. New York, NY: St. Martin's.

Smith, H. L. (Ed.). (1986). *War and social change: British society in the Second World War*. Manchester, UK: Manchester University Press.

Smith, L. (2007). *Young voices: British children remember the Second World War (with the Imperial War Museum)*. London, UK: Viking.

Sollbach, G. E. (2002). *Flucht vor Bomben: Kinderlandverschickung aus dem oestlichen Ruhrgebiet im 2. Weltkrieg*. Hagen, Germany: Lesezeichenverlag.

Sollbach, G. E. (2006). Die (erweiterte) Kinderlandverschickung (KLV) im Zweiten Weltkrieg. In H. H. Ewers (Ed.), *Erinnerungen an Kriegskindheiten: Erfahrungsräume, Erinnerungskultur und Geschichtspolitik unter sozial- und kulturwissenschaftlicher Perspektive* (pp. 31–48). Weinheim: Juventa.

Stargardt, N. (2005). *Witnesses of war: Children's lives under the Nazis*. London, UK: Jonathan Cape.

Stranack, D. (2005). *Schools at war: A story of education, evacuation and endurance in the Second World War*. Chichester, UK: Phillimore.

Süß, D. (2011). *Tod aus der Luft: Kriegsgesellschaft und Luftkrieg in Deutschland und England*. München, Germany: Siedler Verlag.

Tarling, R. (2006). *Managing social research: A practical guide*. Abingdon, UK: Routledge.

Titmuss, R. M. (1950). *Problems of social policy* (Vol. 3). Basingstoke, UK: Palgrave Macmillian.

Tofahrn, K. W. (2003). *Chronologie des Dritten Reiches: Ereignisse, Personen, Begriffe*. Darmstadt, Germany: Wissenschaftliche Buchgesellschaft.

Tosh, J. (2008). *Why history matters*. Basingstoke, UK: Palgrave Macmillan.

Waugh, M. J., Robbins, I., Davies, S., & Feigenbaum, J. (2007). The long-term impact of war experiences and evacuation on people who were children during World War Two. *Aging & Mental Health, 11*(2), 168–174.

Weber, M. (1978). *Economy and society: An outline of interpretive sociology* (Vol. II). Berkeley, CA: University of California Press. (Original work published 1922)

Weber, M., & Winckelmann, J. (1980). *Wirtschaft und Gesellschaft: Grundriß der verstehenden Soziologie.* Tübingen: Mohr Siebeck. (Original work published in 1922)

Weightman, G., Humphries, S., Mack, J., & Taylor, J. (2007). *The making of modern London.* London, UK: Ebury Press.

Welshman, J. (1998). Evacuation and social policy during the Second World War: Myth and reality. *Twentieth Century British History, 9*(1), 28.

Welshman, J. (2010). *Churchill's children.* Oxford, UK: Oxford University Press.

White, J. (2001). *London in the 20th century: A city and its people.* London, UK: Viking.

Wicks, B. (1988). *No time to wave goodbye.* London, UK: Bloomsbury.

Wicks, B. (1989). *The day they took the children.* London, UK: Bloomsbury.

Williams, S., Ivin, P., & Morse, C. (2001). *The children of London, UK: Attendance and welfare at school, 1870–1990.* London, UK: Bedford Way Papers / Institute of Education.

Winkler, H. A. (2011). *Geschichte des Westens–Die Zeit der Weltkriege 1914–1945.* Munich, Germany: C. H. Beck.

Wistrich, R. S. (1995). *Who's who in Nazi Germany.* London, UK: Routledge.

Wortmann, M. (1982). *Baldur von Schirach–Hitlers Jugendfuehrer.* Cologne: Boehlau Verlag.

Wright, J. (2007). *Germany and the origins of the Second World War.* London, UK: Palgrave Macmillan.

Young, K., & Garside, P. L. (1982). *Metropolitan London: Politics and urban change 1837–1981.* London, UK: Edward Arnold.

Zahra, T. (2011). *The lost children: Reconstructing Europe's families after World War II* Cambridge, MA: Harvard University Press.

Ziegler, P. (1995). *London at war.* London, UK: Sinclair Stevenson.

Register of Events, Institutions, Names and Places

Please note that this listing excludes the high frequency terms: Berlin, Hitlerjugend (HJ), erweiterte Kinderlandverschickung (KLV), London, and London County Council (LCC).

Operation Pied Piper, pages 201–203
Copyright © 2012 by Information Age Publishing
All rights of reproduction in any form reserved.

Acknowledgements

Written in London, Hamburg and Cambridge between 2008 and 2011.

I am greatly indebted to the following kind individuals for their valuable contributions, ideas, assistance and patience during the research and production stages of this study:

Professor Dr. Jane Martin

Dr. Kevin Myers

Dr. Stuart Foster

Professor Dr. Gary McCulloch

Dr. Susanne Wiborg

Dr. Vincent Carpentier

Dr. Alan Davison

George F. Johnson

Yvonne Oliver/IWM

Dan Regan

Dr. Peter Cunningham

Hildegund Remme

Dr. Bernhard Bremberger

Jens Fischer

Karl Döbling

Dr. Bettina Reimers

& my wonderful wife and children

Publication Note

Parts of chapters one, two, and three have been previously published:

Journal of Educational Administration and History

(Volume 42, Issue 1, 2010)

Administering "Operation Pied Piper"—How the London County Council prepared for the evacuation of its schoolchildren 1938–1939

They are reprinted here with the kind permission of Routledge.

Photograph Credits

Arrival of London Evacuees at Stevenage, September 1, 1939
   Imperial War Museum Photograph Collection HU 69028

Girls cheering with Swastika flags from train carriage
   Bundesarchiv Berlin Photograph Collection 146-1978-013-14

Crowded London departure with Routemasters, schoolchildren and helpers
   Imperial War Museum Photograph Collection IWM 552-127 (1939)

'Luftnotgebiete – kein Platz für Kinder'
   Bundesarchiv Berlin Poster Collection 003-011-027

Made in the USA
Middletown, DE
21 October 2018